W9-ACS-508

THE EGO AND ANALYSIS OF DEFENSE

THE EGO AND ANALYSIS OF DEFENSE

PAUL GRAY, M.D.

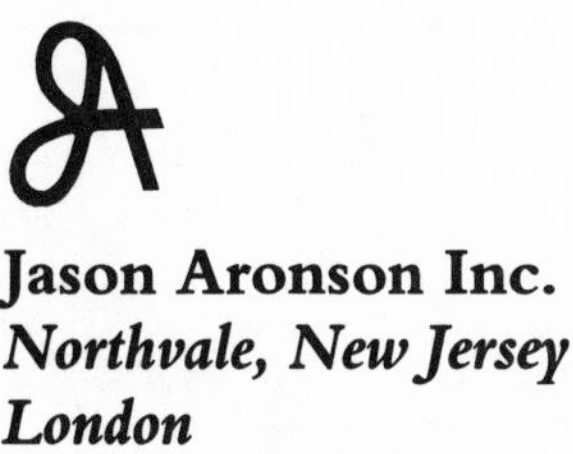

Jason Aronson Inc.
Northvale, New Jersey
London

This book was set in 11 point Bem by Lind Graphics of Upper Saddle River, New Jersey, and printed and bound by Haddon Craftsmen of Scranton, Pennsylvania.

10 9 8 7 6 5 4 3 2 1

Library of Congress Cataloging-in-Publication Data

Gray, Paul, 1918–
The ego and analysis of defense
Paul Gray.
Includes bibliographical references and index.
ISBN 1-56821-192-9
1. Psychodynamic psychotherapy. 2. Ego (Psychology)
3. Psychoanalysis. I. Title.
[DNLM: 1. Ego. 2. Psychoanalytic Therapy. 3. Psychoanalytic Theory. 4. Defense Mechanisms. 5. Conflict (Psychology) WM 460.5.E3 G781e 1994]
RC489.P72G73 1994
616.89'17—dc20
DNLM/DLC
for Library of Congress 93-49005

Manufactured in the United States of America. Jason Aronson Inc. offers books and cassettes. For information and catalog write to Jason Aronson Inc., 230 Livingston Street, Northvale, New Jersey 07647.

To Gerda

Contents

Foreword by Dr. Samuel Ritvo ix

Preface xvii

Acknowledgments xxv

PART I: TECHNIQUE

1. The Capacity for Viewing Intrapsychic Activity 3
2. "Developmental Lag" in the Evolution of Technique 27
3. On Helping Analysands Observe Intrapsychic Activity 63
4. The Nature of Therapeutic Action in Psychoanalysis 87
5. The Analysis of the Ego's Inhibiting Superego Activities 103

6. The Analysis of the Ego's Permissive Superego 129

7. Memory as Resistance, and the Telling of a Dream 151

PART II: TEACHING AND SUPERVISORY GUIDELINES

8. A Guide to Analysis of the Ego in Conflict 173

9. Brief Psychotherapy, Dynamic Psychotherapy, and Psychoanalysis 193

10. The Ego's Predictable Response to the Unfamiliar Analytic Situation 201

11. Reflections on Supervision 207

12. Elements of Supervision 213

13. A Conversation with Paul Gray 221

References 231

Credits 243

Index 247

Foreword

The growing number of psychoanalysts and psychotherapists who know and value the writings of Paul Gray has long awaited the publication of *The Ego and Analysis of Defense*. These writings now become readily accessible for study and teaching. They also give the reader who newly discovers them—or who may have read one or another chapter—the opportunity to study them chronologically. As he does so, he will appreciate that here is a corpus of writings spanning twenty years that is unique in current psychoanalysis for its integrative, progressive developmental quality. Gray does not spin speculative or untried theories in an effort to understand or explain supposedly new observations. He starts with our best-tested and most widely accepted clinical theories, Freud's structural theory, with its focus on the unconscious defense activities of the ego, and his second theory of anxiety, which ascribes that signal function to the ego.

Gray begins his critical study of technique in the first chapter, where he examines the listening analyst's perspective of attention or perceptual focus and shows that there are compelling reasons for preferring to adjust this focus so as to observe closely data limited essentially to inside the analytic situation. He demonstrates the specific advantages this perspective offers in analyzing communications of the patient referring to current or contemplated behavior outside the analytic situation, so-called *acting out*. Paying close attention to the point within the hour when the analysand turns to behavior outside the hour enables the analyst to see how the ego responds to the danger of an emerging drive derivative in the presence of the analyst and, without being consciously aware of doing so, turns defensively to the thoughts of behavior outside the analytic hour. In subsequent papers, Gray addresses the tasks of the analyst in deciding whether, when, and how to intervene in a manner that would enable the analysand to become consciously aware of the nature of the danger from the drive derivative and how he defends himself against it, never losing sight of the fact that this happens in the presence of the analyst, that is, in the context of the transference.

The sharp perceptual focus on listening for and analyzing the ego's unconscious activities within the analytic hour led to this question: Why had the development of analytic technique lagged so when Freud had long before forged the necessary conceptual tools and Anna Freud had shown how to implement them in *The Ego and the Mechanisms of Defense* in 1936? In the paper on " 'Developmental Lag' in the Evolution of Technique," Gray shows, in a work of creative scholarship, why analysts continue to lag in integrating the unconscious portions of the ego, particularly defenses, into a technique that would concentrate on analyzing resistances rather than overcoming them. Despite his new views on the ego and anxiety, Freud retained to the end vestiges of his early hypnotic technique, relying on the transference of authority to the analyst to overcome resistance by suggestion. Gray identifies other sources of the lag—analysts' fascination with the id, the predilection for an authoritative analytic stance, the preoccupation with external reality, the analyst's counterresistance to transference affects and impulses.

In the chapter, "On Helping Analysands Observe Intrapsychic Activity," Gray addresses the difficulties in achieving a major goal of the analytic process, that is, helping the analysand gain full access to those habitual, unconscious, and outmoded activities that serve resistance. He focuses on how the analyst's interventions can be geared to helping the analysand make use of his capacities to observe his own intrapsychic activities. He addresses the concomitant problem for the analyst of choosing a surface, of selecting those elements in the material that may make it possible to illustrate successfully to the analysand that he has unknowingly and involuntarily responded in defensive ways that he and the analyst can identify, enhancing the analysand's use of his self-observing capacities. Surprisingly, this attention to helping the analysand observe how his mind works in resistance and defense is often misunderstood by analysts and viewed as aiding and abetting the defense of intellectualization, rather than enabling the analysand to use his intelligence and capacities for self-observation to further the analytic process.

In the papers on the superego Gray's investigative scholarship reveals that the ambiguity that has long surrounded the technical approach to the analysis of the superego derives from the deeply ingrained tradition that mandated the use of *defensively* transferred superego functions in order to *overcome* resistance, a tradition rooted historically in the fact that the superego was conceptualized as a supraordinate psychic structure before the revision of the theory of anxiety and the recognition of the complexity of the defensive ego. Again, the tradition derived and maintained its authority from Freud's never having relinquished these remains of hypnosis despite his introduction of the structural theory and despite Anna Freud's classic description of the transference of defense in *The Ego and the Mechanisms of Defense*. Gray spells out the technical advantages in approaching the transferred superego manifestations as hierarchically initiated functions of the ego in which the earlier images of authority, whether threatening or permissive and approving, are reexternalized in the defensive effort against the drives. He also shows how essential the moral neutrality of the analyst is to the technique of analyzing the ego's superego functions.

In "Memory as Resistance, and the Telling of a Dream," Gray returns to his 1973 starting point, the analyst's listening perspective, with its focus on the ego's immediate unconscious defense and resistance activities. He conceptualizes and illuminates with clinical observation what is quite possibly the analyst's most difficult and demanding task—increasing the analysand's autonomous access to the ego's unconscious defense and resistance activities at the moment when the ego feels threatened by emerging drive derivatives. At such a moment the introduction of a memory, such as a dream, may provide a displacement into the past from the arena of the immediate present, the very orientation that analyst and analysand need in order to experience and observe the phenomena that occur on the stage of consciousness. The clinical material, though brief, is presented in a way that gives the reader a clear and sharp example of the technique in operation.

In this paper, Gray—almost in passing—makes what I believe is a major contribution to the theory of formation and analysis of dreams, bringing it into line with Freud's eventual view of the role of anxiety in the solution of intrapsychic conflict, a step that Freud seemed reluctant to take in his own late revisions of dream theory. Gray supplants the traditional view of the dream as the fulfillment of a wish with a new definition: "a dream is the ego's response that thwarts the id's attempt to gratify a conflicted wish."

The didactic guide on the analysis of the ego in conflict and on supervision and psychotherapy reveals Paul Gray as a dedicated and inventive teacher who takes great care to conceptualize and articulate his views on the theory and technique of analyzing the ego in conflict. The beginning analyst can feel he is accompanied in this baffling and difficult new undertaking by a sympathetic, experienced mentor who lends a finely tuned ear for sharper listening to the ego's subtle, immediate responses to conflict without having to reach for unconscious or absent content. The guidelines are a trusty *vade mecum*, a state-of-the-art distillation of concept and technique that the analyst can keep in mind.

Those who are concerned that this way of listening to and analyzing the interplay between drive and defense is dry or mechanical and is a threat to psychoanalysis as an art, need only be reminded of the emphasis Gray places on tact and timing, and on care in framing interventions in words that will be understood clearly and that the analysand will find bearable. Success in demonstrating a defensive manifestation to the analysand depends on the analyst's sensitivity to the analysand's receptivity and available capacity for observing with rational attention at the moment of interpretive intervention. At that point the analyst's clarity of conceptualization and communicative skills are of the utmost importance—a daunting challenge to the artistry of any psychoanalyst.

Those who fear that the systematic analysis of defense that starts at the clinical surface results in a dry intellectual exercise need only practice it to confirm Gray's statement that observing the ego while it is in action provides a more autonomous access to vivid affects in remembering and recollecting. When resistances are analyzed rather than overcome and the conscious mind can use its full potential, intense affects can be more fully experienced and tolerated.

After the defensive manifestations have been demonstrated to the analysand, there still remains the analysis of the ego's defensive use of transferences of authority, in other words the ego's defensive use of its superego activities. This is the critical step that distinguishes the analysis of resistance from the overcoming of resistance as the goal of analytic technique. Gray's conceptualization and description of this crucial phase is an essential step in the effort to develop a coherent methodology for analyzing defensive solutions to the transferences of authority, those transferences of defense that are mediated by the reexternalization of the superego. Patients are reluctant to analyze that aspect of transference because it is so effective in protecting the ego from risky revelations. The patient feels safer against the dangers of the instinctual drives if he views the analyst as inhibiting, as were the parents of childhood.

The interventions that are likely to be most effective in analyzing the defensive transference of authority are those enabling patients to examine the experience in the analytic hour, close to the time of perceiving the analyst as the *non-neutral* transference figure they try to maintain for safety against anxiety. Even though Freud's second theory of anxiety made the analysis of these defensive transferences not only possible but essential, analysts have been reluctant to tackle the difficulties of analyzing these resistances, preferring to exploit the transference of authority in the effort to overcome them. Gray's aim in analyzing superego transferences is, once again, to enable the patient to enhance the autonomy of the ego by becoming aware of the discrepancy between the features he repeatedly ascribes to the imagined figure before whom he feels at risk and the neutral, listening analyst. In this way, the patient's own role in remobilizing the fantasy authority image becomes more apparent.

No detail of the analytic process escapes Paul Gray's interest and study. Although nothing is of more practical importance than coping with the resistances to starting analysis, the attention Gray gives to the topic is a rarity in the literature. Recognizing that the resistances cannot be analyzed at that point, he discusses ways in which the positive transference can provide a basis for suggestion in the interest of overcoming resistance to the start of analysis. His mode of preparing the analysand for his or her task is quite different from the usual instruction to lie on the couch and say what comes to mind. He considers how and at what point to begin to orient the analysand to the importance of being able to observe his own intrapsychic activity in the analytic setting so that he can be an active participant in the perception and analysis of resistance and defense.

The concepts and techniques developed in *The Ego and Analysis of Defense* in the setting of essential psychoanalysis have a universal significance for all dynamic psychotherapies and for wider-scope patients as well. As all egos are in conflict and all egos employ defenses, a thorough understanding of the nature of intrapsychic conflict and the ego's responses to it, and the opportunities and limitations of the particular therapeutic situation, enable the therapist to adapt his technique to that situation. Thus, in brief psychotherapy, suggestion is the primary therapeutic action, transference is not examined, and explicit and implicit auxiliary provisions may be offered to the ego and superego. As the therapeutic aim in most psychological therapies is to effect a modification of the superego defense activities of the ego, and since the absence of an analytic situation in psychotherapy does not permit the systematic analysis of these defenses, Gray proposes other ways they can be modified while still working within a conflict/defense model.

In *The Ego and Analysis of Defense*, Paul Gray has taken a large step toward reducing the developmental lag in technique he first called to our attention in 1982. By concentrating on a listening perspective that focuses on the unconscious defense activities of the ego within the analytic hour, he shows us the fascinating intricacies of the interplay between the ego and the instinctual drives. In so doing, he provides the basis for analytic and psychotherapeutic techniques which, while demanding, are a source of pleasure when carried out.

Samuel Ritvo, M.D.

Preface

Many years ago it was my good fortune to be a candidate in an Institute with a curriculum that encouraged an interest in Freudian analytic *theory*. Ever since, my interest in theory led to growing awareness of the discrepancy between theory and practice. What techniques we learned too often supported an increasing preoccupation with meanings of observations and hypotheses about the contexts of the behavioral realities in the lives of our patients. These contexts distracted attention from the observable, on-the-scene intrapsychic realities patients displayed through progressive attempts at verbal spontaneity within the analytic situation. We analysts demonstrated a curious reluctance to apply regularly to our technique, or methodology, that which we espoused in the details of our evolving theory. The optimum technical focus of psychoanalysis was diluted by a familiar form of much of the psychotherapy *of the time* (more later about some contrasts with contemporary psychotherapy).

With the paper beginning this volume, on the technique of focusing the analyst's observing skills, I tried to describe this discrepancy. It was received with far more interest than I had anticipated. Anna Freud's contributions had been especially useful in crystallizing my recognition and elaboration of the inconsistencies. She was the discussant when I presented the paper in London in early 1973. On that occasion her agreeable reception of the paper gave support to my scientific curiosity. Subsequent closer study of the history of analysis brought to my attention much evidence that the problem was not at all new, evidence that was both episodic and chronic. I began a more systematic search to explain these lags.

In collecting my impressions of analysts' counterresistances to consistently applied defense analysis, I became increasingly aware that Anna Freud had tactfully perpetuated a myth when she claimed that her 1936 monograph only summarized Freud's ideas at the time. True, she captured the essence of the evolving direction of Freud's theories, but she had reached beyond him and his implications. She had dared to apply his ideas to the structure of the ego and its inclusion in the analytic method, going further than anyone had done before. I have described how, among her critical reviewers, only E. Kris would acknowledge the originality of her focus. For decades she loyally did not concede this. I sent her a copy of the "lag" paper in which I had disputed her discreet position in the matter by suggesting a limitation in Freud's scope of comprehension of the defensive alterations of the ego as compared with Anna Freud's own elaborations on the subject. Her reply significantly relieved some of my instinctual conflict over my position. She did not at all dispute my stand regarding her father. She replied:

> As you know of course, I agree fully with your principal thought, and as I said, was very interested in the way you develop it. As I see it, the reluctance of analysts to deal with the ego aspects comes from a lack of fascination with the interaction of forces within the mind. . . . I think for you and a good many others it is the constant intertwining battle, the never-ending efforts from one side of the personality to come to terms with the other which is the real analytic pleasure. [Anna Freud, personal letter, October 9, 1979]

A central issue in the discrepancy became conceptually clearer to me. By giving quite short shrift to the ego, our methodology was in fact maintaining several distinguishable functions of the ego in a state of relative inhibition. First, analysts were overlooking a much fuller capacity for self-observation. I had commented on this from the first of the papers, but had not addressed it directly. Another virtually neglected ego capacity was the *extent* to which ego activity portrays its conflict and defense solutions *within the realm of consciousness.* It is there that we may most effectively demonstrate them to the patient. This contrasts with the traditional interpretive overcoming of resistance to "absent content," It was as though analysts had never fully accepted our theory that id derivatives really would continue to press into consciousness as the censoring defenses were being analyzed. Analysts maintained an earlier theoretically supportable requirement (to combat the organic resistance of the death instinct) of repeated naming of the as yet unconscious content, as necessary *in addition to* overcoming the resistance. They continued to carry out the technique of providing two facilitating versions, one in consciousness, one in repression, ostensibly in order to persuade the id to push forward, to work through. The continued need for such a "biphasic" (Stone 1973) approach illustrated the unnoticed phenomenon that the overcoming of resistance was *not an actual analysis of the defenses.* It merely repeated calling the analysand's attention to them.

Not new, but progressively more apparent, was the extent to which a great deal of analytic technique was bypassing the ego. As a result, analysts could not demonstrate fully and analyze the otherwise internalized, primarily defense-motivated portions of the ego labeled *superego.* There was inconsistent, if any, recognition of the dissociation of these elements into the transferences of authority that are precipitated at once when the analytic situation is set in motion. Many analysts were sacrificing the analysis of this major transference of defense to the expediency of overcoming resistance by *using* that transference of authority for *influencing* reduction of defense. Further, his own later theories to the contrary, Freud had not relinquished that practice. The internalizing mutative interpretations of Strachey (1934), and the analytic manipulation of the superego, as recommended by Nunberg (1937), still had, and have, a wide acceptance in practice, if not in theory.

I saw the need for a more conceptualized technical guide to bringing into an analysis a greater awareness of the ego's versatile, and yet therapeutically accessible, roles. We had long understood and widely depended on the fact that when the analysand had repeated opportunity to experience increasing degrees of instinctual derivatives, mobilized by skillful *interpretations*, this could increase the ego's capacity to tolerate those derivatives. Far less recognized was that we could provide such experience as effectively by demonstrating to the patient evidence of the ego's *conscious*, frequently unattended *but not repressed*, clearly observable defensive reactions to conflicted drive derivatives. I offered, in 1986, technical guidelines toward helping *analysands* achieve better observation of these ego responses to conflict.

To emphasize working with observable, verbalized material in an analytic situation is to be responsive to the importance of giving the maturely sized but immaturely experienced ego progressive opportunities to gradually take on varieties of drive derivatives, by providing *experiential* insight, the equally important partner to *cognitive* insight. This differs from the transferentially substituted internalizations and identifications intended by the sometimes quite useful *corrective emotional experience* of certain psychotherapies. Instead it gives to the somewhat atrophied strengths of the ego the capacity consciously to manage workouts, through conscious, incrementally increasing drive-derivative experiences, accompanied by affects. I believe that looking at that experiential component as a *strengthening exercise* is a more neuropsychologically apt description than our ambiguous "working-through." It was also apparent to me that we needed clearer formulations of a theory more illustrative of the therapeutic actions and insights of ego analysis. Two versions of my subsequent approach to that have been published. The paper entitled "The Nature of Therapeutic Action in Psychoanalysis" is more directly relevant to this collection and appears as Chapter 4. The other was included in the Workshop Series of the American Psychoanalytic Association. It was called *How Does Treatment Help? On the Modes of Therapeutic Action of Psychoanalytic Psychotherapy*. It contains much duplication and some wider application of the analytic principles considered in the present volume.

To the perennial predictions for the future of analytic concepts, I would like to add an optimistic trend I have observed in recent years. One can sense some reversal of the inhibiting invasion of psychotherapeutic orientations into analysis. Instead, there are more frequently *informed* uses of ego-conflict-defense techniques in psychotherapy than before. There is a clearer recognition that in many psychotherapy settings some defensive ego activities, in their *immediacy*, are available to close observation and, consequently, can be helpfully demonstrated to patients. This contrasts with the widely used manner in so-called analytically oriented therapy, that attempts, as they say, some interpreting of the unconscious. Furthermore, up to a point, unanalyzed and constructively *used* positive tranference in psychotherapy can support modifications in conflict-defense patterns. I should like to feel that a contributing factor has been increased exposure to concepts and practice in directly observing defensive ego functioning in concurrent analytic cases in one's practice, or exposure to analytic clinical case conferences. Again, the *close-process attention,* useful in the contexts of *both* analysis and psychotherapy, includes in particular the observations, conceptualizations, and interventions by demonstration, referred to above. In the case of analysis these precede and prepare the analysand for the immediate follow-up phase of analyzing the *transference fantasies of authority* that motivate defense in the analytic situation. In the case of psychotherapy such interventions, in contrast to the demonstrations of the observable moments of conflict and defense in analysis, would be less likely to succeed, given the comparative infrequency of psychotherapeutic hours.

There, analysis of superego transference might well be omitted, as the power to influence of that transference of authority had best be preserved in most non-analytic therapeutic situations. Analytically informed psychotherapy has become more frequently a tool for gaining greater insights into debilitating, inhibiting ego modifications, especially those cruelly irrational defensive ego variations that involve the inhibitory activity of turning-on-the-self. With experience in focusing attention on the details of conflict and defense as they appear in the discourse of the patient with the therapist, much more effective support of alternative, more benign modes of restraint of drive derivatives becomes possible. If the ego concepts are understood, extended positive transferential influence can do much in areas of psychotherapy under treatment conditions and/or degrees of pathology which make full analysis unavailable or unwise.

Psychoanalytic ideas and findings will endure in the future even if they become isolated from their origins. The universality of resistance notwithstanding, however, the future of psychoanalytic technique may come to depend on the extent to which observers can find technique to be amenable to research accessible to a wider interdisciplinary and scientific audience. In that regard, I believe that the papers most relevant to the future of analytic technique and to its discrete application to briefer therapies as well are the ones devoted to the analysis of those ego activities that, outside the analytic situation, are more popularly identified with the conscience or superego. If this area of ego function continues to be relatively bypassed, I fear that the amount of *suggestion* remaining necessary to analytic therapies will persist and hence the demonstrable phenomenological potential so essential to valid research will continue to elude us.

The concept of *superego* versus my view of it as another example of the *ego-in-defense* has a long connection with the recognition of the superego's dissolution in the analytic situation (Sandler 1960). Here we are taking a more refined look at Freud's eventual summation: "Just as the id is directed exclusively to obtaining pleasure, *so the ego is governed by considerations of safety*" (Freud 1938, p. 199, italics added.)

Learning to put ego concepts more effectively into analytic treatment, as well as acquiring the essential skill of observing with greater precision the flow of consciousness in the patient's vocalizations, often depends largely on the degree of supervision provided. With that in mind, I occasionally write short orienting pieces, somewhat dogmatically stated. They are attempts at guidelines that I hope will be adaptively modified by the reader in both teaching and learning situations.

Acknowledgments

To recognize all the individuals who made important contributions to my emerging point of view on psychoanalytic technique as identified by certain uncommon emphases, I would need to go back to very early days. So, I begin rather arbitrarily with a brief exposure early in medical school to a remarkable teacher. After one impressive lecture, we lost him to the War (WW II, that is) where he became immensely valuable before returning to become well known as an analyst. Dr. "Hank" Brosin introduced my class to psychiatry with a presentation so impressive to me that for the first and only time in my training I asked the lecturer for a copy of his outline. As I was in the midst of exposures to a sequence of other exciting specialties (and given the nature of resistance), I soon repressed the content and the existence of his notes. Years later, as a graduate analyst I came across them and I discovered they were titled "The Mechanisms of Defense."

My evolving technical preferences and writings, Freudian in origin, coalesced around Anna Freud's (1936) monograph. The writings of Otto Fenichel, Heinz Hartmann, Ernst Kris,

Rudolph Loewenstein, Robert Waelder, Richard Sterba, Leo Rangell, and Charles Brenner all contributed specifically to my thinking.

Two groups have played an important role in maintaining the energy and ferment contributing to my flow of ideas. The first, for over 30 years, is the Center for Advanced Psychoanalytic Studies Group II, and I give special appreciation to Stanley Goodman and Samuel Ritvo for their enduring support. The second is my "Tuesday Group" on graduate studies in advanced technique, whose vitality, intellect, and creativity keep my cerebral synapses alert. I cherish them and all those past and present supervisees who keep my teaching up to the mark.

I would also like to thank the providers of two sustaining formulations that have strengthened my own technical orientation and tap my own writing juices. Lawrence Friedman, in his 1976 paper "Cognitive and Therapeutic Tasks of a Theory of the Mind," develops and summarizes, as does no one else, a key concept for grasping the core of effective facilitation of the ego's capacity for self-observation. A more recent classic, to which I am indebted for its stimulating clarifications so crucial to the possible endurance of ego analysis, is Apfelbaum and Gill's (1989) "Ego Analysis and the Relativity of Defense: Technical Implications of the Structural Theory" portrayal of the role of relative syntonicity of intervention as the key to engaging the ego's widest participation in the analytic situation.

I am grateful to the editor of this volume, Dr. Michael Moskowitz, for his support and helpful advice.

That I dedicate this volume to her does not capture the extent of my indebtedness to Gerda Gray. A wife who brings with her a dowry of editorial skills is more than a writer of scientific papers should expect in life. I have savored the gift of her unending encouragement, and I know that any clarity of expression that accompanies my ideas, I have achieved with her contributions.

PART I

TECHNIQUE

1

THE CAPACITY FOR VIEWING INTRAPSYCHIC ACTIVITY

It is a curious fact that the central, most necessary part of psychoanalytic technique is one of the least discussed, certainly one of the least well conceptualized aspects of psychoanalysis. I am referring to analytic listening or, more accurately, analytic perception. My main purpose in this essay is to examine and sharpen our idea of this aspect of technique in the analysis of adult neuroses. The observations which follow concern that portion of the complex of functions here designated as the analyst's perspective of attention, or perceptual focus, in particular, the uses of such perspectives of attention that are receptive to the derivatives of thoughts or affects or processes of which the patient is unaware.

In addition, I will emphasize a point of view regarding a particular application of the analyst's perceptual focus to a specific task in analytic work: that of analyzing those productions which are intended by the patient to refer to behavior, either current or anticipated, outside the analytic setting. The behavior in question might often qualify for the label of "acting out." In conclusion, I shall consider some possible relationships between the ego's self-observing potential and memory and imagination in general.

I will not here deal specifically with certain other concepts related to the analyst's observing functions. For example, because a coordinated approach to the meaning of the word "empathy" is not yet available (some of our best known papers on that topic are not compatible with each other), empathy as a term and as a concept will be dealt with in a later communication. The use of countertransference as an avenue of observation of the patient's productions is a controversial subject, often discussed with considerable ambiguity, and is also of an order of study different from that of this paper.

Exploring the functioning and uses of the analyst's "analyzing instrument" (Isakower 1957) involves one in what has long remained a complex psychoanalytic frontier. Meanwhile, the continuously expanding importance of ego analysis as a major component of our technique has imposed increasing tasks upon analytic listening or perceiving.

It is certainly true that the most necessary capacity for analytic listening is that complex of functions which allows for the recognition of drive derivatives. Whether this capacity is described as the "unconscious . . . as an instrument" (Freud 1912b, p. 116) or as "listening with the third ear" (Reik 1948) or by one of the various concepts to which the name "empathy" has been attached, the reference is to the essentially nonpurposeful processes. On the other hand, recognition of the *defense against* drive derivatives— that is, ego analysis—usually involves a different kind of perceptual attention and intelligence from that required strictly for awareness of the drive derivatives themselves. The difference is that observation of the ego's defensive ways (usually potentially distinguishable from the drive derivatives) involves not only a greater degree of purposefully directed thinking, but also a different aspect of the analyst's perceptual apparatus. One gets the impression that when this different way of perceiving the ego is unrecognized by the analyst, or is taken

for granted, the resulting interpretations may fail to convey how fully the ego can be observed. When this is the case, how can the patient come to gain a maximum grasp of this part of his own self-observing capacities?

Often the perceptual task required by the patient (as well as the analyst) to capture an ego's defensive detail is ignored by an interpretive intervention such as, "You are disappointed with me" (or angry, in love, etc., i.e., referring only to some drive derivative not in consciousness). The failure to observe and spell out in an explicit way how the drive element is kept from consciousness thwarts an optimal contribution toward the patient's eventual capacity for overcoming defenses voluntarily. The patient has not been taught to perceive or intellectually to comprehend these details of the ego's functioning. Even if direct references to the instinctual element (i.e., not including in the interpretations the appropriate ego analysis) do bring it into consciousness, a degree of passive permission to experience what has been forbidden may substitute for the greater amount of work required of the patient if he has to assume the added responsibility of perceiving *how* his ego avoids his psychic reality.

Given the talent for the kind of perception (attentiveness) which is receptive to drive derivatives, or a heightened capacity for such perception as a result of learning, the analyst must strive to maintain this perception in spite of a variety of "distractions." For convenience, the distractions may be divided into those which are unavoidable because they are necessary, and those which are potentially avoidable and unnecessary for the progress of analysis. Among the former are such things as perceiving and noting the details, as manifest details, of the analysand's memories, fantasies, or dreams—that is, observing the content of and details of the functioning ego, including the form and content of the defenses; or—to cite a different order of distinction—maintaining a portion of attention on the time in order to appropriately conclude the hour. The considerable range of avoidable distractions include those carried over from experience with

psychotherapeutic situations, or from analyzing children or adolescents, or "widening scope" patients, including the borderline or psychotic. Also included are the many countertransference and counterresistance uses of attention. Conspicuous examples of the latter are listening for the purpose of unsublimated voyeuristic gratification, or being unable to perceive transference derivatives out of some fear of them.

Discussions of analytic technique often fail to point out that those uses of attention which the analyst carries over from experience with patients other than adult neurotics often lend themselves, during an analytic hour, to strengthening the analysand's defenses. I suggest that the counterresistance use of unnecessary forms of "perceptual focus" is especially tempting against oral-sadistic derivatives, especially when these derivatives involve the transference. A common example of this occurs when aggressive derivatives, emerging toward recognition via various displacement upon the analyst and utilizing real and fantasied perceptions, are prematurely interpreted in genetic terms. The analyst is spared a more intense and elaborated form of the negative transference, and as the focus of attention is turned away from the analysis of the defenses still present, much of the resistance is preserved.

Analytic tradition has better prepared us for the necessity of dealing fully with the patient's defenses against erotic developments in the transference than it has for defenses against aggression toward the analyst. But it is probably more than the fact that aggression in analysis has a more recent history that explains the frequency with which it is insufficiently analyzed. Paradoxically, aggressive components of our patients' productions often are the most readily recognizable—but recognition and analysis are not the same. I believe that the analyst is faced with a qualitatively different task in achieving neutrality in the face of verbalized aggression as compared with verbalized erotic wishes. The ego qualities necessary in an analyst for achieving neutrality in the face of aggressive analytic content are less specifically considered

in training and in literature than are those required for the most effective analytic attitude toward transference love.

The particular misuse of the analyst's perceptual focus that is central to this discussion is a failure to maintain the view that the patients' productions are to be used as avenues to the functioning of their mind. Because of such failure, the analyst is often unable to convey to the analysand that the analyst's primary goal is always the analysis of the patient's psyche, not the patient's life. I am referring to the possible effects of the analyst's shifting attention away from the *immediate* psychical implications of what the patient is saying or manifesting. This does not mean confining attention only to transference manifestations, or omitting details of manifest content.

For example, let us take a patient who refers to some clearly competitive situation and then expresses some passive form of response to it. It may be valid to point out to the patient that he characteristically deals this way with competition in his life. On the other hand, if he can be shown that the passive trend he adopted *while talking about the particular situation* represented a form of defense *at that moment,* he will be in a better position to work toward analytic changes of such character traits.

One of the determinants of the analyst's perceptual focus will be the particular form of his "neutral" position. Anna Freud's (1936, p. 28) observation that the analyst "takes his stand at a point equidistant from the id, the ego, and the superego" has been virtually the only explicit guideline for over 35 years. Invaluable as this precept is, judgments about equidistance vary considerably among analysts. When faced with the possibility of transference aggression, the analyst may be tempted to shorten the distance from the patient's superego.

Attention to superego function in technical approaches that are not strictly analytic may necessarily involve either authoritative superego function on the part of the analyst, or at least call for mobilizing superego function in the patient to control dangerous acting out. In contrast, with adult neuroses, analyzing the patient's superego is *not* for the immediate purpose of strengthening control, but for uncovering such operations of the superego as unconscious demand for punishment, pathological function during the analytic hour for autosadistic gratification or defensive turning of aggression against the self, or simply controlling emergence of certain free associations.

Again, with nonanalytic approaches, a therapist may need to supply for the patient supplementary ego functions for purposes of reality assessment. To extend these same technical devices or attitudes to adult neuroses should not be necessary, and if the patient is treated as if it were, it can be regarded as a parameter that will limit the depth or degree of completeness of the analysis. In fact, the need for supplying supplementary ego functions provides a useful indicator regarding the clinical assessment of the patient's ego and suggests a corresponding modification of the therapeutic goal, at least for that particular analysis with that particular analyst.

The well-known adage "the analyst stands for reality" is often misinterpreted to mean that the analyst must concern himself with orienting the patient in some general ways regarding worldly realities. It is more technically useful to say that for the neurotic patient in analysis there is a particular external reality reference during the hour which he recognizes or distorts, and that reality is the analyst. As Stein (1966) points out,

> Our approach differs from other psychotherapies in that we explicitly *avoid* reality testing—at least in the usual sense. We need not tell our patients that they have misjudged a life situation, nor do we as a rule give in to the temptation to correct a misapprehension of some analytic event. Instead, we attempt to correct, by analysis, those distortions of self observation which become evident *in the analytic situation.* [p. 276, italics added]

Clinical illustrations can be a mixed blessing. Optimally, they clarify an otherwise ambiguous concept; but if the analyst's formulations or interpretations are involved, there is a risk of appearing to support a model way of saying something, rather than indicating only a particular aim or goal. The following examples are intended only to illustrate distinctions between an analytic perceptual focus on things "inside" the analysis and one that is concerned with details "outside" the analysis. For this reason they are trimmed to such an extent that any serious use beyond that is precluded.

EXAMPLE 1

A young woman given occasionally to impulsive decisions or arrangements, after about six months of analysis achieved a deepening degree of involvement in the analytic process. Part way through an hour, she began to speak of her success in overcoming shyness at work. She said this was allowing her, during the past several days, to persuade her boss that the company could in fact pay her way to a neighboring state for a week during the coming month for research purposes that would be valuable for the company. She remarked upon the pleasure the experience and travel would provide for her.

I silently observed, among other things, that within the idea she had just expressed was the thought of her being at some distance from the analytic setting and from the analyst. It can be surmised from the material that the patient was also referring to memories of currently contemplated behavior—to an impulse which, if it persisted, might in fact carry the patient briefly away from the analysis in the near future.

Assuming I was stimulated by the patient's remarks to comment or interpret, let us compare some possible responses:

(a) Point out to the patient that this would interrupt her analysis;

(b) Suggest that it would be important to analyze such an impulse before carrying it out, in order to know whether it is determined primarily by analytic reasons;

(c) Or, on the other hand, use could be made of what had just preceded these remarks—it was in this instance an expression of mild disappointment over the difficult location of the analyst's office. For instance, I could show the patient that her thoughts of being many miles away followed immediately the expressions of disappointment. This detail could then be analyzed. Thus, it might be revealed that she is indicating in this way that disappointment and criticism connected with the analyst are being experienced as unsafe; or some other equally important dynamic meaning of the *reference* to the trip could thus be demonstrated.

For either (a), (b), or (c), many variations would be possible, depending on the stage of the analysis, the analyst's style of phrasing his remarks, and so on, yet a significant distinction can be made between (a) or (b) on the one hand and (c) on the other. In (c) the perceptual focus is in terms of an immediate danger (of the emerging drive derivative) *in that hour*. The patient could perceive that the analyst's perceptual focus was on the psychological phenomena (i.e., the psychic realities) occurring at that moment, "inside" the analysis, and not on aspects of potential behavior (acting out) at another time and place, that is, "outside" the fundamental analytic setting.

It is not implied that the thoughts or plans about which the patient spoke necessarily originated at that moment in the hour. As suggested, they largely included memories of recent impulses. These thoughts very probably coincided with an "outside" reality, consisting of an idea or plan of several days' duration, which may in fact have developed over that time out of fears mobilized by the analysis. Further, it is not suggested that responding to the patient in a manner such as (a) or (b) might not effect some reaction on the part of the patient *useful* to the analysis. The point is that, by being concerned in (a) and (b) with aspects of "outside" reality, an unnecessary reference to the patient's behavior outside the analytic setting would displace the important analytic happenings of the moment. Thus, a defense against something immediate would be provided, or reinforced and compounded, by inviting a less than analytic orientation on the part of the patient.

Formulations or responses of the analyst along the lines of

(a) or (b) that do result in an inhibition of the impulse to interrupt the analysis, do so for a reason that is not clearly analytic. Typically it can be largely out of compliance. On the other hand, assuming that the trip, as behavior, actually was significantly connected with the analysis, a similar result achieved by the approach (c) has a greater chance of success because of *actually reducing the patient's resistances.* This is brought about by working directly with the relevant instinctual issues, which were, of course, reflected in the immediate hour by the trend in the patient's productions.

It is easier to restrict one's attention to the "inside" realities of the analysis if one respects the patient's enormous capacity for distortion in relating reality events. Such distortion occurs increasingly in the flow of associations, provided we do not hinder the deepening development of the transference neurosis or "transference neurotic attitudes" (Greenacre 1966, p. 746). We work toward allowing the ego to permit the drive derivatives an increasing freedom to take such liberties with perceptions of external realities—in fact, at the beginning of the analysis we often specifically advise the patient to attempt to avoid concern over the accuracy of mental productions as he observes and reports. We are more interested in his "honesty" in reporting what is taking place in his psychic reality than with what actually takes place outside the analytic setting.

Because of the influences of the fundamental rule of analysis, the analysand's communications to the analyst should be recognized and allowed as compromise formations (Brenner 1966, Freud 1912a). Once the analytic process bears increasingly on the analysand, his experiences, and productions in the analytic hour become influenced in much the same manner as dreams are influenced (A. Freud 1936).

EXAMPLE 2

A 40-year-old man, one year in analysis, began, midway in an hour, to relate a memory associated with events from the day before. He spoke of his wife's becoming explosively irritable over a trivial occurrence. He told of her yelling at him criticisms that hit on an especially painful set of memories. After describing this in detail, he recalled that some anger welled up in himself. He began to speak of how he had controlled his outward response by reminding himself that she was premenstrual at the time, and further, that on the previous night he had been sexually ungratifying to her in a way she must have found very frustrating.

This was a patient whose fear of his aggression in general was severe. His resistance to aggression against the analyst was only slightly worked through. Because of what had occurred earlier in the hour, I knew his associations included a displacement of potential criticism or anger having to do with me. The memory reported referred manifestly to a recent episode in which his narcissism had been cruelly hurt. However, the displacement from me to his wife failed to achieve any significant degree of conscious mobilization or expression of aggression even at the safer location. As one can see, additional defensive measures occurred as he began to describe the memory, which was the new location of the drive derivative. That is, his fear of revealing to the analyst his aggression against women (at the moment, his wife in particular) forced him *to recapitulate, in memory,* avenues of bringing his aggression under control: reason, thoughtfulness, self-examination.

At this point two technical choices may be considered: an "inside" or an "outside" focus of attention regarding the defensive issue of his fear of aggressive feelings and thoughts about a woman, at the moment, his wife. For the sake of brevity and because it is not necessary to the illustration, we shall not concern ourselves with the issue of fear of aggression against the analyst. It was not neglected in the analysis, being dealt with somewhat later.

It could be surmised that in this man's actual relationship with his wife he had to defend himself repeatedly against consciousness of strong aggressive feelings against her. In the associations quoted, he was probably giving a summary of how he typically kept out of mind various degrees of sadistic impulses against her, for example, reaction-formation, turning on himself, passivity, symptom formation, and so forth. It might appear, therefore, that the present circumstance provided an opportunity to point out to the patient how he had been required yesterday to deal with his thoughts and feelings in relation to his wife. The rationale for this might be that if the patient could gain insight into an aspect of his relationship with his wife, or insight into how he deals with his aggression in his daily life, he would stand a better chance of becoming less afraid of his aggression. The perceptual focus in such remarks would be toward an ostensible episode in the patient's life from the previous day. The focus is "outside" the hour. To a degree, the analyst has now become involved in the life of the patient; an "external" reality is being, by implication, defined. Separately, but also of importance, *the displacement in time*—yesterday—is being strengthened. I would hasten to agree that these aspects are all compatible with interpretations that could result in therapeutic gain, as is regularly true of much that is "applied psychoanalysis," psychoanalytically oriented psychotherapy, and so on. My thesis, however, is that what has just been described as "outside" is peripheral to what is fundamentally psychoanalytic and consequently can unnecessarily dilute or distract from the analytic process and, in addition, strengthen the resistance against drive derivatives during the analytic hour and also against the degree of transference neurosis which might otherwise be achieved.

In this example, the "inside" perceptual focus was, in fact, conveyed by showing the patient that, as the association to a potentially provocative view of his wife came to mind, rather than experience *at that point, in the hour*, a degree of anger against her, he was required, because of fear of having and revealing such feelings in my presence, to recapitulate an emotion-controlling sequence.

In brief, during an analytic hour in which this patient had to avoid anger with his analyst, his solution was a displacement to a memory of another figure who had aroused his aggression. In the presence of the analyst, even in the displacement, the experience of aggression again became unsafe, and the immediate solution was further control—almost to the point of assuming a masochistic orientation. Any reference on the part of the analyst to the memory material, as if he were speaking of the outside event itself, would not only neglect observations about the location of the drive conflicts of the moment and the details of the defensive measures being employed, it would also be taking as literally true something almost certainly distorted, condensed, and out of context.

The analysand must eventually believe the analyst is confining his interest in him (and his mind) to the analytic setting. It is to be hoped that in time the patient will recognize that his many transference wishes for wider interest of the analyst are at odds with his need for a truly neutral observer with whom the greatest exposure can be risked. If the focus of attention is "outside," the way the patient experiences the analyst is shifted. He is experienced as involved in the patient's *life*, concerned beyond the analysis of the patient's mind, and the patient's sense of the analyst's neutrality likewise shifts. To the extent that the patient incorporates the analyst in this newly involved sense, he sacrifices some of the potential autonomy over his own mind. This is in contrast to what he can potentially achieve if he incorporates the analyst only for the task of gaining an understanding access to his unconscious mental processes and content.

The inevitability of a significant degree of such misidentification of the role of the analyst occurs in the following way and need not depend on any actual lack of neutrality on the part of the analyst. Attention to an "outside" orientation necessarily keeps active, for the patient, certain aspects of control of behavior, which are less relevant and even inimical to optimum analytic conditions "inside" the hour. The superego may be stimulated to reinforce defenses against the drives. When the patient contemplates memories of an external reality only in terms of dealing with the actual situation, he cannot afford to suspend certain of his usual superego functions or reality demands. He can gradually come to suspend these functions in a transient, voluntary way, in exchange for a differing set of realities, under the circumstances of a successfully conducted analytic situation. It is a common form of defense during an analytic hour for a patient to focus on the meanings of some current life experience away from the analyst, in order to support resistance to transference. The relief gained through such displacement is usually readily recognizable. Another factor sometimes overlooked is that the patient, by evoking the illusion that the outside situation with certain realistic dangers is being confronted, can mobilize superego regulation of the amount of affect permitted in consciousness at the moment. The familiar concept "reality-bound" involves this process.

When the analyst shifts his perspective of attention to examining the patient's thoughts on events and issues outside the analytic office *as realities*, rather than attending to them as details of the patient's stream of thought, he strongly risks tilting the point of view of the patient's ego toward an interest in *controlling behavior*, rather than toward a more fundamental analytic interest, namely, that of gaining as much voluntary access as possible to the various reaches of his mind. The increasing element of control over possible action that occurs when the patient experiences his productions in a reality-oriented context usually is unconscious. His observing superego, if intact, is automatically more careful about what is safe to experience. The objection that such an emphasis may produce an analysis that takes place "in a vacuum" need not be a concern. If successfully allowed to focus on the analyst through adequate development of the transference, the impulses and affects are concerned at such times with an actual and present, though distorted, object and have to be gradually experienced as consciously controllable.

In the reality of the analyst's presence, patients are often allowed gradually to experience impulses toward the analyst by virtue of the physically restraining aspect of the couch—both the instruction to remain upon it, and the immobility of the position itself. Patients at times can allow themselves impulses under these conditions which, in a more mobile position under other circumstances, could not be kept from action.

One encounters technical recommendations for involvement in the external lives of analysands, for example, encouragement or advice toward initiating sexual intercourse, to confront phobias, for grown children to move out of a parental home, to separate from a spouse on a trial basis, to undertake a particular piece of work. I share the opinion of others, such as Brenner (1969) in the instance of treatment of phobias, that these manipulations, intended to overcome resistance by force, inevitably change the circumstances of the analytic situation and necessitate a different kind of goal from that which we may strive to attain in a neutral setting.

One way of viewing the advantage of focusing the analysis on the mind of the patient rather than on the study of the patient's behavior is that the patient can come to share the recognition with the analyst that, unlike behavior, *thinking has no limitations*.

I have been considering how unnecessary attention to reality outside the "analytic stage" of the hour can strengthen the resistance against the patient's involvement in the analytic process. In defining the "analytic stage," I would include all the external environment of the immediate analytic setting within range of the patient's perceptual capacities, that is, the analyst and the physical surroundings, in addition, of course, to the patient's internal perceptions.

Certain contemporary events or crises that superimpose on the analysis important emotional burdens, such as the loss or serious threat of loss of a loved one, naturally are explicitly recognized as realities "outside." The resulting emotional task of the patient naturally extends inside his analytic hours, and the analyst is confronted with the attending processes, such as grief. The analysis of any defense against the patient's facing such a process may provide a better understanding of the patient's traditional forms of resistance. However, the direct benefits that the stable presence of the analyst and the analysis provide for the patient during such times are probably to a considerable extent, and unavoidably so, rather psychotherapeutic ones.

In addition to contributing to the deepening of the analytic process and to a more precise analysis of impulses which may also relate to acting out, I think greater "inside" attention may contribute toward another worthwhile goal. If a patient is deprived of the opportunity to fully develop his potential for truly experiencing his mental processes as "only thoughts," (rather than, for example, contemplated action, or action itself), he has missed a chance to achieve a greater degree of conscious control over pathologic stimulation of unwelcome affect. Ideally, and I believe this is a potential for the normal ego, an individual should have a choice of whether he will regard his inner life as pertaining at any given moment to external reality, or, on the other hand, as a manifestation of his psychological or mental functioning. He should have voluntary discrimination between outer and inner reality. In fact, this is precisely what we ask a patient to do when we call attention to the derivatives in his stream of thought, away from the external meanings toward the intrapsychic issues.

To the extent that this choice is made possible, the human mind becomes increasingly free to discover or release from neurotic inhibition the constructive uses of those functions ordinarily involved in fantasy. Creative imagination, as a concept, does not have to confine itself to the world of the artist or the genius. In its more mundane forms it facilitates reality testing in seeking solutions for everyday problems, as well as providing adaptational directions for dealing with life and death issues.

Extending the topic of the uses of memory within the technique of analysis, I would like to suggest a further refinement. In times during analysis when attention may focus upon the patient's so-called past, we are primarily attempting to clarify *memories* of the past, not necessarily the external realities of the past.[1] This is not at all to suggest that the external events or

---

[1]In this connection, recall from Freud's (1899, p. 322) paper concerning screen memories: "It may indeed be questioned whether we have memories at all *from* our childhood: memories *relating to* our childhood may be all we possess."

conditions are of any less importance as genetic factors, but to recognize that it is the uncovering or reconstruction of the precise way such things have been stored in the patient's psyche that accomplishes the analytic result. These recordings are the still present, *structuralized* psychic realities we are attempting to make available to conscious ego influence.[2]

The eventual important unconscious psychic realities may be condensations of experiences that, in a conglomerate form exist as a repressed "event," but need not correspond with precise reality of the past. If, as the analysis proceeds, reconstructions of these psychic realities are achieved, then the patient is free, if he so chooses, to concern himself with documentation of the actual realities, or to apply his judgment in assessing the validity of these early perceptual impressions. As we know, it was the way these early events, external and internal, were perceived that contributed to the structure of the subsequent conflicts.

We are used to viewing the question, "Is it a memory?" as if we were inquiring, "Is that the way it happened?" As a result, if while analyzing we focus our perceptual attention too much on the "event" (which in non-analytic situations is obviously of legitimate clinical interest), it may tend to distract our attention from how the patient perceived what we are referring to as a possible memory. When the issues inherent in the possible memory are made available, the patient's freer ego capacities may permit him to make new accommodations to them; these should not have to depend on the "facts" of historical actualities, but rather on the working-through in respect to the memories, mnemic registrations with which the patient is eternally burdened. This does not exclude the possibilities for recovery of evidence distinguishing between real events and fantasy, nor does the discussion here attempt to deal in any way with issues

[2]And a later observation: "The phantasies possess *psychical* as contrasted with *material* reality, and we gradually learn to understand that *in the world of the neuroses it is psychical reality which is the decisive kind*" (Freud 1917a, p. 368).

such as the relative etiologic importance of actual events as compared with fantasied ones. The capacity to distinguish between things perceived as "real," in the sense of being external, and things perceived as fantasy remains an important function for the ego to be able to exercise.

At this point, a parallel may be apparent to the analyst's perceptual focus regarding more recent outside realities, discussed earlier. I believe the rationale is the same in both instances. In the instance of contemporary memories, I indicated that optimally the patient should come to make a conscious use of the ego's capacity for perceiving what is on his mind in either a psychoanalytically inside or outside sense. In the case of the more distant past, however, in contrast to the contemporary past, I believe it is unnecessary to expect the *patient* to recognize this perceptual distinction. As earlier memories are recovered, abreacted, worked through, and so on, the patient more or less spontaneously comes to view their importance as psychic realities rather than something only for "reliving."

I believe that once the analyst (or potential analyst) has become an important object for the patient for real as well as transference reasons, behavior occurring within the duration of the analysis is registered with memory traces that in some way include the analyst. These traces that are partly linked with the analyst become a permanent part of the patient's storehouse of experiences. When these particular experiences are treated primarily by the analyst as *experiences*—actual events outside the immediate psychoanalytic hour—rather than as the inner psychic realities with which the patient's defensive functions are concerned, it then becomes, because of the fixed (structural) affinity with the analyst, especially likely for the patient to perceive the analyst's focus of interest as having to do with the way the patient lives his life, rather than the way his mind functions. That the memories acquired during an analysis may always include as part of their structure some aspect of the analyst could be an important factor in the dramatic repetition of many aspects of a previous analysis that occurs when such individuals subsequently undertake an analytic re-exploration. These repetitions have been described in some detail by Pfeffer (1959, 1961).

There are certain natural tendencies that can lead to focusing on the patient's productions in terms of the "outside" realities to which they happen to refer, and away from their immediacy and complexity as "inside" manifestations. I do not think that these tendencies necessarily warrant the label of countertransference issues, although they may lend themselves to forms of counter-resistance. Because there are varying degrees of sublimated scoptophilic interests involved in the work of analyzing, thinking of the patient's productions in terms of actual events may for some tend to be a more interesting level of attention. Anyone who has conducted psychoanalytic supervision has had the opportunity to observe in some supervisees a conspicuously heightened sense of pleasure and shift in mode of presenting the material when speaking of what "happened" in the patient's contemporary life, in contrast to when he is focusing attention on what the patient has said in terms of its meaning as part of the patient's stream of thought.

Not all analytic patients are equally capable of achieving the perceptual or experiential distinctions required by some of the technical observations discussed here. At the present time I am not sure whether this is primarily owing to certain differences in cognitive ability—especially limitations in the area of concept formation (often the ego's defenses, which have to be understood by the patient before they can be perceived, are relatively complex)—or whether the limitations are in the nature of ego inhibitions, variabilities, or deficiencies, or perhaps combinations of all of these. The possession of such a capacity is probably part of what we mean when we speak of "psychological mindedness," as well as being an aspect of intelligence. Certainly, it is true that capacities to grasp some of the focus distinctions in order to bring the ego to bear on them are often defensively interfered with. Some patients remain "reality-bound," not only to avoid a greater freedom of thought generally, but because of a virtual inability to "look inward" when such looking has become instinctually involved as a scoptophilic activity.

The preceding observations suggest a technical approach which attempts to provide an opportunity for developing the patient's self-observing capacities to their greatest potential. While both capacity and potential vary, most patients who come for analysis have a reasonable potential in this regard. I think that virtually all analysands who have been judged suitable for analytic training are potentially capable of making the introspective discriminations which have been discussed.

Today, for various reasons, reanalysis of analysts is not as widespread as Freud (1937) and many others have urged, and this is a highly regrettable trend. On the other hand, to an increasing degree, emphasis is placed upon the importance of trying to provide the potential analyst, within his therapeutic training analysis, with as much capacity for eventual self-analysis as possible. These encouragements have rarely, if ever, been accompanied by specific suggestions within our technique for furthering this goal. The guidelines have usually consisted only of reminders that the training analysis needs to be more thorough than the nontraining analysis.

Many highly developed skills make use of ego processes that are utilized quite out of the range of consciousness and, in many instances, out of the range of available understanding. Certainly, the basic discoveries and concepts of psychoanalysis were developed without an understanding of many of the ego processes that eventually came under consideration. However, if one attempts to make a historical examination of the development of the practice and theory of psychoanalytic technique, certain trends emerge. Of particular interest is the trend against the analyst's unnecessarily pre-empting the ego functions of the patient undergoing analysis. In the early days of analysis, hypnosis stood as the maximum degree of the analyst's assumption of ego functions for the patient. Through the years the patient has been required increasingly to assume responsibility for the existence of the various mechanisms of defense and other aspects of resistance. Concurrently there has been an increasingly explicit recognition given to providing opportunity for the necessary ego exercise, so that the patient might master his responsibility.

By projecting such patterns of technical development into the future, it should be possible to anticipate particular areas in which further development of technique can theoretically take place. Gradually increasing recognition given to the study of self-analysis (Fleming 1971, Kramer 1959, Ticho 1967) may suggest a trend toward technical interests at the other end of a spectrum which began in the early period of analysis with hypnosis. Contemporary ways of referring to the analyst's task, such as Kohut's (1968b, p. 550) "self-analysis with the aid of the analyst," are relevant to the natural evolution of psychoanalytic technique.

Just as it became necessary for the analyst, in order to bring about the patient's potential sense of responsibility for resistance against the analytic process, to identify and then clearly describe the mechanisms of defense of the ego, so is it becoming necessary and possible to conceptualize the functioning of the ego in a wider variety of ways, so that these too can be brought into the ego's awareness and thereby subject to greater degrees of regulation.

The emphasis here has been upon those ego functions that are involved in the process of self-observation. Ego functions that have become drawn into compromise formations might, for practical purposes, be regarded as handicapped by conversion symptoms within the ego itself. Obviously, unless an analysand can be made to recognize the existence and form of those mental processes which are called into play during the task of analysis, including some of the ways in which his perception of "what is on his mind" takes place, those symptoms would hardly be analyzed and the involved ego functions would not be brought back under the control of the patient. Herein lies the opportunity for making the fullest use of mental functions related to self-observation. That these functions are studied and positively exploited to a lesser degree than many other capacities of man probably derives from their history of narcissistic involvement—in both a genetic and traditional sense. Kohut has eloquently discussed the problems confronting the analyst (and patient) who would approach narcissistic elements with respect for their developmental potential, rather than emphasizing them only as defensively self-centering (Kohut 1968a). Nevertheless, we must recognize that it is always this self-contemplating part of the patient's ego upon which we are primarily dependent and which we try to "split" off so that analysis can possibly take place.

Making the patient aware of some of these internal processes at times is primarily educative, for it may never have occurred to the individual to look at such parts of himself. More characteristically, resistance moves in against such knowledge, and the resulting learning inhibition requires analysis.

To be able, voluntarily, to explore ideas and significantly regulate the dosage of affect accompanying those ideas is to give the process of "trial action" a greater versatility, and one which is probably within the capacity of the unhampered mature ego. This requires capacity for neutralization of affect, rather than resorting to mechanisms of defense.

CONCLUSION

In summary, this has been a consideration of that aspect of analysis of the neuroses concerned with the listening analyst's perspective of attention or perceptual focus. A preference has been indicated for adjusting this focus so as to observe data limited essentially to *inside* the analytic situation. Elaboration of this point of view included illustrating specific advantages that it offers in the analysis of communications of the patient referring to current or contemplated behavior *outside* the analytic situation, sometimes labeled as "acting out."

The preceding have been considered in terms of the evolution of psychoanalytic technique—the increasing understanding of the role of the ego, the diminishing importance of measures of suggestion and persuasion, the increasing awareness of the importance of not pre-empting the patient's ego functions during the course of the analysis.

It is suggested that the ideas that are stressed are also in the interest of improving analysands' capacities for eventual self-analysis. I believe that greater effectiveness of psychoanalytic technique in increasing the ego's autonomy lies in further discoveries about the functions with which the normal ego can perceive itself.

2

"DEVELOPMENTAL LAG" IN THE EVOLUTION OF TECHNIQUE

An important element—if not the most important element—in comparing one analyst's technical approach with that of another lies in identifying, in more than usual detail, the manner or choice of the analyst's *forms of attention* during the conduct of the analysis. In a previous essay (Gray 1973) I examined and described elements of such focus—by the analyst and in due time by the analysand—that have evolved in the course of the developing practice and theory of analysis of the neuroses, or to express it more realistically, *might well be expected to have evolved.*

Anyone interested in the technique of classical analysis who has observed clinical presentations, experienced supervisions both passively and actively, and has taken part in those activities both "at home" and away becomes aware of distinct variations in the way different analysts focus upon patients' productions. Moments in our literature that provide suitable details further convey an impression of the existence of such a spectrum of practice. Thanks to a mitigating "scientific tact," to borrow a phrase attributed to Freud (Sterba 1978, p. 191), this state of affairs has usually resisted close scrutiny, and admissions of such variations are often accompanied by an attempted explanation that there are of course "differences in *style.*"

It has for some time been my conclusion, rightly or wrongly, that the way a considerable proportion of analysts listen to and perceive their data has, in certain significant respects, *not* evolved as I believe it would have if historically important concepts concerned with the defensive functions of the ego had been wholeheartedly allowed their place in the actual application of psychoanalytic technique. Study of the literature reveals that although for the most part they are quite brief, observations concerning delay in applying ego theory to technique are not new (Hartmann 1951, Sterba 1953, Stone 1973, Waelder 1967). Rather than review them here, I shall include references to them at those places where I feel they have particular application.

In this paper I am proposing the hypothesis that the above observations are manifestations of what I call a *developmental lag* in fully assimilating and applying certain of the information that has been acquired about the ego's importance in the therapeutic effectiveness of the psychoanalytic method. I shall restrict the term "developmental lag" to that of a convenient metaphor, borrowed from the long-familiar analytic terrain (rather than from the varied, more specialized contemporary uses of "developmental"). If in time it should appear to have a somewhat more legitimate place in this present context than as a mere metaphor, I shall not be disappointed.

The standard explanation for the relatively slow emergence of conceptualizations about the ego holds that it was a matter of precedence, governed by time, expressed usually as: in the beginning there was interest in the repressed *content*, and naturally it took time to come to perceive the nature of the ego in its complexity. If my thesis is valid, that there exists a universal *resistance* to truly assimilating certain concepts concerning the ego, then the standard explanation, lending as it does an appearance of an even rate of development to our theories, may not be adequate. It also follows that Freud would have shared this resistance.

For the time being, I shall reserve judgment as to whether the evidence for and characteristics of this lag are the consequences of an organic limitation in the ego's capacity to perceive itself, or due to a potentially modifiable resistance, borne out of intrapsychic conflict. Since I lean toward the latter, more optimistic perspective, I shall examine some of the data which I take to support the hypothesis that there exists a developmental lag and offer some speculations concerning psychological motivations for such a lag.

I

The first significant and far-reaching step toward modern ego-involving psychoanalytic technique was abandoning the use of hypnotic trance (Freud 1910). This step was decisive; classical analysis has not returned to the full use of hypnotic influence, primarily because "results were capricious and not lasting" (Freud 1917b, p. 292). As we know, coinciding with and contributing to this development was the discovery that the patient's conscious, voluntary cooperation could be enlisted to overcome repression. Although the initial manifestation of this cooperation was essentially the patient's attempt to free-associate, it soon became technically important to call the patient's attention to the existence of a resistance to do so. A brief transition period occurred, during which a supplementary laying on of hands was part of the persuasive method; nevertheless, the trend was definitely in the direction of making more use of the relatively autonomous aspects of the patient's psyche, in effect avoiding bypassing important components of the ego.

Although there does not seem to have been an explicit formulation of these trends, I believe they allow for an inference or hypothesis that *the therapeutic results of analytic treatment are lasting in proportion to the extent to which, during the analysis, the patient's unbypassed ego functions have become involved in a consciously and increasingly voluntary co-partnership with the analyst.*[1]

Coinciding with the phasing-in of the knowledge that resistance in analysis was not directed primarily against recall of traumatic past events, but against the emergence into consciousness of live impulses—with their attendant wish or fantasy components—came a second major element affecting technique: the principle that the important work of analysis lay primarily in working with the patient's resistances. Part and parcel of this trend was a rather slow acknowledgment that resistances themselves, although not part of the repressed, were in fact unconscious. Because this recognition is often cited as the stimulus for the formation of the structural theory, the illusion is created that this recognition was a rather late "discovery." Waelder (1967), in a discussion of defense mechanisms, points out that "It was first in *The Ego and the Id* that Freud stated *clearly* that parts of the ego were unconscious too . . . ," but adds, in a footnote, "Against this it may be held that Freud referred to defense as unconscious in one of his earliest papers: 'symptoms arose through the psychical mechanism of (unconscious) defence—that is, in an attempt to repress an incompatible idea . . .' (1896, p. 162)." Waelder continues, "But the unconsciousness of defense was then neither explained nor elaborated and applied in theory and technique and Freud referred more than twenty-five years later to unconscious guilt feelings as a 'new discovery' (1923, p. 27). Thus, while the passage proves that the idea was present, or germinating, in Freud's mind, it can hardly be maintained that it was already part of psychoanalysis as a common and communicable body of knowledge or theory" (Waelder 1967, p. 354; italics added).

Waelder adds other evidence that, from the beginning, Freud showed the need to pay attention to the ego in work with patients. Waelder credits Anna Freud with the crucial step from the early aim in technique of *overcoming* the resistances, to the

---

[1]Thereby including what in a perceptive and practical study by Gutheil and Havens (1979) is felicitously called a "rational alliance."

contemporary aim (I would say the *ostensible* contemporary aim) of understanding and learning how to control them. He does not comment on the subsequent irregularities or the inertia in the application of Anna Freud's innovation; nor does he refer to the possibility of any ubiquitous internal conflicts contributing to the slow emergence of ego applications to technique. The suggestion he offers is only that the relatively slow pace was influenced by the unappealingly teleological nature of the ego concepts. Waelder's observations indicate how Freud early on gave evidence of perceptions that might have led sooner than was the case to a greater attention to, and a more effective use of, the ego in technique.

From 1913 to 1917 Freud's papers contained more specific statements about psychoanalytic technique. They remain the most profound, incomparable contributions to the subject, yet there is evidence within them regarding the "lag." I believe there is specific importance to my thesis in Freud's style of referring to earlier ideas while simultaneously adding newly developed ones. It could be argued that, in general, Freud never entirely abandoned *any* of his previously held positions. He appears, at times, to have added new ideas somewhat in the manner of his miraculous archeological "dig."

> Now let us, by a flight of imagination, suppose that Rome is not a human habitation but a psychical entity with a similarly long and copious past—an entity, that is to say, in which nothing that has once come into existence will have passed away and all the earlier phases of development continue to exist alongside the latest ones. [He then lists many coexisting structures.] And the observer would perhaps only have to change the direction of his glance or his position in order to call up the one view or the other. [Freud 1930, p. 70]

While trying to find special implications in certain inconsistencies and ambiguities in Freud's statements relevant to technique, one also ought to keep in mind the sometimes offered explanation that Freud hesitated to write about technique because he wished to avoid putting such knowledge in the hands of unqualified individuals. Could this have contributed to an illusion of lag? I believe a more significant element is involved than either a reluctance to abandon a cherished position[2] or some measure of restraint in spelling out details of technique. I believe that Freud was in fact *ambivalent about the trend of involving more of the patient's ego during the analysis*—a trend in technique for which he was, of course, responsible.

Freud (1913), in discussing the nature of communications to the patient and speaking of sources of information about what exists in the patient's repressed unconscious, says, "It is not difficult for a skilled analyst to read the patient's secret wishes plainly between the lines of his complaints and the story of his illness." However, Freud condemns analysts who through early direct interpretations "arouse . . . violent opposition in [the patient]"; further, "As a rule the therapeutic effect will be nil; but the deterring of the patient from analysis will be final." Of himself, he states, "In former years I often had occasion to find that the premature communication of a solution brought the treatment to an untimely end, on account not only of the resistances which it thus suddenly awakened, but also of the relief which the solution brought with it." He includes an apparently unequivocal precept: "Even in the later stages of analysis one must be careful not to give a patient the solution of a symptom or the translation of a wish until he is already so close to it that he has only one short step more to make in order to get hold of the explanation for himself" (pp. 140–141, *passim*). Here the trend to work with material near the surface is so clear that the recommended interpretations even bear resemblance to what Bibring (1954) was eventually to call a "clarification."

[2]I am aware of Kuhn's (1970) illuminating account of the general difficulty encountered by scientists in paradigm change. I believe that the difficulties encountered by scientists in accepting paradigms that deal with dynamically unconscious elements compound those described by Kuhn.

Freud's main point here is the futility, and often harm to analysis, of an emphasis on the imparting of "knowledge" to patients about their repressed unconscious. He nails this point down by implying similarity between technical reliance on direct interpretations of the analyst's impressions of the repressed contents and that of telling the patient factual information about traumas, which has been gleaned from relatives. Following a clinical illustration, Freud concludes he had "no choice but to cease attributing to the fact of knowing, in itself, the importance that had previously been given to it and to place the emphasis on the *resistances*. . . . Conscious knowledge was . . . powerless against those resistances" (italics added). Freud then overrides the trend he has just been espousing by adding, "For the sake of complete accuracy, however, it should be added that the communication of repressed material to the patient's consciousness is nevertheless not without effect. It does not produce the hoped-for result of putting an end to the symptoms; but it has other consequences. At first it arouses resistances, but then, when these have been overcome, it sets up a process of thought in the course of which the expected influencing of the unconscious recollection eventually takes place" (p. 142). In an inconsistency here, Freud has maintained room for his previous approach of establishing by interpretation a "record" or impression, in consciousness, of what is presumed to exist as a separate record in the repressed unconscious (Freud 1910, p. 42), and in so doing, he again gives credibility to "deep" interpretations.[3]

Later, Freud (1914) indicates that making interpretations "from the patient's free associations, what he failed to remember" is a technique of the past. Now the analyst

> contents himself with studying whatever is present . . . on the *surface* of the patient's mind, and he employs the art of interpretation mainly for the purpose of recognizing the resistances

---

[3]By "deep," I mean here interpretations of repressed unconscious material which present the patient "with thoughts that he had so far shown no signs of possessing . . ." (Freud 1909, p. 104).

> which appear there, and making them conscious to the patient. From this there results a new sort of division of labour: the doctor uncovers the resistances which are unknown to the patient; when these have been got the better of, the patient often relates the forgotten situations and connections without any difficulty. [p. 147; italics added]

The "two-records" approach and deep interpretations have apparently now been laid to rest. Strachey's classic contribution in 1934 was a brilliant attempt to summarize and synthesize almost everything up to that time pertaining to the therapeutic action of psychoanalysis. It contained many technical implications and recapitulates Freud's progress beyond the earlier technical practices of approaching the id more directly. Strachey referred to the early approach of *naming* in order to establish a registration in the consciousness of an otherwise repressed trend of "objectionable" thought, stating that "It was only if these two impressions could be 'brought together' (whatever exactly that might mean) that the unconscious trend would be 'really' made conscious." He then reviewed the progress made in giving more attention to the resistance, indicating that ". . . it was at this point that the *practical* lesson emerged: as analysts our main task is *not so much to investigate the objectionable unconscious trend as to get rid of the patients' resistance to it*" (p. 276; italics added).

Despite an extraordinary capacity for grasping the extent to which various lines of psychoanalytic thought had progressed at that time, Strachey failed to make the decisive observations Anna Freud made soon after. I think that his failure to do so was another measure of the elusiveness of the applications to technique of the pertinent ego concepts.

Hartmann (1951) provides one of the most explicit statements in the literature on the existence of a lack of integration between psychoanalytic theory and psychoanalytic technique. His central point, "the lag is . . . on the side of technique [rather] than on the side of theory and of psychological insight" (p. 143), refers to insight about the ego. Apropos Freud's technical papers under discussion above, Hartmann regards the occurrence of Freud's explicit attention to the priority of working with resistance "without at first realizing all its implications for ego psychology" as indicating one time when theory lagged behind technique. It is true that Freud's conclusion that the analyst contents himself with studying what is on the surface of the patient's mind, and uses interpretation mainly for dealing with resistance, was to be conceptually enhanced with the eventual formation of the structural theory. However, his concurrent theory provided adequate support for this technical advance. Freud (1915) states, "indeed . . . if [an idea] is not inhibited by the censorship, it regularly advances from one position [*Ucs.*] to the other [*Cs.*]" (p. 175). Here is a theoretical concept sufficient to support any developing priority for analytic attention to the resistances.

Twenty-three years after the important 1914 technical statement, however, Freud resurrects the earlier approach in his paper, "Constructions" (1937b), when he describes communicating to the patient extensive reconstructions to create an impression in the patient's consciousness "so that it may work upon him" (p. 260). It is almost as though the refinements of ego analysis, which by then had been elaborated from Freud's own observations by Wilhelm Reich, Anna Freud, Richard Sterba, Otto Fenichel, and others, had never taken place. To my knowledge, only Stone (1973) has taken notice of this major inconsistency, when he spoke of "Freud's early, never fully relinquished biphasic process" (p. 47).[4]

Since those resistances, which in Freud's writings later became the mechanisms of defense, had early been assigned to some version of the ego, it follows that whenever he did give precedence to working on the resistance he was of course speaking of working on or dealing with the ego. Many of his descriptions or recommendations sound almost modern (i.e.,

---

[4]Stone refers to a pre–Anna Freud "cultural lag in the sphere of resistance analysis. . . . "

post–Anna Freud), if one fails to realize that Freud was not speaking of analyzing the ego in the manner eventually conceptualized. To "work upon," to "overcome," to "deal with" the resistances involves technical measures that are often different from those used in *analyzing* defenses. Yet Freud was unequivocal in his recognition that the key to effective, lasting therapeutic results lay in reversing the pathological alterations that the defense mechanisms had wrought on the ego. This is illustrated by his observation: "Indeed we come finally to understand that the overcoming of these resistances is *the essential function of analysis and is the only part of our work that gives us an assurance that we have achieved something with the patient*" (Freud 1917b, p. 291; italics added).

What was it that Freud, if he was not *analyzing* the defenses, had primarily relied on to influence the ego? I have touched on the persistence of the biphasic technical device of interpretatively establishing "two records." There is a more fundamental factor that should be explored.

Dropping full-scale hypnosis or hypnotic trance from psychoanalytic technique did not result in the exclusion of suggestion—a partial hypnosis[5]—to *influence* the patient. Just as strong positive transference was the earlier vehicle for the trance-hypnosis which entirely excluded the ego's participation, so positive transference became the vehicle for *influencing* the patient's participation in the analytic process. The *authoritarian* element, although applied with a different emphasis, was nevertheless preserved. In lieu of a not yet developed technique for *analyzing* the defenses, Freud retained the force available for "influencing" and "overcoming" them, namely the power of suggestion: no longer utilizing the trance, but using the related device of relying on the *ego-disarming* quality of the positive transference. Freud (1917b) acknowledged this:

[5]Both Ferenczi and Bernheim regarded hypnosis as only a form of suggestion. For a full consideration of the matter, see Gill and Brenman (1961).

> If the patient is to fight his way through . . . resistances which we have *uncovered* . . . he is in need of a powerful stimulus which will influence the decision in the *sense we desire*. . . . At this point what turns the scale . . . is . . . simply and solely his relation to the doctor. In so far as his transference bears a 'plus' sign, it clothes the doctor with *authority* and is transformed into *belief* in his communications . . . [p. 445; italics added]. The change which is decisive for a favourable outcome is the elimination of repression. . . . This is made possible by the alteration of the ego which is *accomplished under the influence of the doctor's suggestion*. [p. 455; italics added]

Prior to a more detailed grasp of the ego's mechanisms in its defensive role, the continued use of a partially hypnotic influence was a necessary technical adjunct. Judging from the last quotation, the use of suggestion to overcome resistances appears to have continued for Freud, and has to the present time continued for many analysts as an accepted part of their work, giving further evidence of the lag in integrating knowledge of the ego into psychoanalytic technique. I would not dispute that suggestive influence may be to some degree inevitable in any human interaction, but I am referring to dependence on it and a fostering of it in the analytic situation. Many practitioners who may not be particularly interested in sorting out therapeutic factors in their analytic work and who do not knowingly use suggestion might object to any implication that they were doing so. However, the analyst who makes interpretative remarks referring to unconscious matters of which the patient cannot become aware—instead of referring to ". . . a preconscious derivative which can be recognized as such by the patient *merely by turning his attention* toward it" (Fenichel 1941, p. 18; italics added)—has left the patient to take the interpretation "on faith" and is still making use of the "two-record," biphasic method. This is an authoritative approach that relies heavily on suggestion to influence rather than on analysis of the resistance. Recent critical examinations of some of the processes and factors subsumed or hidden under references to "therapeutic alliance" (Brenner 1979) should help clarify this little-discussed area of persistent hypnotic-suggestive influences in analytic technique.

Clearly, not only Freud had a tendency to draw back from fully applying to technique the acquired knowledge of the ego's role in attaining therapeutic action. Recurrent observations stressing therapeutic advantages in giving the ego a more prominent position in the overall task of making the unconscious analytically conscious are often treated as if they were discoveries or new points of view rather than elaborations on parts of Freud's own earlier observations. Memories of references to the ego's unconscious defensive activities tend, with time, to undergo retroactive blurring or distortion, so that a rereading of some of the "classic" contributions on the subject can produce some surprises. Reich is an early contributor among those associated with the uneven emergence in analytic technique of priority for "defense before drive" analysis. Reich's contribution is generally remembered for his rather extreme concept of "armoring" and the rather heavy-handed technical measures involved, matters which are in fact largely found only in the *later* part of his classic paper, "Character Analysis" (1928); there the difficulties he speaks of encountering, with patients we would likely include today in the categories of narcissistic character disorders or narcissistic personality disorders, are formidable to be sure. However, his thoughtful and detailed suggestions pertaining to the analysis of defenses of the more clearly neurotic conditions very closely resemble many of Anna Freud's eventual observations. Anna Freud was certainly not unmindful of Reich's early contributions. However, that Freud himself does not once mention Reich's early, reasonably presented technical recommendations may be difficult to explain entirely in relation to Reich's later fall to unacceptability with his eventual analytically foreign ideas. I am of course implying that there was something about the nature of ideas that gave such priority to resistance *analysis* that Freud treated with reservations.

Anna Freud's (1936) monograph, with its clarity and detail

regarding the ego's function in relation to the instinctual drives—in particular during the analytic process—went beyond Reich in elaborating the analysis of the transferences of defense. Only one of the several early reviewers, Ernst Kris (1938), captured the essence of her insights and recommendations. He referred to them as "something *entirely new*, not only in point of form, but in the penetration of the material." He alone drew attention to her calling for "a change in the method of observation" (p. 139; italics added) to provide a more effective technical approach. The phrase Anna Freud used was "change the focus of attention" (p. 20). An even, hovering attention, tuned via the analyst's unconscious primarily to the drive derivatives, was no longer sufficient to satisfy the technical requirements. Kris not only made note of her new way of analytic listening, but in a unique and prophetic observation anticipated that "the *change in the mode of observation might* pass unnoticed" by other analysts (Kris 1938, p. 139; italics added). Unfortunately, he failed to comment on why analysts might be so resistant to this development. However, he continued throughout his career to implicitly support the increased importance of ego analysis by a deemphasis on the therapeutic value of highly specific reconstructive interpretations (Kris 1956).

Almost twenty years later Sterba bore witness to the accuracy of Kris's early prophesy. Sterba is among those few who openly recognized and accepted the greater technical demand imposed on the analyst when there is more explicit perception and interpretation of the patient's ego. His early contributions (1934, 1940) indicate his consistent interest in this area. He may have anticipated some of Anna Freud's recommendations. Later, Sterba expressed concern over the shallowness of many of the contemporary analysts' comprehension and use of Anna Freud's recommendations:

> It is my impression the importance of this newest addition to our science has not been sufficiently recognized and that it has not yet penetrated the thinking and therapeutic technique of

> most analysts. It is easy to understand why this is so. We are still very much impressed, even fascinated by the id contents which psychoanalysis enables us to discover. The working of the ego is so inconspicuous and silent that we are hardly aware of it. . . . We never can catch [the unconscious defenses] at work; we can only reconstruct them from the result. While one can listen with the "third ear" to the utterances of the id, it needs a most refined instrument to register the workings of the ego defenses. It has been my observation that it is a most difficult task to teach students to pay attention to these mute and subterranean workings of the ego. Even the experienced analyst must constantly exercise self-discipline in order to remain aware of the ego's defense measures in therapy. . . . [J]udging from my experience as a teacher, from our scientific meetings and from the current literature I find too little real influence of Anna Freud's studies, although often lip service is paid to them. "Mechanism of defense" is used glibly to indicate the advanced state of one's analytic thinking, and "identification with the aggressor" is mentioned in order to display consideration of the ego. I believe it will require a great deal of time and effort on the part of training analysts to make Anna Freud's discoveries of the silent activities of the ego penetrate general analytic thinking and improve psychoanalytic technique so that it will consist of id-plus-ego analysis, applied alternatingly. [Sterba 1953, pp. 17–18]

Sterba could validly make these same observations today.

We can see that among the internal factors at work in the slow adoption of technical modifications, such as Anna Freud describes, are numerous misperceptions of what is meant by *defense* or *ego analysis*. One of the more common is expressed, "Of course analyzing the defenses is important, but one must analyze the drives also." This perspective fails to recognize that to observe a defense—much less to demonstrate its existence and motive to the analysand—is, with rare exception, not possible without having perceived and referred to the id derivative against which it is directed. Another distortion: "Interpret defense before drive" is frequently rendered as, "At the beginning of the analysis one is concerned with defenses, but then one gets down to the *real* analysis"—another example of how knowledge of the ego in neurosis slips away. It is as if Freud had not observed, the patient "meets us with a violent and tenacious resistance, *which persists throughout the whole length of the treatment*" (Freud 1917a, p. 286; italics added).

There have been singular attempts to correct such distortions, notably by Fenichel (1941), who demonstrates so clearly that reference to the defense, and then to the drive derivative defended against, typically takes place within a single interpretation. Appropriate defense analysis does gradually strengthen the ego and bring change in the intensity or predominant form of defense. However, to conceptualize a technique which after a while would not have to work with the ego appears either illusory or implies the use of a degree of hypnotic-suggestive influence which would prevent the ego from full participation in the analytic process. Freud's (1915) observation, ". . . we shall . . . assume that to every transition from one system to that immediately above it (that is, every advance to a higher stage of psychical organization) there corresponds a new censorship" (p. 192) has rarely been grasped as a recognition of the hierarchical concept of the defensive functioning of the ego during the analyzing process. It is a theoretical point that when taken seriously guides one to work technically from the side of the ego throughout the analysis. Freud (1913) came very close to expressing such a conclusion. He obviously recognized the important distinction of the evolving technical approach from that of the early authoritative id-content interpretive emphasis:

> If the patient starts his treatment under the auspices of mild and unpronounced positive transference it makes it possible at first for him to unearth his memories *just as he would under hypnosis*, and during this time his pathological symptoms themselves are quiescent. But if, as the analysis proceeds, the transference

> becomes hostile or unduly intense and therefore in need of repression, remembering at once gives way to acting out.[6] From then onwards the resistances determine the sequence of the material which is to be repeated. *The patient brings out of the armoury of the past the weapons with which he defends himself* against the progress of the treatment—weapons which we must wrest from him one by one. . . . We have . . . made it clear . . . that we must treat his illness, not as an event of the past, but as a present-day force. [Freud 1914, p. 151; italics added]

Fenichel refers to the general inertia in translating observations regarding resistance into technical development. He stated, "One of the stimuli to the development of so-called 'analytic ego psychology' was insight into the fact that *resistance* [author's italics] analysis is the real therapeutic agent . . . the volume of the literature concerning the newly gained psychological insight is incomparably greater than the number of papers which seek to *utilize this insight to contribute to an improvement of psychoanalytic technique*" (Fenichel 1941, p. 106; italics added). In addition to referring to Anna Freud's work, he spoke of one paper by Nina Searl (1936) which attempted to "clarify what it means to *analyze* a resistance in contradistinction to refuting a resistance."[7] Since then it continues to be just as rare to find papers specifically concerned with that issue.

Freud's treatment of the developments in defense analysis in the mid-thirties deserves special attention. When Anna Freud spoke in Philadelphia in 1973, she said she had prepared her (1936) monograph in honor of her father's 80th birthday. She indicated it was to be a summary of her father's ideas on the

[6]Here Freud uses "acting out" in its original form, that is to say, within the analytic setting.

[7]Why this gifted writer's contribution, with its many helpful guides to understanding some of the principles and techniques of defense analysis, has remained virtually untouched is a mystery and is probably germane to my thesis. In a sensitive tribute to another "neglected classic" of Searl's, Scott (1976) suggests that in late life there may have been parallels with the development of Wilhelm Reich's career.

subject. Kris and others would of course see it otherwise. Freud himself made reference to this work in only two of his papers. First, there was a brief comment in anticipation: "An investigation is at this moment being carried on close at hand which is devoted to the study of [the ego's] methods of defence: my daughter, the child analyst, is writing a book upon them" (Freud 1936, p. 245).

After the monograph appeared, Freud had time to write six more papers. In only one of these—"Analysis Terminable and Interminable" (1937a)—does he speak of her work (pp. 236, 238), seemingly crediting her with the essential ideas she expresses. Section V of Freud's (1937a) paper, if read carefully, reveals evidence of *a change in Freud's way of regarding the analyst's approach to observing ego resistance* as compared with the approach that characterized some of the important developments within his outstanding early technical statements. Let us compare his earlier and later comments.

"The patient's resistance is of very many sorts, *extremely subtle and often hard to detect*" (Freud 1917a, p. 287, italics added). This opinion is quite in keeping with Anna Freud's eventual description of the ego's defenses, activities so subtle that they "can only be reconstructed" (A. Freud, 1936, p. 2) after the mechanism has taken place. And this is in keeping with Sterba's remarks that "it needs a most refined instrument to register the working of the ego defenses" (Sterba 1953, pp. 17–18). Later, however, we find Freud (1937a) saying of resistances, "The analyst recognizes them more easily than he does the hidden material in the id" (p. 239); I regard this as a lapse.

The most revealing evidence that at this time in his life Freud did not see eye to eye with Anna Freud's clarifying and probably original concepts concerning the technique of defense analysis—more exactly, the analysis of transference of defense—lies in his discussion of the "alterations of the ego" which have been brought about by the mechanisms of defense. Here is where he elaborates upon the idea of "resistance against the uncovering of resistances." Freud had said for so long that mechanisms of defense are automatic, dynamically unconscious activities of the ego, that to some extent his phrase was redundant. However, Freud uses the phrase in the context of discussing massive increases in resistance on the part of the patient when the analyst approaches *dealing* with the resistances:

> One might suppose that it would be sufficient to *treat them* [the ego's defenses] *like portions of the id* [italics added] and, by making them conscious, bring them into connection with the rest of the ego. . . . But what happens is this. . . . The ego ceases to support our efforts at uncovering the id . . . , negative transferences may now gain the upper hand and completely annul the analytic situation. The patient now regards the analyst as no more than a stranger who is making disagreeable demands on him, and he behaves towards him exactly like a child and does not believe everything he says. If the analyst tries to explain to the patient one of the distortions made by him for the purpose of defence, and to correct it, he finds him uncomprehending and *inaccessible to sound arguments* [italics added]. Thus we see that there *is* a resistance against the uncovering of resistances. . . . [Freud 1937a, p. 239]

I would argue that what Freud describes is a classic example of an analytic patient who has experienced an interpretation that has been too "deep." Freud has described the reactions of an ego that has had to cope with the threatened emergence of frightening degrees of id derivatives too soon. This is, in fact, one of the very problems that led Freud (1913) earlier to recognize and emphasize the value of working from the surface and withholding interpretation of symptoms or wishes until the patient "is already so close to it that he has only one short step more to make in order to get hold of the explanation for himself" (p. 140). This trend led eventually to the contemporary concept of the ego.

Following *Inhibitions, Symptoms and Anxiety* (1926a), Freud's interest in detailed attention to the *nature*—not the existence—of resistance appears to have diminished. As described above, he later shows an apparent recurrence of a predilection for the earlier "two-impressions" interpretative approach, which depended strongly on the authoritative, hypnotic-suggestive influencing potential of transference in overcoming resistance.

Individuals influenced by Freud during his time have shown that they could evolve differing technical approaches, offer theory to support their approaches, and yet maintain that they were strictly following Freud's guidelines. Reich (in his early phase), Anna Freud, Sterba, and Fenichel all chose to emphasize rather similar perspectives, clearly deriving from certain of Freud's contributions. Nunberg, also as a bona fide Freudian, developed a technical and theoretical approach that differs in important respects from these others. He placed less confidence in an ego-analytic approach intended to facilitate and develop in the analysand an autonomously cooperating and participating observing ego. On the contrary, Nunberg (1937) continued to take the persistence of the hypnotic type of influence as the necessary component of the analytic process:

> For . . . making conscious what has been reproduced in repetition [in analysis], the patient obviously needs the cooperation of . . . that part of his ego which in the transference is siding with the analyst. In obedience to the analyst's request to remember—to repeat—experiences from the past, the patient's ego braces itself for the readmission of the repressed into consciousness. . . . *The ego's reaction is similar to that which occurs in hypnosis, where, in obedience to our compliance with the hypnotist, even unpleasurable suggestions are accepted and carried out.* The obedience is reproduced owing to libidinal ties belonging to the oedipus complex. [p. 169, italics added]

Nunberg, appearing to follow a practice of facilitating removal of resistance by authoritative reinforcement, is described by former supervisees as having encouraged the use of direct, deep interpretations for resolution of certain near-panic anxiety eruptions.[8]

On the occasion of the 30th anniversary of the publication of Anna Freud's monograph, Arlow (Panel 1967) raised important questions related to the fate of the defense theory over the previous three decades, and inquired as to why there was such a lack of emphasis on *psychic conflict.* Lustman attributed the move "away from a focus on conflict, anxiety and danger . . ." to the emphasis on developmental psychology. In another panel 11 years later, "revisiting" the monograph, Arlow, by raising some of the same questions, was able again to underscore the need for better scrutiny of this area.

II

I borrowed the phrase "developmental lag" to characterize a puzzling reluctance to apply certain ego concepts to the method of psychoanalytic technique. I shall now take further advantage of the metaphor and examine the implied "conflicts" in terms of particular "fixations" at earlier periods of development in analytic theory and practice. I shall also consider the resulting "resistances" to progress in this area in the face of certain burdensome consequences encountered by the analyst who makes ego analyzing a constant part of his technique. Selected are only four so designated fixations: (1) fascination with the id; (2) predilection for an authoritative analytic stance; (3) preoccupation with external reality, including past as external reality; and (4) counterresistance to transference affects and impulses.

---

[8]Friedman (1969) examines the "paradoxes" created by the analytic approach that attempts to eliminate transferences while regarding them as simultaneously necessary for the alliance involved in the analytic work itself. He perceptively describes the approaches that explicitly regard the hypnotic factor as essential, and compares them with points of view that increasingly emphasize the use of rational aspects of the ego.

Fascination with the Id

Analysts are often reluctant to give up or dilute the degree of gratification they so commonly experience when they seek, perceive, and name drive derivatives of another human being. In analytic practice, when this source of the analyst's gratification becomes conspicuously intense, we ordinarily recognize it as some form of countertransference or perhaps a limitation of the analyst. With appropriate regulation, it may become one of the sublimations in analytic work, through the effective resonating use of the analyst's unconscious as he senses instinctual derivatives of a patient. This is not to suggest that there is anything inherently wrong with gratification experienced in connection with applying analytic technique. I am suggesting, however, that the analyst who invests a greater amount of his attention to the non- (or very much less) instinctualized ego activities must significantly sacrifice some of the above source of gratification in the work. Sterba, as recounted earlier, reminded us of the analyst's being "impressed, even fascinated, by id contents." Stone (1973) refers to "the strange magnetism which the verbal statement of unconscious content exerts on analysts . . ." (p. 47).

The common tendency to find gratification in naming id content raises a question about the varieties of sublimation that are characteristic for different analysts and that contribute to their technical preferences. Has this naming been a rather universal tendency, not only because of its frequent therapeutic (but perhaps not always lasting) result, but also because in itself it is an instinctually gratifying working experience to which would-be analysts have traditionally been drawn?[9] If so, what are the sublimations that may serve a greater attention to ego observa-

---

[9]Sterba (1941), in a discussion on irresponsible interpretations, illustrates how common the tendency is among those who have even an elementary knowledge of the unconscious to become "wild analysts outside of the analytic situation," suggesting that a compulsion toward "naming" of id content is an easily aroused trait.

tion? A supervisee who was keenly perceptive of instinctual derivatives—a good "third ear"—had the intellectual and imaginative capacity of also comprehending ego defense details, but was bored by them. He found it difficult to resist giving direct interpretations, even in the face of an observable increase in the patient's resistance or of a patient's passive or masochistically motivated complying confirmation of such an interpretation. Driven to improvisation, I drew on my knowledge that the supervisee was an excellent chess player—a game where his capacity for restraint regularly took precedence over immediate gratification. I openly discussed with him the question of sublimation in relation to his priorities in interpretation. I suggested he try to let himself be as confident with a more systematic ego-including analytic "game" as he was about his chess moves, hoping that he might thus find that aspect of the work less boring and derive a different kind of sublimatory gratification, even though sacrificing his thrill in direct id interpretations. My efforts were only partially successful.

Predilection for an Authoritative Analytic Stance

Analytic neutrality is a more complex task than is often recognized. The achievement of an amoral attitude toward the hourly productions of an analysand and the avoidance of personal reactions to transference impulses are requirements that are taken for granted. The sacrifice of gratification from authoritative experiences is another matter. Such gratification may reasonably accompany many legitimate and effective forms of psychotherapy. Given a dichotomy between the role of authoritarian, hypnosis-related suggestion and defense analysis in modifying resistance, it is tempting to speculate that former hypnotists might be biased in their eventual choice of a technical approach. Both Freud and Nunberg began their psychological careers as hypnotists; both were profoundly impressed by the response of the hypnotic subject. The power to manipulate another's psyche can provide a strong narcissistic gratification. However, since there are experienced hypnotists who also strive in their psychoanalytic work for nonsuggestive approaches to resistance, a hypothesis of hypnotist predilections as accounting for the exercise of an authoritative technical approach does not seem to be supportable.

It is not only the "playing God" type of authoritarian role that must be sacrificed to a neutrality which allows an optimal approach to analytic material from the side of the ego's defensive activity. I have in mind something closer to the authoritarianism inherent in a parental role—even a benign parental role. I am not speaking of the analyst who gives interpretations in a dogmatic, commanding, or authoritative tone. I am referring to the analyst who, in effect, says, even gently, "What you really feel (mean, etc.) is such-and-such, because I perceive it that way," or, 'this is the way it is." It is an analyst who does not invite the analysand to use his observing ego to share the analyst's perception of the data. Such an analyst is apt to be experienced by the patient as an authority, not as an observer who treats the patient's observing ego as of potentially equal value to his own. Treating a patient's ego with the respect of equality obviously does not mean that the patient will always hear it that way; the transference may have it otherwise. But if the patient's eventual perception of a kindly scientific neutrality is prevented by an actual authoritative approach, the patient will be handicapped from achieving the eventual measure of autonomous self-analytic skill of which it is potentially capable. The benignly authoritative roles which I believe are inimical to effective *analysis* of defenses may of course have useful, even essential, functions in the intensive treatment of many patients for whom consistent defense analysis would be too burdensome (i.e., many patients with narcissistic disorders, borderline conditions, some very severe neuroses, most children, and many adolescents).

Patients have various motivations for trying to keep the analyst in an authoritative position. Usually these are recognized and dealt with as transference phenomena. Let us select one such motivation that may elude transference recognition and hence make "rational alliance" with the patient's observing ego difficult, and in some instances impossible. That is a *tendency or need for incorporative or internalizing types of identification.* Although Strachey's (1934) classic paper offered a model for therapeutic action that tried to integrate much of the analytic theory and practice of that period, Klein's influence on him appears to me to have resulted in a paradigm, limited and limiting in its application.[10] His description of the gradual replacement of the primitive superego by the incorporation of the contemporary image of the analyst was to a significant degree modeled on the process of hypnosis. The essential difference was that his "mutative" process involved repeated, small increments of introjection, as compared with the massive incorporation in hypnosis. It is likely that therapeutic action by internalization comes about in many valuable analyses, but to consider this as the ultimate therapeutic factor for *all* analyses significantly limits the development of a technical approach that could offer greater opportunity to many patients for more autonomous ego growth. Fenichel, in his reply to Strachey's original paper, said, ". . . I think he uses the concept of 'introjection' in a wider sense than is legitimate. When I recognize that what someone says is right, it does not necessarily mean that I have introjected him" (1937, p. 24).

If one is to provide opportunity through psychoanalysis for therapeutic change not due primarily to internalizing processes, what elements of change can we rely on? For the time being, I suggest that the essential cognitive and experiential factors involved in such an analysis of neurotic conflict can conveniently be categorized and understood within the concept of *learning process.*[11] This is cognitive process, in respect to the patient's *comprehension* of the analyst's observations concerning the ego

---

[10]I believe that the resemblance between Strachey's description of the process of "mutative" interpretations and Kohut's (1971) "internalizing transmutation" is more than superficial.

[11]See Meissner (1973) for distinctions between identification and learning process.

and id aspects of the neurotic conflicts, and an experiential process, in respect to the patient's discovery that his ego can *tolerate and control* the increments of drive derivatives.[12]

Although some patients, pathologically and defensively, react more than others to the analyst with incorporations, probably all show some regressive tendency in this direction. To the extent that the analyst presents himself, through his remarks, in an authoritative or parentlike manner, the nonincorporative learning modes of acquiring insight are significantly compromised. The analyst who makes direct interpretations of id derivations without approaching them through the defense relies primarily on the suggestive power of the positive transference to overcome resistance. In addition, he risks moving in the direction of "wild analysis" (A. Freud 1969, p. 34). In so doing, he facilitates the internalizing processes and limits the patient's opportunity to learn with the fullest possible participation of the ego. Some patients have incorporative tendencies and needs that may well exclude change through acquisition of significant areas of insight; therapeutic changes have to depend on what is possible. However, the clinical impression of what is "needed" by the patient is often slanted by that part of one's natural parental potential to take some satisfaction in being incorporated by someone who is in one's "care."

I invite us to reflect briefly on the spectrum of contemporary "wider scope" modifications or "alternative approaches," sometimes with authentic, sometimes with ostensible psychoanalytic aims. Most of these have offered technical recommendations designed to contribute therapeutic factors considered essential to the treatment process. Almost without exception these models provide aspects of parental roles. Some, in addition, include the specific importance of a traditional aspect of "the doctor." One thing that they appear to share is a reliance on interpersonal influences. I do not argue against the validity of

[12]See Hatcher (1973) on "experiential" and "reflective" self-observation in relation to insight.

these therapeutic contributions. I do believe, however, that in each instance the theoretical formulation has been based on a particular category of patients.

It is within the experience of most analysts to work with patients for whom the technical efforts must take into consideration that the problems to be dealt with extend beyond neurotic conflict; not infrequently, the therapeutic objectives must accordingly be modified. The approaches I referred to above contain valued sources of guidance in providing such modification where it may be needed. Those patients whose egos *are* suited to an approach that does not require interpersonal therapeutic ingredients should not have to be deprived of the opportunity for greater autonomy.

Preoccupation with External Reality, Including Past as External Reality

It is common clinical knowledge that some people, when confronted with a therapeutic approach that asks them to look inward, become "reality-bound." I suggest that this defensive method, in less blatant forms, plays a greater role in psychotherapeutic interactions, and in analysis in particular, than is ordinarily recognized. Freud (1917a, 1917b, p. 368) speaks of manifestations of this problem regularly encountered in analysis: He observes that if a patient is confronted with the fact that he is expressing things that contain fantasy material, "his interest in pursuing the subject further suddenly diminishes in an undesirable fashion. He *too* [italics added] wants to experience realities and despises every thing that is merely 'imaginary.' " It is at this point that Freud, after expressing the technical dilemma of when to choose to direct the patient's attention to the intrapsychic importance of his productions, makes his oft quoted statement, "The phantasies possess *psychical* as contrasted with *material* reality, and we gradually learn to understand that *in the world of the neuroses it is psychical reality which is the decisive kind*" (1917b, p. 368).

Freud is explicit about the technical difficulty of assisting patients to contemplate psychic productions—whether they be fantasies, memories, or abstractions—as a *reality*, as an *immediate event* to be observed. In saying "He too," Freud appears to recognize a corresponding problem in the analyst. I do not believe he specifically approached this issue again.[13] With the subsequent development of clearer concepts regarding the ego's defensive mechanisms, the task of focusing on intrapsychic realities could become more comprehensive, though even more demanding than before.

A common challenge in analytic focusing is in having to observe that what is manifestly a recollection has a function separate from memory, of *immediate* importance—an intrapsychic event—in the associative stream of thought. Let me add to previously mentioned reasons for this, that developmentally and because of continued wishes that it be so, memory and fantasy are closely linked. With the ordinary occurrence of something being recalled, the individual experiences the phenomenon as a *reference* to something that happened in the past, something that is perceived as a former, recent or distant past reality, *external* to the intrapsychic here-and-now. Analysts know, however, that their patients' memories may serve other purposes. The memory may, for instance, be of primary importance as an "association," because of a topic or detail within it; it may serve as a displacement away from the analyst or someone else; it may come to the patient's mind as a screen; it may serve as a source of nostalgic gratification, etc. In brief, what has taken place with the appearance in consciousness of a memory is an immediate, internal *psychic event*, which potentially can be perceived by both analyst and patient in several ways. Although analysts do know this very well, there is nevertheless, and for a variety of reasons, a great temptation to yield to the natural tendency of giving memory a

---

[13]Freud (1899) elaborated on the principle of other uses of memory, beyond those of accurately recording the past, in his early paper on "Screen Memories."

priority in its function as referring to *past external reality,* over its role as an *internal event of immediate intrapsychic importance* (see Gray 1973). Analytic supervision provides endless opportunities to observe analysts presenting process notes, during which, unwittingly, they drop their perceptions of memories in the material as psychic events, turn to the ordinary way that memories are listened to, and speak of the external events to which the memories refer. The analyst lapses into telling the supervisor what the patient "did" in his daily life rather than what the patient remembered and verbalized only *manifestly* referring to such events. To the extent that this tendency on the analyst's part predominates over focusing on the occurrence of memories as a part of the mind's display of activity as it struggles with the ever-present task of ego–id conflict, the resistance is thereby supported. Further, if it is a tendency that is tacitly (or passively) encouraged by the supervisor, a counterresistance in the analyst will be supported. What is not as apparent is a tenacious attraction to this tendency, conveniently viewed here as a "fixation."

When memory is experienced in the ordinary way, there is a fleeting illusion of nearness to the particular moment in the external world that has been recalled. We recognize sustained forms of this in acts of reminiscing. This illusion of nearness to an external reality is to some extent true regardless of whether it refers to an occurrence that ostensibly happened yesterday or many years ago.[14] External reality, in contrast to psychic reality, is the phylogenetically more familiar ground upon which we seek solutions and gratifications, move away from distress, and bring about changes.

The analyst's knowledge of the genetic backdrop, of the infantile temporal origins, often may encourage this bias toward continued listening to memory only in terms of its reference to the past. And thus, whenever the past is vividly described, it may evoke the illusion, for the listener as well as for the experiencer,

---

[14]For elaboration on the role of the *actuality* or *presentness* of the past in mental life, see Namnum 1972.

that one is close to an external reality. This in turn can, blatantly or subtly, cause the edging out of any concurrent focusing on the details of the less conspicuous internal psychic conflict—the "then-and-there" activity of the ego (A. Freud 1936, p. 14).[15]

It is not surprising that after all these years, the universally preferred stereotypic view of psychoanalysis remains, that it is a procedure that consists of a search for memories of the past, rather than one devoted primarily to the gaining of voluntary controls over previously warded-off instinctual impulses. It is difficult to know to what extent Freud, in his later years, revived his never altogether dormant interest in "the past," and in particular the concept of "historical truth," because of certain preoccupying realities, namely his health, his age, and especially, his emigration. In the 1935 "Postscript" to his "Autobiographical Study" Freud wrote:

> Shortly before I wrote this study it seemed as though my life would soon be brought to an end . . . ; but surgical skill saved me. . . . In the period of more than ten years that has passed since then . . . a significant change has come about . . . ; interests which I had acquired in the later part of my life have receded, while the older and original ones become prominent once more. . . . This circumstance is connected with an alteration in myself, with what might be described as a regressive development. [pp. 71–72][16]

Freud's "regressive development" may have been manifested by the return, in some of his very late writings, to forms of interpretation he had ostensibly set aside over twenty years before and thereby contributed significantly to the developmental lag. Here I am referring, among other things, to his use of

---

[15]Kanzer (1952) provides illustrations of how focusing on the past can obscure recognition of transference elements, in Freud's analysis of the Rat Man.

[16]For additional views about Freud's emphasis on past realities, see Schimek (1975) and Jacobson and Steele (1979).

the large-scale, direct interpretation reconstructions. This is not to be taken as an across-the-board antireconstruction position on my part. There are varieties of reconstructions that I find quite compatible with and essential to the technique of competent analysis of defenses against specific drive derivatives.

Counterresistance to Transference Affects and Impulses

Counterresistance refers here to ways of the analyst's perceiving and conducting an analysis so as to stimulate or reinforce resistance beyond that degree which occurs due to the internal conflicts mobilized by the task of free association. In a strict sense, counterresistance might well be confined to ways that are unconsciously motivated within the analyst. Some counterresistance, of course, exists chiefly because of less than skillful technique. Be that as it may, it is the unconsciously motivated form directed against the full emergence of analyst-cathected affects and impulses that I include as one of the fixations that contribute to relative neglect of analyzing the ego and its defenses.

Historically, it was not uncommon for the analyst to make genetic interpretations of observed unconscious material relating to the analyst, without providing the patient with an opportunity to work through the full awareness of those affects or impulses toward the analyst. The patient's resistance to this particularly advantageous experience was thus supported.

This resistance-supporting tendency persists, although to a lesser degree. We see it whenever the analyst interprets the genetic aspects of barely or newly, yet cautiously conscious, transference of id derivatives (as distinguished from interpreting genetic aspects of transference of defense) without having made sure that the patient had worked through virtually all of the defenses against experiencing those derivatives in their immediate form, toward the analyst and others (see Gill 1979). The analyst who does provide the latter experience will, of course, have to be subjected to drive derivatives of a more detailed and intense variety. Inevitably this will expose *all* of the ways in which the analyst has been or is being perceived, fantasied *and* real. It is, therefore, gratuitous to make a special technical point of getting the patient to verbalize his observations of and reactions to "the real relationship" (Greenson 1967). Actually, it is especially *because* the patient's "real" perceptions of the analyst will be *included* in the material, particularly as defenses against the act of perception (Lustman 1968) are diminished, that the analyst's counterresistance to observing and analyzing the ego's activities is easily aroused. It is difficult for analysts to overcome narcissistic self-protection against having their actual characteristics—appearance, ways of speaking, ways of thinking (as these become apparent), and so on—accurately perceived by the patient as a part of effective analytic process. It is a challenge, when this problem occurs in supervision, to transmit this principle successfully without inflicting a narcissistic wound.

CONCLUSION

Freud's phrase, "There is resistance to uncovering resistances" could well refer to an ubiquitous reluctance to consider, perceive, and conceptualize—both to oneself and to one's analysand—the detailed workings of the ego in its defensive measures against specific drive derivatives.

Many obstacles the analyst meets in making observations about the ego's defensive activity occur because of, or are reinforced by, the fact that there is something to be gained by the analyst—as distinct from the patient—in *not* making such observations. The gains range from enhanced instinctual satisfactions to relief from conflicts. Some of the conflicts have to do with the analyst's narcissistic vulnerability to the patient's id; some are superego-induced conflicts within the analyst which compromise his neutrality. Essentially the conflicts resemble the intrapsychic conflicts of neurosis itself and qualify often as a form of countertransference. A burdensome byproduct of the widening-scope applications of analysis is increasing emphasis on the therapeutic uses of countertransference. Given the trying aspects of the work with many such cases, this trend has often been a matter of attempting to make a virtue out of a necessity, and historically has made an appearance whenever analysis moved toward the treatment of nearer-psychotic pathology.

I have reserved one obstacle until last because I do not think it lends itself to the metaphor of a *fixation* and because there is not much to say about it. This obstacle concerns an inner tendency to maintain a natural or at least a maturely typical state of virtual ignorance of those functions of the ego that potentially enable it to observe itself. Freud (1900) first called attention to the fact when he discussed analyzing one's dreams: "Practice is needed even for perceiving endoptic phenomena . . . from which our attention is normally withheld; and this is so *even though there is no psychical motive fighting against such perceptions*" (pp. 522–523, italics added). Over thirty years later, addressing his unseen "Lecture" audience, Freud (1933b) wrote more specifically about the ego:

> I must . . . let you know of my suspicion that this account of mine of ego-psychology will affect you differently from the introduction into the psychical underworld which preceded it. I cannot say with certainty why this should be so. . . . I now believe that it is somehow a *question of the nature of the material itself* and of our being unaccustomed to dealing with it. In any case, I shall not be surprised if you show yourself *even more reserved and cautious* in your judgement than hitherto. [p. 58; italics added]

Evolution has provided man, in spite of repression, with numerous ways of becoming aware of much about his unconscious *id* activity—through dreams, art, literature, etc. Eventually, to these was added psychoanalysis. To borrow a concept from Jonas Salk's *Survival of the Wisest* (1973), the capacity of Freud's ego for certain new perceptions brought forth a "metabiological mutation" that speeded the evolutionary change of man in ways which, for better or worse, have transcended those changes brought about by the course of "biological" mutations. It is an interesting question and relevant to this discussion whether, were it not for an interest in *analyzing* neurotic conflicts, there would have been occasion for man to try to perceive his own unconscious *ego* activity and make it part of his consciousness. In the evolution of our capacity to perceive demonstrable ego mechanisms in their detailed roles in neurotic conflict, we are not assisted as with the "cooperative" qualities of the drive derivatives, which strive to find us. The workings of the id are, in many ways, available for those who wish to study them—even in settings that are not analytic situations; the defensive activities of the ego can hardly be captured in "closeup" except in an analysis that includes a consistent attempt to develop an increasingly autonomous capacity for an ever-freer intrapsychic spontaneity, reflectively observed and verbalized. Let us not be dissuaded by limiting factors from further evolution of our psychoanalytic technique in the realm of neurotic conflict.

3

ON HELPING ANALYSANDS OBSERVE INTRAPSYCHIC ACTIVITY

A major goal of the analytic process is to help the analysand gain full access to those habitual, unconscious, and outmoded ego activities that serve resistance. There is, however, a paucity of methodology available for achieving this goal. I have discussed elsewhere (Gray 1982) some forms of counterresistance to this challenging task. An earlier article (Gray 1973) dealt with particular ways in which analysts, by focusing their observing skills, can favorably influence their own access to the analysand's unconscious defense-against-drive processes. Here I explore specific techniques for helping the analysand make better use of those observing skills that are essential for systematic analysis of the resistances to free association, as well as valuable in the development of a self-analytic capacity.

The crux of the difficulty in making the unconscious ego conscious is that the elements the analyst wants to bring into awareness are not "driven" toward the analysand's awareness, as are the id derivatives. Even-hovering attention and skillful, id-resonating interpretations in a transferentially enhanced authoritative atmosphere are, by themselves, relatively ineffective in bringing into the patient's awareness the unconscious ego activities that carry out repetitive forms of defense as resistance. To observe the simple or intricate defenses at work against specific id impulse derivatives, the analysand requires a form of observation distinguishable from the "experiential observation" (Hatcher 1973, p. 388) that serves free association (Eissler 1963).

I am interested in methodology for drawing more fully on the relatively autonomous capacities of analysands to strengthen both their motivation for and their work in analyzing. Nowhere are these autonomous capacities more necessary than in learning how to observe and comprehend one's intrapsychic process. Out of a range of measures that, I believe, can help the patient make use of these capacities, I have selected only two areas for discussion. The first area is a primarily cognitive, educative endeavor, while the second deals with the analyst's skill in creating the best working opportunities for analysands to become familiar with their capacity for self-observation. I am aware that one cannot do full justice to the often overlapping, or even simultaneous application of, technical measures in practice.

STRENGTHENING ANALYSANDS' MOTIVATION FOR DEVELOPING A CAPACITY FOR INTRAPSYCHIC OBSERVATION

Although patients may possess the optimum motive for entering into psychoanalysis, namely, a wish for relief from some form of neurotic distress, it does not follow that they are at once motivated to undertake the observing tasks required during the analytic hour (Friedman 1969, Hatcher 1973, Kris 1975). In this discussion, I consider two forms of self-observation: (1) that required for the task set by what we have traditionally called "the fundamental rule"; and (2) that which is necessary as the patient attempts to perceive in close retrospection the phenomena that occur as manifestations related to intrapsychic conflict—specifically, those conflicts and solutions mobilized by, and occurring during, the analytic situation. Gradually, the analysand's second observing task can occur during the process of the defense reaction itself (see final clinical example later).

To teach analysands the first of these observing tasks, the analyst presents them with a relatively clear concept: that they must strive to set aside reasonable and moral judgment, permit a flow of inner spontaneity, and observe and put into words unreservedly "what comes to mind"—think out loud. This task of free association evokes resistance, which expresses itself by making difficult the comprehension of what is to be attempted. Sustaining that comprehension remains one of the extended efforts of the analysis. An added burden for analysands is learning that in order to undertake the second task, they must—at intervals determined by the analyst's interventions—attempt to enter into a rational observing alliance with the analyst. This reorienting from free-associative attention to an experience of what the mind produces, to an objective "intellectual contemplation" (Sterba 1934) only sets the stage for a less familiar and usually unwelcome examination of *how* the mind works.

Regarding the second observing task, what Kris (1975) referred to as "the ability of the ego to . . . observe its own functions," (p. 267) typically is initiated by inviting the analysand to think back about a just completed mental activity that the analyst has reconstructed. Turning attention toward something just spoken or momentarily felt—something that "occurred" in the immediate past, but is now preconscious (yet close enough to the surface to be retrieved)—is not easy for the analysand. It takes practice just to learn that one can do that sort of thing.

Clearly, this complex second observing task we ask the patient to undertake requires, as in the case of free association, a good measure of motivation. Traditionally, motivation for the work of analyzing—sometimes distinguishable from the wish to "be analyzed"—relies heavily on response to or compliance with transferentially endowed authority; that is, it stems from a fear of punishment or a need to express devotion and gain love. This use of aspects of the positive transference (Fenichel 1941, Freud 1917b, Gill 1982, Gray 1982, Nunberg 1937) is a form of suggestion that is still widely used to overcome resistance. It is usually more accepted in practice than acknowledged in theory. Many analyzable patients have a capacity and a tendency to cling to this particular motivational source. Analysts who depend on it usually assume it will be relinquished near the end of the analysis. This is not necessarily the case. In my experience, a patient can also (and to greater advantage) derive motivation throughout the analysis from progressively acquiring a reality-based rationale for proceeding in a particular way toward a real gain (as differentiated from a fantasied gain) and, in addition, from learning through repeated observation that this particular way gradually accomplishes what it sets out to do, as the ego gains nondefensive strengths. In practice, there is always a mixture of rational and irrational motivating factors. My interest lies in identifying technical ways of reducing the irrational, that is, the use of suggestion, and increasing the rational use of autonomous learning as early in the analysis as the patient's characteristics permit.

Having so far dealt largely in principles, I shall now move closer to practice. In building a rational motivation in analysands for undertaking the tasks of observation, I want to provide them with a working concept of how those difficulties that made analysis the treatment of choice are manifestations of involuntary solutions to certain unconscious conflicts—conflicts that, in the beginning, neither the patient nor the analyst are able to identify, let alone resolve. The extent to which this working concept can be used varies with the analysand's available rational attention and his usable intelligence, and requires a sensitive and empathetic assessment by the analyst to determine how much the patient is able to digest at any one time. At some point, I would hope to convey to the analysand that the particular reasons why these conflicts have been kept out of the patient's awareness have been operating, in one way or another, since early in his life, when he was not yet old or strong enough to be able to work them out consciously. Once the patient understands in this general way the psychological nature of the difficulties, the analyst can usually describe how the analytic situation contributes to a resolution of the problem by the way it is conducted in order to gain access to those obscured conflicts. In my orienting comments about the functioning and aims of the analytic situation, I speak of the *two* kinds of self-observing that will become essential. In this paper, I give less attention to describing the task required in free association, there being not much I can add to what analysts already know and have long practiced. I do include the following observations, though. Where appropriate, I explain the difference between free association in analysis and free communication, to which the patient may have become accustomed during some previous therapy. Sooner or later, I also convey the information that the patient can potentially and actively participate in influencing the degree of freedom with which things come to mind—that is, in the "flow" into consciousness—and that we are aiming for an increasingly greater spontaneity in this regard. (In analytic language, which I would not use with analysands, I try to acquaint them with their capability for bringing about a *degree* of facilitation of regression in the service of free association, by a voluntary, intentional use of the ego's capacity for this.) Further, I make clear that I am talking about an effort *toward* free association, since interferences regularly take place while we are working to carry out this task. I point out that it is precisely the study of these interferences and the obstacles to putting the observations into words that provides us with greater access to what is now out of reach and which contributes to the patient's problems; and that the *nature of the obstacles* to free association will be intimately connected with the *nature of the problems* or conflicts that brought the patient to treatment.

This motivating orientation helps some patients—especially where the form of a previous psychotherapy contrasts sharply with analysis—to understand basically why the analyst does not need to spend "equal time" interpreting the patient's contemporary life outside the analytic situation in order to be therapeutically helpful; the essential conflicts and issues will reveal themselves *in the analytic situation* as the work continues to give access to inner spontaneity. (This does not mean "transference only" and does not in any way mean ignoring the full range of thoughts, feelings, and impulses *referring* to the analysand's contemporary life.) Again, these guiding conceptualizations are parcelled out in accordance with the analysand's capacity to comprehend them. How soon and how much will vary from patient to patient; with some, they can be offered during the initial interview. Again, the intention is to provide, as early as possible, a rational basis for the motivation to develop the ability for self-observation, rather than to depend on an irrational basis of working for the analyst, a motivation that sacrifices a fuller development of autonomous faculties.

Having provided a basis for rational understanding of the point of the analytic process, the analyst is in a better position to bolster patients' motivation further as he gives them repeated opportunity throughout the analytic process to become familiar with their autonomous "tools" (Loewenstein 1982, p. 214) of observation. Quite apart from arousing resistance, the effort to observe what spontaneously comes into one's awareness often encounters the inherent difficulty of an unfamiliar task. However, self-observation of the process of the mind's intrapsychic activity at its encounter with and defensive solution to conflict—conflict not ordinarily in the scope of attention—makes an even stranger demand (Freud 1933b) on the autonomous ego apparatus. Therefore, it is important to provide patients with clearly documented examples of their resisting minds at work. With repeated experiences, patients gradually learn that they can bring these activities more and more under conscious management. All of this contributes to a greater sense of what is involved in undertaking a freer inner spontaneity. It also lends positive motivation to the search for the meanings, present and past, of those involuntary defensive responses.

I anticipate that my description of this approach may stimulate the objection, "Doesn't this contribute to intellectualization?" My reply is: Any communication by the analyst, or contemplation of a task by the analysand, can be turned into intellectualization if that is a significant defense of the analysand. This would be equally true if one discussed "the fundamental rule" with the analysand, or, at some other time, how to approach a dream usefully. Certainly it is intellectual but so is any intervention at the point where the analysand can rationally comprehend it. I would argue that the intellect used as a defense is to be analyzed, not avoided through manipulation by not making demands on the analysand's intelligence. It is what the patient does with the information communicated that is important. Thus, any defensive intellectualization the patient may engage in should itself become a subject for the same technique described before. My thesis is that a technical orientation which encourages the analyst to describe the characteristics of the things that are observable, and which also provides rational, constructive *reasons for doing so,* can potentially arouse analysands to be willing to use their perceptual equipment more fully. To paraphrase Friedman (1976), by gradually familiarizing analysands with the characteristics of those identifiable processes within their verbalized thinking that are responses to conflict, the properties of otherwise unconscious ego activities become "objectified" and hence more accessible for repeated observation.

Some analysands can shift quite readily from observing what is in their awareness (for purposes of free association) to the rational observing focus of the analyst's comments. Other analysands experience difficulty at different points in the process of this shift. Patients whose participation is handicapped in this area may have general inhibitions against a rational alliance with the analyst, or there may be specific autonomous functions that are compromised. For them, the analyst may have to turn the analytic attention away from the study primarily of what the analysand has been saying to take up an examination of the very functions, the "tools," which the patient is neglecting, keeping the analysis from being, as Hartmann regarded it, a *shared* "scientific investigation" (Loewenstein 1982, p. 220).

The more clearly we analysts can conceptualize for ourselves the detail of the analytic work of observing we may wish to have patients undertake, the greater the likelihood that we can facilitate their learning to do so. Let us look closer at the autonomous ego functions analysands need in order to observe the conflict-motivated defensive activities of their egos.[1] As analysands are interrupted by the sound of the analyst's voice, they must draw back from the more spontaneous and less rational mode and must now take up objective capacities. In this new and more rational alliance (Gutheil and Havens 1979), they may sequentially undertake the following: (1) rationally attend to what the analyst is saying; (2) recognize that the interpretive intervention implies an invitation to turn objective attention back over the reconstructed or recounted sequence of material the analyst has offered as evidence of a conflict the patient encountered during the attempted spontaneity and to which the patient's mind automatically responded with a protective, defensive solution; (3) comprehend that the motivation for the conflict solution was due in part (and this part will be explored) to the fact that while the analysand was revealing thoughts and feelings to the other person in the room, some fantasied risk of doing so arose; (4) analyze that irrational risk (a bit more each time) and through understanding it gradually reduce the automatic need for the patient to inhibit, by the specific means indentified, those

[1]I am virtually equating manifestations of *resistance* with those manifestations of *defense* that are stimulated by the task of free association. I believe that such a theoretical perspective, though not exhaustive, is practical in comprehending and observing resistance during the analytic process. Except for the examples I give in the clinical illustrations, I shall not further elaborate varieties of defensive solutions to conflict. I am in agreement with Brenner that "the ego can use defensively whatever lies at hand that is useful for that purpose" (Brenner 1982c, p. 75). Defenses are not limited to "special mechanisms." For comprehensive views about defense and/or resistance manifestations see earlier contributons—Freud (1926a), A. Freud (1936), Gero (1951), and Loewenstein (1982); see also Gill (1963), Schafer (1968, 1973), and Stone (1973). For more recent contributions see Abend (1981), Brenner (1976b, 1982), Rangell (1983), and Wallerstein (1983).

particular elements that had shortly before come into conflict; and (5) return attention to the essential task of permitting a more spontaneous access to the inner self, in particular, allowing greater freedom to let emerge those conflicted elements, the inhibition of which had just been explored.

I wish to comment briefly on the first and fourth of the aforementioned stages. In regard to (1) "rationally attend to what the analyst is saying," precisely at this point, as suggested earlier, certain pathological problems may limit, transiently or indefinitely, any success in engaging the analysands' observing attention to their intrapsychic activity. For example, some of the persons Kohut (1971) designated as having narcissistic personality disorders hear the analyst give attention to an aspect of what they have been saying that goes beyond what they manifestly wished to communicate, and they become traumatized. This narcissistic wound handicaps the patient's observing capacity immediately, and any specific attention to the ego's activities becomes impossible. Understandably, Kohut (personal communication) indicated that he used free association with such patients less and less frequently. Others so limited are patients Sterba designated as having "a permanently unified ego" (Sterba 1934, p. 120) and whom he regarded as incapable of achieving an observing "dissociation" or "split" (Freud 1933b, p. 58). Obviously, clinical and theoretical observations concerning limitations in applying this technical approach, which stresses collaborative development of the analysand's observation of manifestations of mental activity during conflict solutions within the analytic hour, deserve extended attention. I shall add here only the impression that patients who are severely passive generally present more difficulty in enlisting an observing alliance of the kind being described. This can also be true for a long time with people who have an excessive need to distance themselves from any form of close cooperative experience.

In regard to (4) "the analysis of the irrational risk," it is in the area of analyzing the inhibiting irrational fear that I see a primary application of genetic interest; this is in the service of analyzing the resistance against identifiable trends, ideas, memories, affects, impulses, *whether or not they pertain to the analyst.* It is here that I see the value in reconstructing, where possible, the conditions of originally perceived danger (A. Freud 1936) that forced the analysand at an earlier time to abandon the freedom or capacity to be aware of and/or to reveal his desires, impulses, wishes, appetites, and to turn to defensive, automatic, immature but adaptively available means to resolve the intimidating conflicts—all of which resulted in inhibiting the now dreaded impulses by removing them from consciousness. I am aware that these remarks about genetics and reconstruction may not be central to enhancing the analysand's motivation for intrapsychic observations. I include them because I do not wish their absence to stimulate questions that may deflect attention from the difficult subject of self-observation of ego activities.

In summary, in this first section I have described ways of enhancing analysands' motivation for realizing and developing their skills for observation of certain crucial intrapsychic activities as they are brought into play during the analytic process. In the context of an available rational alliance, the analyst provides a basic, essentially ego-syntonic rationale or direction, emphasizing analysis of resistance against identifiable instinctualized mental activities. This primarily educational provision is followed up during the course of the analysis by interpretive interventions that give the analysand—from earliest opportunities—repeated observing experience of those ego activities that occur in the face of specific intrapsychic conflict phenomena. The objective is, of course, to make possible, through insight and experience, the gradual exchange of previously automatic, unconscious defensive activities, which were acquired adaptively during immaturity, for voluntary, more mature forms of control and a more realistic perception of the patient's internal and external environment.

I do not underestimate the predilection of some patients for utilizing, through suggestibility, less stable acquisitions, such as incorporative identification of the analyst's aims, rather than permitting themselves to learn and to use those concepts more and more autonomously. I am aware that what the patient learns about these things in the beginning of the analysis may be subjected to all the distortions that transference resistance can impose, in the same way that patients can neurotically modify all the other information they learn from the analyst, be it the appointment times, the dates of the analyst's vacations, the fee arrangements, or the carefully spelled out versions of "the fundamental rule." It is my experience, however, that without such a conceptual foundation, the patient's task of making conscious in an increasingly stable way the capacity to observe the ego's functions becomes more difficult. Typically, analysands gain in motivation when they understand what observing equipment they possess and how and for what purpose to use it. Let us leave the issue of motivation now and turn to the second area, that of trying to enhance the *effectiveness* of the analysand's observing experiences.

COOPERATING WITH ANALYSANDS' SELF-OBSERVING ACTIVITIES

The effectiveness with which patients can use their capacity for observing ego activities depends primarily on the nature of the burden the analyst's interventions place on them. The context in which such cooperative effort takes place surrounds those manifestations of intrapsychic conflict that occur during the analytic hour, "inside" the analytic situation. Although I feel that there are advantages to working in this context whenever possible (Gray 1973), I am not suggesting doing so exclusively (Gray 1984); I am trying here to describe more clearly how to do it.

Obviously, a discussion of where and in what way the analyst decides to focus analytic attention must deal primarily with choice of a surface. I say "a" surface rather than "the" surface because, although there is wide agreement on analyzing "from the surface," surface means different things to different analysts. I regard as an optimum surface for interpretive interventions a selection of those elements in the material that may successfully illustrate for analysands that when they were speaking, they encountered a conflict over something being revealed, which caused them involuntarily and unknowingly to react in identifiably defensive ways. By "successfully illustrate" I mean to succeed in directing analysands' attention to things they can grasp in spite of never ceasing resistance. The interpretive task is to estimate sensitively the patient's ability to comprehend, in order to make a formulation that is not too superficial, yet does not stimulate more reactive defense (Fenichel 1941).

To the extent that analysts are able to use an optimum surface, they will provide analysands with the best chance to use their self-observing equipment. So far, this rather simple expression of aims and general process fails to disclose a variety of obstacles that can make the task complex and challenging. Let us examine some of the most prominent difficulties.

Analysands are not familiar with the nature of the activities in which the mind-at-surface quietly engages while they are speaking. Indeed, they are barely even aware of the existence of these activities. For instance, the natural orientation of their thinking is restricted to regarding the things they say as references solely to what they have been talking about. Patients must learn that they can yield this natural stance as they gain familiarity with another function of their mind, a function that consists of their living out a piece of mental behavior while they are speaking, and must also learn how and why they are doing so. The educational help described earlier will assist significantly with this, but experiencing and practicing these skills is obviously essential. Part of the manifestation characterized by "there is a resistance to uncovering of resistances" (Freud 1937a, p. 239) often results from the analyst's failure to provide the analysand with the best opportunity to perceive the resistance.

Examples

During the early hours of an analysis, an analyst told a female patient, in very clear and appropriately spoken terms, that something the patient had just expressed had interrupted and replaced an uncomfortable preceding thought. The analysand, quiet for a few seconds, then responded in a serious and thoughtfully unprovoking tone, "What is it that I am supposed to do with that?" The analyst dealt with this by replying, also in a thoughtful tone, that the patient wished the analyst to do the thinking for her. Although there eventually would be times in the analysis for such an interpretation, it was not helpful at this point; for, in fact, the patient did *not* know how to try to make use of what the analyst had said. In a subsequent hour, following similar remarks by her analyst, the analysand, now more cautious, did manage to say that she "really" did not know what to do with his observation. This time, the analyst was able to say that by his comments he was trying to provide an opportunity for her to notice that in attempting to be spontaneous and candid in expressing her thoughts and feelings, she had reached a specific place that became difficult—there was some conflict—and suddenly she had turned to another line of thought, as if she had taken refuge in it. He added that if in retrospect she could confirm this, then she might be free, by "going back" to that difficult place, to try to understand with the analyst's help what sort of "risk" had inhibited her. If she could do this, she might not have to avoid such conflicted thoughts or feelings. Within the bounds of what her resistance permitted, she was subsequently able to begin the task of gradually bringing into her awareness how currently unnecessary were her ego's unconscious, reflexive, defensive activities.

Not wanting to distract us from looking at the method, I have deliberately left out of my account the particular content of the material that the analysand had found too risky to become more aware of and to put into words. Let us now look at some examples with more "content." In passing, we can note that the term content may apply equally well either to the defense or to the drive derivatives defended against (Loewenstein 1982). Hence, a polarization of defense analysis with content analysis really only obfuscates an area already difficult to spell out.

There are countless examples in which the analysand arrives at critical or aggressive thoughts toward someone else and suddenly replaces them with self-criticism. This can be demonstrated easily to a patient. I have listened to a case report in which the analysand began to learn from the analyst how to observe his intrapsychic behavior. He grasped with such vividness his way of suddenly turning on himself in order to protect various objects that he said it was "like making a U turn." The analyst usefully adopted this simile to designate for the patient the progressively more subtle and complex versions of the "U turn" that continued to occur.

In another example, an analysand was able to follow the analyst's illustrations of turning on herself as a solution to conflict over some derivative of aggression. She was now increasing her capacity to study additional details of how this defense was being carried out. The analyst had recognized these details much earlier, but because of resistance and *because of their complexity*, to include them in the surface then being examined would have put too much of a burden on the analysand's observing apparatus. Now the patient could go beyond the observation that she was afraid to criticize the analyst and would escape by picking on herself. She found it possible to comprehend, where it could be demonstrated, that she carried this out by instantly *identifying with the victim* (Orgel 1974b) or potential victim of her feared aggression and, in increasingly elaborate detail, masochistically brought upon herself all of the cruel impulses she was *afraid to feel toward someone else*. She now began to understand very clearly the phenomenon of stopping her active observing and reacting toward another by becoming some part of that person. Needless to say, this learned capacity for observing *identification* as it took place within the analysis became valuable far beyond the specific form it took in the activity of turning on herself.

It can be instructive to the analyst to notice the specific ways that an interpretive intervention may *fail* to help the analysand's observing capacity and to see where the resistance has defeated the attempt.

Near the end of an hour, a woman permitted a new, less guarded level of recall and reexperiencing of resentment against a brother, a brother on whom she fondly depended but who had chronically traumatized her as a youngster. She recounted an episode during which she had observed an inappropriate, "crazy" behavior of her sibling. With this material, an edge of bitter resentment emerged. Although her memory had reached a new degree of vividness, she finally interrupted the flow with a form of defense—in essence, a reaction-formation, consisting of breaking off the description of the sibling's provocative behavior and moving quickly to recall instead the sibling's sad remorse subsequent to his behavior. This latter recollection was accompanied by a feeling of sympathy, rather than the previous growing resentment, and did not provide the analyst with any further disclosure of the bizarre, perverse cruelty of the sibling. The analyst then intervened to point out how the sympathetic feeling she was experiencing *now*—although also a part of her relationship with her brother—had come to mind in this instance and in a familiar way, interrupting her recall of the behavior she had described as "crazy." He pointed out further that the resentful feelings had vanished. The analyst drew her attention to the implied risk associated with the presence of the listening analyst, had she continued to pursue the original train of thought, imagery, and feeling.

Often, after such an interpretive intervention, the analysand would be able to return to the uncomfortable point of the defensive interruption and there to recognize the sense of discomfort or conflict, to "take it on," to explore that sense of danger to a greater extent, and to make possible the analysis of more detailed increments of the inhibiting fantasy which set off the defense. For her, one important fantasy connected with the danger was that if she continued angrily and vengefully to recall and expose more of her sibling's behavior, the analyst would cease to listen analytically and, instead, would feel shocked and disgusted and would behave in a specifically punitive manner. Also, with exploration she often recognized something more about the dangerously conflicted conditions that had prevailed early in life, when she became a distraught, emotionally traumatized witness, provoked among other things to angry, vengeful impulses toward her brother—impulses she so feared revealing that she was compelled to forget them. In this instance, she managed her forgetting by means of a complex form of reaction-formation, which, as a character trait, was now being repeated in the form of resistance.

During this particular hour, however, her resistance was especially heightened because of an approaching, longer than usual weekend interruption, and she regressively gave up some of her previously gained observing ability. Instead of exploring what had occurred during the hour, she continued to insist that her brother had "in fact" not "meant" to behave so badly and should have been better treated by those about, including the patient, and that further there was nothing more that had happened. "That was all."

In view of the heightened resistance of this analysand, the analyst could have made a less burdensome, more useful choice of surface by selecting and speaking only about her need to stop exposing the observed details of the sibling's egregious and bizarre behavior she had always kept in protective secrecy. Alternatively, he might have spoken only about her need to stop aggressive feelings that were mobilized in relation to the traumatizing events she was recalling and describing. In other words, it would have been more useful if the analyst had referred to one defended derivative at a time, rather than to two. Eventually in the analysis it was demonstrated that additional drive derivatives were being defended against, but then, as now, I was trying to refer only to those conflicted derivatives that could be usefully demonstrated for her observing ego.

I shall include one more consideration for improving the analysand's observing capacity. We depend not only on the attitude we convey in our manner of speaking and the sequence of references—that is, "defense before drive"—but also on our *choice of words*. Analysts hardly need reminding of the value of thoughtfully worded interventions. There are, however, some useful ways of conceptualizing aspects of this part of technique, if we wish to study the detail of reaching the analysand's observing functions. When we choose our words most wisely, we lessen the burden on analysands' rational listening, comprehension, and observation in three ways. First, we respect their egos by choosing language that does not strain their fund of knowledge; second, we choose so that we do not stimulate their conflicted instinctual drives; and third, we try not to attract their superegos into substituting a judgmental attitude for an objective one. Since a satisfying discussion of this area would be lengthy, I shall settle for brief examples of each of the three categories, in the hope of stimulating further thought on the subject.

First for the ego area: if the analyst uses a word that for the patient has a lifetime of meaning different from the one intended by the analyst, a sort of mini culture-shock may result. A common example is the analyst's use of the word "feel" or "feeling" to refer to an *unconscious* instinctual derivative. It may take the form: "I believe that you are feeling angry with me for being late (or going away, etc.)." I have in mind occasions when the analysand is in fact not "feeling" any such thing. It may be quite true and important that the analysand is at that point defending against reacting to a disappointment, but that is different from feeling something. An analyst's "suggestion" may temporarily melt the resistance and a feeling may *then* occur; on the other hand, such wording of the intervention may lend itself to the resistance and the analysand can quite accurately say that there is no such feeling. The word "feeling" is so ingrained as a reference to something of which one is aware that to use it otherwise does not provide a very good chance for the analysand to join the analyst in observing a useful surface. It would be easier to join the inquiry if, for example, the word were put in a familiar context by approaching from the side of the defense. For instance, one might ask what does it mean, in the face of a potentially clearly disappointing event, that the patient is *not* feeling disappointment in the analyst? It might be even better if the analyst can describe the *way* in which the chance of such a feeling is being involuntarily avoided.

Second, for the instinctual stimulation area: here words that are sometimes characterized as "seductive" apply. These are words that effect a transient "melting" of the resistance and add an impetus to the drive. An example would be if the analyst, referring to an intimate object of the analysand, uses the first name, or even pet name, of that person in a "familiar" way, thereby creating a momentary alliance based on the fleeting illusion of a shared familiarity with the mentioned figure. The analyst might avoid the seductive illusion by disclaiming any such shared familiarity, for example, by using the words "your wife" or "your husband," "your friend Harry," "your companion Jane." This would preserve the analysand's autonomous task with the effort required to think objectively in that context. Thus, patients' independent responsibility for their object relationships would remain more clearly in their own hands.

Third, for the superego attracting area: here, words are used that although quite accurate for the occasion in their dictionary definition, have become, over the years of parlor-analytic use or even legitimate therapeutic manipulation, rather pejorative in meaning. Such words instantly invite the superego into the scheme of things, and objective observing gives way to a moral judgment. Sometimes this superego invasion is so insidious that the analysand's appearance of seeking insight masks an inhibiting resistance-supporting "mental health morality" (Hartmann 1960). Examples here include references that characterize analysands as regarding themselves "special" or "entitled." At some point, it is appropriate to bring these attitudes into consciousness, but the analyst can refer to them without muddling rational attention by using words that arouse the superego.

Finally, we come to some "working" examples. The effectiveness with which analysands can come to use their observing equipment—provided they have been allowed to practice—can be very impressive, even when it involves very quick, subtle defensive activity.

A man who had been overstimulated by his mother, and especially by his father, was given to clinging to his thoughts, feelings, longings for particular women in his life, in order to keep away from the dangers connected with positive feelings for his analyst. At one point, when working through some of these fears, he recalled the day he had first telephoned me. He said, "When I heard you saying 'yes, I can see you . . . will next week be all right . . . or is it more urgent?,' I was so moved that tears came to my eyes." At this point, some emotion came into his voice; there was a very short pause and he continued: "It was a time when I was still living with R (a sister with whom he had been very close) . . . it was in the country . . . but I was so depressed, and something about your willingness to see me . . ." (the emotion had left his voice by the time of this last remark). At that point I drew his attention to what had just taken place. I pointed out that what he had just spoken last was said rather differently—with less feeling—than he had permitted himself when he first began to recall and think about me. I showed him further that he had apparently run into difficulty with those feelings about me and that his familiar solution was to reach—ever so briefly, but it was there—for thoughts about a gratifying woman. He was able to attend to this, to think back briefly and review for himself what he had inadvertently done. He could now sense that he had stopped himself from being moved emotionally toward stronger feelings for me. He could take advantage of the evidence that he was afraid of these feelings. With some conviction, he said, "If I don't do that, I will want to be with you all of the time . . . I *won't* become that dependent."[2]

In another example, a woman who in many ways used her masochism to shield herself from the dangers of revealing or

---

[2]For some expansion of this clinical example, see Chapter 4, this volume, pp. 94–100.

asserting her phallically associated aggression spoke at one point of an individual who had repeatedly disappointed her: "That man . . . (*angrily*) I'm pissed off at him . . . (*very slight pause*) he is always dumping on me." Although she was still upset, but because she had acquired the capability of being closely observant upon intervention, the analyst interrupted her before she could go on, and reconstructed what took place. He pointed out her need—by thinking of the man "dumping" on her—to turn partly on herself what she had actively permitted toward another just an instant before when she said, "that man—I'm pissed off at him." She was thoughtful for a moment and then recalled a recent exchange with a woman friend. In the memory, the patient is saying of another man: "I said 'I'm pissed at him' . . . and then, with a viciousness that surprised me, I said, 'What I want to say to him is FUCK OFF!'"

I cite this example, of course, to show that because of practice in using her own observing equipment effectively the analysand is capable, when shown, of seeing how she could switch virtually in mid-sentence—in the immediacy of process—from an aggressive stance to a masochistic position. For our purpose, it is beside the point that she was also defending, by displacement, against transference impulses toward her analyst, or that through the process of gaining insight into the nature of her resistance and permitting a clearer version of her aggression, she needed to bring another woman into the picture momentarily (her mother always tolerated anger toward men and toward her father in particular). It is also beside the point that she had not yet spoken of the still live fantasied danger of expressing aggression toward men in front of me. We can observe all this in the example, and in practice the analysis would deal with it in due time. I elaborate these elements in an attempt to attenuate an easy diversion from our focus on the elusive area of observation of the ego's activities during neurotic solution to conflict. In this often less familiar and for some less interesting area of technique, one must sometimes compete with the listener's attention drifting toward other fascinating aspects of the clinical material not being addressed.

Finally, here is one more brief clinical example of what I mean by the analysand's eventual ability for a more autonomous self-observation. A woman who, through repeated shared observations, had learned about a particular defensive solution to her fear of her aggressive phallic impulses, said the following: "Yesterday, my mother spent 20 minutes on the phone carping about my father, she always . . . (*pause*) . . . but I did the same thing today on the phone with my sister, so who am I to . . . (*stops here*) . . . (*slowly*) . . . I can see what I am doing . . . (*pause*) I start to protect her again by taking it out on myself . . . what I want to say . . . my mother behaves like a bitch."

Here we can see where multiple skills of more or less simultaneously observing id contributions, conflict, and ego solutions all come together for a moment of conscious self-analysis.

Almost 50 years ago, Sterba's classic observations (1934) regarding the *fate* of the ego as one of *therapeutic dissociation* provided analysts with a valuable concept of how the observing ego plays an important role during the analytic process. I believe we can move beyond the implications of the word *fate* by thinking of the changes in the self-observing ego as more than a kind of inevitable byproduct of the analysis. Systematic attention to self-observation, when clinically appropriate, can become a more explicit aim of analysis of the neuroses. It should become an integral part of analysis of the ego's manifestations of resistance through its forms of unconscious, defensive activities in the face of analytically mobilized conflict. Whenever this is successfully carried out, I believe we have secured "the best possible psychological conditions for the functions of the ego" which, as Freud said (1937, p. 250) is "the business of the analysis."

4

THE NATURE OF THERAPEUTIC ACTION IN PSYCHOANALYSIS

My subject is broader than might appear at first glance. Whether or not one personally prefers to apply the psychoanalytic method only to a restricted group of patients, the reality is that today a wide range of clinical problems are treated with a variety of approaches many consider to be "psychoanalysis." The therapeutic action in the analytic treatment of this spectrum of patients varies not only with the particular methodology applied, but also with the psychological nature of the analysand. I *do* mean the therapeutic action varies, not the opinion of what takes place, although that is an added complexity. That patients differ in their capacities for change presents further problems. In addition, individual patients, depending largely on their pathology, have characteristic propensities for certain kinds of therapeutic action. Since I am responding to a request for my personal view of the topic, I shall not provide, at this time, a review of contributions by others who have usefully conveyed their own conceptions (Abrams 1980, Blatt and Behrends 1987, Joseph 1979, Kohut 1984, Loewald 1960, Modell 1976, Panel 1979, Strachey 1934).

A frequent problem when examining the subject of therapeutic action is how to avoid repeating the parable of the blind men examining an elephant. I shall try to identify the positions from which I approach the creature.

I shall describe in what follows (1) the theoretical and clinical context for my comments, as well as the therapeutic aims or kind of analytic "help" I have in mind; (2) some of my thinking and forms of attention during my work with the patient, followed by some notes of a closely monitored analytic process illustrating my own choices of therapeutic actions; and (3) certain advantages and possible disadvantages inherent in this approach.

1. The theoretical and clinical framework within which I examine therapeutic action is the analysis of those problems that arise when instinctual derivatives, searching for more adequate discharge, encounter conflicts that force the ego to turn primarily to unconscious, rather than conscious, solutions. As further clarification of my focus, I emphasize what I regard as the fundamental clinical issue, namely the patient's basic need to avoid anxiety.

I shall speak of therapeutic actions in terms of psychological concepts. Although I am aware of hypotheses that modern neurophysiology provides about therapeutic actions, some virtually at a cellular level, I shall not address those here. In defining the area of therapeutic actions I include reference to clinical conditions for which such action is most relevant. Here I must be unsatisfyingly brief. I include the extensive range of neurotic symptoms or character traits that develop primarily to prevent intrapsychic conflict from mobilizing anxiety. These conditions may be accompanied at times not only by anxiety symptoms, but by a considerable scope of other distressing affective states which serve as alternatives to or protection against anxiety: exaggerated guilt, shame, low self-esteem—or narcissistic defenses against the latter—as well as of depressive reactions.

For those therapeutic actions I shall illustrate, the treatment has the broad therapeutic aim of reducing the patient's *potential* for anxiety, as differentiated from merely reducing anxiety. Diminishing the potential for anxiety, via analysis of unconscious infantile fears, decreases the patient's *need* for symptomatic regression.

I distinguish between, on the one hand, conditions or components necessary for a context in which change can occur, and, on the other hand, the analytically sought-for processes of therapeutic change themselves. I am aware that it is not always easy to distinguish between these two areas. Although a patient must be conscious, attentive, and have some degree of rapport with, relatedness to, or interest in the therapist's contribution, for an analytic result to be possible, these essential prerequisites are not the essence of the therapeutic actions of the analyses to which I refer.

2. Before approaching the clinical material, I want to describe the particular form of attention to which I give priority, to provide a basic ground for understanding my brief sample of process material. In order to be better understood I shall risk appearing to describe the obvious.

In listening to the patient, I focus on the flow of material with an ear for evidence, at the manifest surface level, of some identifiable expression of an instinctual drive derivative. This might appear from the patient's words alone—what is actually being said—or it might be evident from one or more of the many sounds or nuances of affect accompanying the words. I have in mind particularly affects deriving characteristically from libidinal or aggressive sources. My working assumptions are that (a) these drive derivatives are constantly trying to maintain access to consciousness; (b) they have no inherent resistance to doing so; and (c) if and when they are involuntarily interfered with, it is as the result of some conflict the ego is sensing. The drive-inhibiting solution is meant to stop the conflict from mobilizing anxiety. As long as the drive derivative that has drawn my attention continues unabated, I tend to restrain interventions. I wait for this particular instinctually associated trend to continue into the patient's awareness as far as the patient's ego can tolerate it. Once there is evidence that the patient has encountered a conflict over this trend, for which the ego initiates a form of resistance, my interest is in assessing if and how best I might be able to call the patient's attention to the event—the sequence—which has just taken place. Another of my essential assumptions is that the conflict the patient has encountered is crucially heightened by a fantasy, that to put into words what comes to mind in the presence of the analyst is to create some kind of risk—some consequence which will arise from or within the analyst (Gray 1986).

There is a further piece of theory accompanying me through this activity with the patient: I regard such inhibiting fantasies of danger as repetitions of the images of childhood authorities—or their subsequent versions—that first served to inhibit the impulses now trying to surface during the analytic situation. These are images we recognize as eventually internalized for superego purposes. They are the same images one *always promptly reexternalizes on accepting a relationship with another individual who imposes (or even appears to impose) a task or threat of uncovering unconsciously defended impulses and emotions*. Once reexternalized, they qualify as transferences. In the analytic situation, they become a major aspect of transference as resistance (Gray 1987). Their analysis makes up not only a crucial part of defense analysis, but more significantly, the analysis of that specialized part of ego functioning we regard as superego. This is one of the conceptual points to which I shall return in accounting further for my particular perspectives on therapeutic action.

Anna Freud (1936) observed that the defensive activities of the ego were "carried out silently and invisibly" (p. 8) and could only be reconstructed after the activity took place. From today's vantage point it would be more useful to say that these defensive activities are silent and invisible *to the patient*—that is why we refer to them as unconscious. They need not be so to the analyst if he is closely attentive to them, nor eventually to the patient if they are sufficiently demonstrated.

I characterize the kind of phenomena that alert *my* analytic listening as those moments when I observe that point of intrapsychic stress which forces the ego to interfere with the emerging material, stopping the conflicted drive element from intruding further into consciousness. One could call such a moment a "breaking point," in that the ego, resorting to a way of unconscious functioning developed for childhood purposes and now regressively repeated, does effect a "mini-breakdown" in mature functioning. At such moments, there is invariably a "change of voice" (R. Gardner, personal communication); of course "voice" here is used in its broadest connotations. It may be a blatant, dramatic, sudden difference from what occupied the moment before; or it may be an exceedingly subtle alternative. In either case, it is a change that, with practice, is evident to a listening analyst's focus of attention. It does not depend on the analyst attending to his own unconscious.

Obviously, I am trying to implement and maintain a principle of drawing more and more of the patient's ego into conscious participation in the analytic process. After the original shift away from the use of hypnosis, Freud found it necessary to preserve a "remnant of hypnosis" to increase the patient's strength in overcoming resistance, and also to "persuade" and "convince" him of the "truth" of the interpretations. However, once the role of anxiety in the neuroses was revised and the defensive versatility of the ego increasingly conceptualized, the technical possibility of analyzing without depending on suggestion has been more within our grasp. As I have stated elsewhere (Gray 1987), some degree of suggestion is ubiquitous in any human interaction. Nevertheless what many individuals can learn through rational attention, if given the opportunity to use more and more objective ego capacity in the service of grasping intrapsychic reality, is a far cry from insight gained under hypnotic-suggestive influence. For analysts to pay technical attention to improving a patient's capacity for more mature observing, and consistently to analyze symptomatic compromise of ego functionings that perpetuate immature avenues for change, can go a long way toward reducing the short-changing role of suggestion.

I shall begin the clinical material with a closeup look at some increments of therapeutic change in a man as they take place during part of an analytic session. The patient was in treatment essentially for problems of unconscious conflict over competing successfully in a variety of career and social activities. A primary underlying factor was intense anxiety over his (usually unconscious) potential for aggression. Prominent among his neurotic solutions to such conflicts were regressions to passive and inhibited states. These passive states were associated with a background of early stimulating events with his father, which had aroused both competitive homosexual impulses (to dominate or possess his father's masculine advantages) and passive homosexual impulses.

Because of intense fear of his aggression, the patient's passive longings tended to surface more readily. However, because his particular passive wishes threatened to put him in a helpless and overpowered state, these longings ran into conflicts of their own and, in turn, aroused defenses. Though unmarried, the patient was capable of passionate, intimate, yet uncommitted relationships with women. It became clear during the analysis that he sought such relationships more compulsively when he was in danger of becoming affectionately dependent upon a man. This last description of one of his character traits—out of the many things that could be said about him by this time in the analysis—is included because that particular defense informed an observation I make in the case material that follows.

Increasingly, the patient had become aware that the conflicts he experienced while trying to free-associate were significantly influenced by the presence of various, usually at first preconscious, fantasies of incurring some risk at my hands, because of what he might reveal. These intimidating images came to include my not respecting him; my laughing at or ridiculing him; and especially my judging him ineffectual, weak (small). Increasingly, these images took on more aggressive consequences such as my becoming provoked into a shouting rage, leading to some danger to his body. Two generalizations were possible: first, these intimidating images corresponded to certain early views of his father. Although his father was generally a kindly, benevolent person, the boy had also selectively viewed him as inhibiting the boy's freedom to display himself to advantage, or as competing for advantage. Second, these inhibiting images arose during those hours or moments associated with the patient's need to turn away from some *active* or aggressive line of thought or feeling toward someone other than himself. He could thereby achieve an inhibition of the feared thoughts by reaching for a transferred image that would threaten to put *him* on the receiving end of some kind of aggression. Repeated demonstrations of these data, and especially sharing with him the evidence that during our work together his ego was exploiting these inhibiting images for purposes of resistance, had allowed him increasing control over the need to inhibit himself constantly by clinging to a powerful authority.

It is helpful to know that the patient, by the time of this example, had acquired considerable skill in reflecting on details of what he had been saying or experiencing whenever I invited such observations. I shall now describe the process during an hour when he was beginning to allow greater access to certain positive feelings for me which, although defensively motivated, were in themselves potentially frightening.

He spoke briefly of wishing to know more about me than I revealed during our work together; he had long avoided any active curiosity in this direction. He then paused briefly, almost imperceptibly, and his tone took on a different quality—a moment of "change of voice." He now spoke of the day he had first telephoned me (he has displaced to the past), and continued, "When I heard you saying, 'I can see you. . . . Will next week be all right, or is it more urgent?' I was so moved that tears came to my eyes" (in the displacement the conflicted active curiosity has given way to a more passive, dependent mode). At this point his feeling could be clearly heard. He paused very briefly and continued—now without the emotion (another "change of voice")—"It was a time when I was staying with my sister (a sibling with whom he was very close) . . . it was in the country, but I was so depressed, and something about your willingness to see me. . . . "

What appears to have happened is that briefly into his somewhat freed-up curiosity—his active wish to acquire some knowledge of me—he experienced conflict; to appear to want to possess something of me was too dangerous. The solution was to inhibit his active role by turning to a passive, dependent relationship with me and to put *himself* on the receiving end of my activity, manifestly *my* professional curiosity and attention. However, this became rapidly too threatening, and he turned to another familiar defense. Although a sequence of defenses is now apparent, and theoretically could be pointed out to him, it is more useful, more manageable for a patient, better for his self-observing capacity, to focus on the *last* defense, because it is the "nearest" one, the one with which the patient is momentarily coping. Therefore, I drew his attention to what had just taken place. I pointed out that what he had spoken last was said rather differently—with less feeling—than he had permitted himself when he first began to recall the telephone conversation and to think about me. I showed him, further, that when he had run into difficulties with those feelings about me, a familiar solution occured; it was to reach—ever so briefly, but it was there—for a thought about a gratifying woman. He was able to attend to this, to think back and review for himself what he had just done involuntarily. He could take advantage of the reconstructed evidence that he was dealing with a conflict over these feelings, that in a familiar way, they had entered consciousness and he had then dynamically interrupted them. As he now thought back on what had just taken place in his mind, he *felt* the discomfort connected with the instinctualized part he had unknowingly avoided. He said with conviction: "If I don't do that [defend himself as he did] I will want to be with you all of the time." Now the libidinal derivative came through more freely, was held briefly and usefully in awareness, but not surprisingly soon encountered a new limitation. So, reaching again for defense, he quickly added: " . . . and I *won't* become that dependent." This provided us with another opportunity to explore further increments of a spectrum of fantasies of danger associated with a passive relationship with an older man, fantasies which at the moment were *helping defensively* to keep him at a distance from additional libidinal impulses.

Not to analyze such highly influencing, transferred fantasies of authority, either intimidating and inhibiting him on the one hand, or forgiving and approving on the other, would be to leave the defensive superego aspect of the ego fundamentally unaltered.

The patient drew upon a number of sources in transferring these superego functions. He regressively activated and in "panoramic procession" (Greenacre 1959, p. 485) reexternalized them upon the analyst in order to support the resistance against accepting a *morally neutral* opportunity for self-discovery. The sources included pregenital events of separation from a periodically hospitalized mother, early surgical instrumentation, and misperception and misinterpretation of what happens to dependent individuals, females in particular, when they are passive to a male.

In examining this material from the standpoint of the goal of *reducing the potential for anxiety*, I shall emphasize several therapeutic actions which were accompanied by change toward a more *maturely effective functioning of the patient's mental apparatus.*

Let me start with a sequence of insights the patient was gaining into the workings of his mind. He learned by repeatedly attending to his analyst's descriptions—reconstructed from the patient's just spoken words—that he could grasp the concept of what to look for and could thus retrospectively recognize defensive activities that occurred on the surface of his mind; he could *comprehend the familiar evidence* that they served to relieve some approaching sense of risk because of what he was beginning to expose. Here one can identify both *conceptual* and *perceptual* components as essential to the insights involved in this aspect of the therapeutic action. By my observing and sharing with him how his mind at times unwittingly responded to the presence of certain elements, he slowly acquired a usable conceptual and observational sense of defensive mental actions of which he had been unaware. It is important to note that the interpretive interventions consistently approach material from the *side of the defense*, and refer to a surface-near derivative that has already been allowed into awareness and *then* (following conflict encountered) has been repressed (used here in its broad sense of dynamically removed from consciousness). Although the derivative has been clearly identified, its importance is not stressed in a confrontational manner. In this way the patient does not experience at once the burden of such conflict and so does not *need suggestion* to manage the self-observation. The patient then has more opportunity to use his ego's more autonomous self-observing capacity. The need for suggestion in order to face the resistance is more apt to be present when the analyst tries, through *an* interpretation, to confront a drive derivative not yet in consciousness but sensed to be not far below the surface. All too often the analyst uses authority to *overcome* the resistance sufficiently to bring the drive derivative into consciousness; as a result, the ego's often highly detailed role in enforcing the repression is less likely to be subject to the important perception, examination, and exploration of its history.

These insights usually led to increased understanding of those early times in the patient's life when he had needed to develop such automatic reactions, and extended the sometimes reconstructed knowledge of the original needs for defense—now resistance—that was one of the essential aspects of our work. In addition, as he once more *exercised the regained use of his objective self-observing functions,* formerly used by his superego for critical inhibiting purposes only, he added another kind of insight—

insight gained by *experience.* As he used these atrophied pathways of objective, more reality-attuned observing capacities, he achieved greater consciousness of *having* such a capacity and of his *increasingly autonomous access to it.*

Eventually, this man learned he could notice these habitual reactions within his mind, without my first having to draw his attention to them; he could observe them *as they occurred.* Patients at this stage of experience have said "I can see what's coming"; "I saw what I was doing"; "I know what I'm doing"; "I'm doing it again"; etc. None of these need be self-critical observations; to the contrary, they may be accompanied by amazement and a sense of self-discovery. For this patient, such observations contributed steadily both to his growing capacity for self-analysis and to further therapeutic action.

Further therapeutic action comes from the subsequent use, preferably at once in the analytic situation, which the patient made of the therapeutic gains just described. When he followed up the observations and comprehension of the formerly unconscious solutions of his ego-in-the-face-of-conflict by returning via reflection to these sites in his thinking and speaking in order to reengage the moment of the "break-point" or "change-of-voice" he was able to take on some of the discomfort that the conflict aroused. This use of the previously gained insight in his efforts to further his task of *verbalized spontaneity* opened up the possibility for an additional insight, namely, elaboration of the motivations for these avoidance phenomena. His awareness that he was mobilizing part of the conflict by attempting to put private thoughts into words *in the presence of the other person in the room*, made it possible for him to recognize that the conflict he was now experiencing was connected with a fantasy that some disturbing consequence could arise from these disclosures. Each new occasion of comprehending something that had been taking place unconsciously within him for years, and *each new experience of actively using these insights in furthering the analytic task and process, increase ego strength for objective self-confrontation.*

Increasingly undistorted id derivatives succeeded in entering his awareness, as he gained insight into the defensive motivation for, and the current inappropriateness of transferring, the restraining childhood images of authority as he had perceived—and partly created them—prior to the superego solution to his oedipal conflicts. Again, each new bit of such systematically gained access is accompanied by the important, *experientially acquired insight* into the reality that his adult ego is in fact capable of consciously, willingly managing the restraint or discharge of his instinctual life. Both the fact and the sense of his growing strength in the face of previously warded-off wishes and live impulses constitute this second phase of therapeutic action. This aspect of therapeutic action is a form of *learning* of his capacity for ego strength *through the experience* of gradually, autonomously exercising his control over the impulses being reclaimed. This process optimally does *not* depend on internalizing a new fantasy of a more permissive authority, a less mature learning process because internalization processes, typical of superego formation, rely primarily on unconscious mechanisms, illusory in nature. The anxiety-relieving and civilizing measures appropriate to childhood and adolescence can be improved by providing opportunities for more mature therapeutic actions during adult analyses. I am, of course, aware that some patients with severe intrapsychic compromise may rightly require a degree of interpersonal sharing which, of necessity, lends itself, very valuably, to a greater amount of internalizing solutions.

3. In discussing certain advantages and disadvantages of the methodology described I shall first reiterate my opinion that the two major factors influencing therapeutic actions are, on the one hand, the psychopathology, or more precisely the personality structure, of the patient predisposing him to certain predilections for change, and on the other hand, the analyst's technical approach reflecting in considerable detail his theoretical orientation. My own approach, exemplified in a limited way in the clinical example, stresses an observing, listening, focus which tries to perceive, primarily via the spoken material, evidence of

drive derivatives that *have reached the patient's awareness* and that have *then* developed enough conflict to stimulate the ego to a defensive/resistive solution, the outcome of which is the removal of the drive element from consciousness. At appropriate moments and with acceptable words, I invite the patient to share in observing what has taken place. The analytic inquiry moves toward understanding the motivations for such intrapsychic activity; the genetic history of these resistances usually contributes to the insights that lead to processes accompanying change. One specific advantage of this method is its greater dependence on confirmable observation, rather than on data depending considerably on the analyst's use, at least initially, of references to his own unconscious. Since my theoretical stance is one of choosing to believe there are no unconscious id forces "drawing down" mental elements from above, my working hypothesis, on which my technique depends, is that consistent, detailed analysis of the forms and motivations of the ego's surface-near manifestations of resistance against specific drive derivatives will *of itself* allow gradual, analytically sufficient ego assimilation of the warded-off mental elements as they are able to move less fearfully into consciousness. An advantage of central importance here is that aspects of the ego which have been operating out of control, in particular the superego functions, are gradually brought into the patient's awareness; to expand our time-worn adage, where unconscious ego was, conscious ego, as well, shall be.

I anticipate there are some analysts who fear the disadvantage of a loss in this approach. They are the ones who, in dealing with the resistance, have depended to a considerable extent on helping the patient to bring to the surface drive derivatives, not yet in consciousness, through timely and accurate interpretations of their hidden locations. Such an approach, while itself often highly gratifying for the analyst in its art, can make the task of turning instead to a rather meticulous registering of the sometimes fast-moving surface changes presented by a defense-motivated ego seem, at first, too demanding; such conscious attention to the surface detail of conflict and solution can appear uninviting, perhaps too "rational." My response to this ostensible disadvantage is not to see it as a question of having to abandon an analytic methodology that gives a somewhat greater role to using one's unconscious resonance for id derivatives, but to see the matter as one of acquiring an alternative within one's technical repertory. The more direct, broader uses of interpretation of instinctual derivatives continue to be of value with patients who virtually cannot free their observing capacities from domination by the ego's superego functions, or for psychoanalytically oriented psychotherapy where one assumes that interpretive work is, of convenience, going to deal with resistance by means of considerable authoritative transference influence. For such patients extensive familiarity with the ego's defensive measures and the acquisition of self-analyzing skills are much less possible, and therapeutic actions depend much more on incremental mutative internalizing of a benevolently perceived authority.

5

THE ANALYSIS OF THE EGO'S INHIBITING SUPEREGO ACTIVITIES

Much ambiguity surrounds the technical approach to the superego during the analytic process. I shall argue here that the cause lies in two related circumstances. First, there is the deeply ingrained tradition in technique that expediently mandated the use of transferred superego (not always so labeled) influences in order to overcome rather than analyze resistance. This was especially true during the years before the role of conflict in resistance was understood. Second, the superego itself was conceptualized *before* the revision of the theory of anxiety and the resulting recognition of the ego's versatile defensive complexity. By then the superego had achieved status as a structure supraordinate to the ego, rather than as a manifestation of the ego's active defensive solutions to unconscious conflict. In addition to these two, I shall hypothesize about some less central influences.

As documentation, I intend to examine evidence in some of Freud's work. In attempting to reduce some of the ambiguity, I shall draw on relevant literature from Freud's later contemporaries, as well as on more recent authors. There will follow some views of my own on what I mean by *analysis* of the superego and on the theory and practice of analytic technique in relation to the superego.

I

In 1919, Freud was on the verge of a decade of writings (1920, 1923, 1926a) that would turn around much of the comprehension of intrapsychic processes and eventually would change, in widely varying degrees, much of the conceptualization of technical access to those processes. Yet, in 1919, he stated the case for analytic methodology in the following manner:

> We have formulated our task as physicians thus: to bring to the patient's knowledge the unconscious, repressed impulses existing in him, and, for that purpose, to uncover the resistances that oppose this extension of his knowledge about himself. Does the uncovering of these resistances guarantee that they will also be overcome? Certainly not always; but our hope is to achieve this *by exploiting the patient's transference to the person of the physician, so as to induce him to adopt our conviction* of the inexpediency of the repressive process established in childhood and of the impossibility of conducting life on the pleasure principle. [p. 159, italics added]

The essence of the analyst's power that makes the "inducing" possible was bestowed on him by a transfer to the analyst of images of parental authority from childhood that the patient had meanwhile internalized. Freud (1923) would later describe this primarily defensively motivated internalization as an "alteration" of ego function and name it *superego*. By 1919, the expedient of therapeutically "exploiting" with suggestion this reexternalization (with whatever accompanying technical shortcomings) had become the most effective tool thought to be available in the analyst's repertoire for coping with the crucial obstacle to treatment, the resistance. Despite later providing newer ways for himself and other analysts to comprehend intrapsychic processes, Freud continued in many ways to hold fast to his technical mode of 1919, retaining that "remnant of the hypnotic method" (1913, p. 133). It is interesting to note here that Anna Freud (1969), in *Difficulties in the Path of Psychoanalysis,* reminded readers that in Freud's last decade he did begin to speak of *how* the analyst might go about the "undoing of alterations . . . present [in the ego] as results of the defensive process" (Strachey 1964, p. 213). Freud either chose not to acknowledge or did not recognize (Gray 1982) the important technical measures that Anna Freud (1936) had by then evolved with her perception of the undeveloped trends in her father's contributions.

Faced at times with a disappointing, but hard-earned and long-cherished technical orientation. Freud moved further into his quest of the mysteries of resistance. Impelled especially by the challenge of clinical observations of an apparently unconscious need for punishment, Freud (1920) grappled with what he saw as exceptions to the pleasure principle. As he proceeded in *Beyond the Pleasure Principle*, he created for himself as well as for his followers a not uncharacteristic dilemma: he stated two divergent points of view regarding the nature of instinctual drives in their movement toward consciousness and gratification. The distinction between them is important because, during the ensuing years, we have tried to accommodate to his inconsistency. What is significant here is that one's attitude toward superego function in analytic treatment can be influenced according to which point of view one follows. The first position is in keeping with the eventual conception of neurosis based on conflict between the ego and the instinctual drives, and it could have made the habitual *necessity* for suggestion in technique obsolete (Waelder 1956). Freud's (1920) first position was that

> we must above all get rid of the mistaken notion that what we are dealing with in our struggle against resistances is resistance on the part of the *unconscious* . . . that is to say, the "repressed"—offers no resistance whatever to the efforts of the

> treatment. Indeed, it itself has no other endeavour than to break through the pressure *weighing down* [italics added] on it and force its way either to consciousness or to a discharge through some real action. Resistance during treatment arises from the *same higher strata* [italics added] and systems of the mind which originally carried out repression. [p. 19]

This unequivocal statement is a precept with which most analysts might agree.

Freud was to repeat this near the end of his writings (1940): " . . . the unconscious . . . comes to our help, since it has a natural 'upward drive' and desires nothing better than to press forward across its settled frontiers into the ego and so to consciousness" (p. 179). Anna Freud (1936) echoed this point of view: "We know that the id impulses have of themselves no inclination to remain unconscious. They naturally tend upward and are perpetually striving to make their way into consciousness and so to achieve gratification . . . " (p. 29).

Freud's second position, on the other hand, finds suggestion as essential to analytic technique, in order to overcome "organic inertia." Freud's (1920) clinically complicating hypothesis, the death instinct, based as we know on the hypothesis of "*an urge inherent in organic life to restore an earlier [inorganic] state of things*" (p. 36), led to this second position.

Freud spent a major portion of the same paper, in which he had stated the first position, developing the theory which relegated a significant portion of the resistance to a factor "beyond" those that could be identified and analyzed by interpretation and which would require a "working through." This latter called for a continued essential use of suggestion, a "use" that depended on suspending the analysis of those aspects of the transference which, a few years later, would be specified as associated with the superego. This new "beyond" factor was the "repetition-compulsion" that Freud (1926a) also characterized as the "*resistance of the unconscious*" (p. 160). It is not well known that Freud specifically attached both of these concepts to his hypothesis of the "death instinct."

Although the idea of an "organic" element in repression was actually not entirely new to Freud (1897), it burst forth in 1920 with great emphasis. At the same time, Freud had reservations that he did not particularly heed. His previous concept (1914) of "working through" appeared to be concerned only with "fixation" inertia. In this earlier observation, what Freud called a "compulsion to repeat," a "way of remembering" (1914, p. 150), was not contaminated by organic resistance and could have foreshadowed what eventually was conceptualized as conflict within a structural model. One needs to keep in mind here what Schur (1966) said about Strachey's translation:

> The distinction between "*compulsion to repeat*" and "*repetition compulsion*" gets lost, unfortunately, in Strachey's translation of the German word *Wiederholungszwang.* The term "compulsion to repeat" is used throughout without an editorial note explaining the distinction between these two concepts. There is a basic difference between the empirically valid observation of a compulsion to repeat and the theoretical concept of a repetition compulsion as an overriding regulatory principle of mental functioning. [p. 159]

In 1914 Freud even included what I believe was a most far-reaching, even "modern" characterization of repetition, an essential portrayal of his eventual theory of intrapsychic conflict. I quote it here, and shall return to it later: " . . . as the analysis proceeds . . . the patient brings out of the armoury of the past *the weapons with which he defends himself* . . . " (p. 151, italics added). Nevertheless, in *Beyond the Pleasure Principle* (1920), for better and/or worse, confronted by puzzling, tenacious resistances in analyses, Freud extended a lifelong preoccupation with death into the far-reaching theory of the death instinct (Schur 1972). His frustration at the time is clear: " . . . the analysis of the ego has made so little headway . . . " (Freud 1920, p. 53). Understandably, he was driven to characterize certain chronic severe forms of resistance as having a "hint of . . . 'daemonic' power" (p. 36). He freely displayed his own ambivalence about this new and radical explanation: "What follows is . . . often far-fetched speculation" (p. 24); "It may be asked whether and how far I am myself convinced of the truth of the hypotheses that have been set out in these pages. . . . I am not convinced myself . . . " (p. 59). Sterba (1982) quoted Freud's personal remarks: "It has been said that I am trying to force the death instinct upon analysts. However, I am . . . like someone who has to leave the house and leaves a toy behind so that the children will have something to play with while he is absent" (p. 116).

At the very end of *Beyond the Pleasure Principle,* Freud (1920), appearing unsatisfied with the hypothesis of his paper, sensed "a host of . . . questions to which we can at present find no answer. We must be patient and await fresh methods and occasions of research. We must be ready, too, to abandon a path that we have followed for a time, if it seems to be leading to no good end" (pp. 63–64).

However, Freud did not abandon the path he was following. In 1930, speaking of his ideas on the death instinct, he stated that although they were "only tentatively . . . put forward . . . in the course of time they have gained such a hold upon me that I can no longer think in any other way" (1930, p. 119).

Intrinsic to the concept of the death instinct was the simultaneous evolution of Freud's theory of aggression. We should not ignore Freud's prior, long-standing ambivalence about the presence of aggression as a primary drive. As he himself recognized, "I can no longer understand how we can have overlooked the ubiquity of non-erotic aggressivity and destructiveness and can have failed to give it its due place in our interpretation of life" (1930, p. 120). Although Freud in 1930 recognized and elaborated the relationship of suppression of aggression to the production of guilt, that is, the essential aspect of the superego in its use of the mechanism of turning aggression on the self, it is possible that his conflicting views on aggression acted as a determinant in his failure to bring the superego into sharper focus as exemplifying the major defense against aggression. For if the superego were to be truly analyzed, aggression would return with all its potential intensity to the jurisdiction of the ego. Freud may have been wary of this potential when he chose a theory that made aggression virtually an atypical, "secondary" instinct (Strachey 1961, pp. 61–62), as its aim was thought primarily to serve the organism's "return to an inanimate state" (Freud 1937a, p. 246).

Characteristic of Freud's doubts over a primary role for aggression was his suggestion that, after all, "there *might* be such a thing as primary masochism" (1920, p. 55). To his very last months, he was still ambivalently preoccupied with the problem of aggression, writing in a letter to Marie Bonaparte, May 27, 1937: "The whole topic [aggression] has not been treated carefully, and what I had to say about it in early writings was so premature and casual as hardly to deserve consideration" (Jones 1957, p. 464). Then, as though tempted to let go of it finally, he wrote:

> The turning inward of the aggressive impulse is naturally the counterpart of turning outward of the libido when it passes over from ego to objects. One could imagine a pretty schematic idea of all libido being at the beginning of life directed inward and all aggression outward, and that this gradually changes in the course of life. *But perhaps that is not correct.* [pp. 464–465, italics added]

In a subsequent letter to Bonaparte, June 17, 1937, he wrote: "Please do not overestimate my remarks about the destructive instinct. They were only tossed off and should be carefully thought over if you propose to use them publicly" (p. 465).

In summary, the death instinct theory, as we shall see later, was destined to continue to insinuate itself into psychoanalytic theory in a manner that contributed to an ambiguity regarding the degree of analyzability of the resistance. It lent an aura of "beyond" analyzability to elements that were to become associated with the superego. Guilt was seen partially as a "natural" expression of an instinctual need, rather than as a defensive alternative to aggression.[1]

Beginning with "The Ego and the Id," Freud (1923) again made another hypothetical construct that he then developed in at least two ways, each with differing technical implications. This time it was the superego construct itself. With the structural theory, Freud indicated that he had "embarked upon the analysis of the ego" (p. 36). There is ample evidence that, in the first instance, Freud began by picturing the superego *as one of the functions of the ego*. Had he continued in this manner, I believe that he would have found a natural place in the scheme of the ego's versatile complexity for including the superego with the growing list of the ego's activities pertaining especially to defense.

In his most definitive approach to the superego, Freud (1923) spoke of that complex of functions as "a grade *in the ego*, a differentiation *within the ego*" (p. 28, italics added). In discussing the process of superego formation, he used the phrase "alteration *of his ego*" (p. 29, italics added). Later, Freud would speak of "alteration" in the ego as specifically resulting from the *ego's* "defensive mechanisms" (1937a, p. 238), Describing the formation resulting from the identifications arising out of the oedipal conflict, Freud said: "*This modification of the ego . . . confronts the other contents of the ego as . . . super-ego*" (1923, p. 34); by 1927, "It [the ego] harbours *within it* . . . a special agency—the superego"

[1]Efforts to refute the death instinct theory and/or the repetition compulsion include Fenichel's (1941) unequivocal statement that "after elimination of the defense, the energies of the warded off instincts accrue again to . . . the ego . . . and . . . the 'repetition compulsion' vanishes completely . . . " (p. 111). See also Brenner (1959); Grunberger (1971), Lichtenstein (1935), Novey (1962), Orgel (1974a), Schur (1966, 1972), and Sternbach (1975). On the other hand, for those who continue to accept the death instinct, see Klein (1946–1963), Nunberg (1956), and Ostow (1958).

(p. 164, italics added). However, Freud's indecision regarding the superego's status is clear: "The super-ego owes its special position in the ego, *or* in relation to the ego . . . " (1923, p. 48, italics added).

In the second instance, Freud leaned more often toward "the differentiation we have made of the mind into an id, an ego, and a super-ego" (1923, p. 40, italics added). Later, Freud (1926c) was to elaborate: " . . . the mental apparatus is composed of an '*id*', . . . of an '*ego*', . . . and of a '*super-ego', which develops out of the id*" (p. 266, italics added).

Further evidence of the degree to which Freud held the superego to be independent of the ego lies in his description of those resistances allegedly *not proceeding from the ego*. These two were (a) "*the resistance of the unconscious* . . . arising from the id" (1926a, p. 160), which he had linked to the death instinct and the repetition compulsion (Freud, 1920) and for which he reserved the necessity for "working through,"[2] and (b) resistance "*coming* from the *super-ego*" (1926a, p. 160). Similarities in his discussion of these two concepts of resistance again suggest the conceptual separation of the superego from the ego. There is an implication that at bottom, in its manifestations of "the need for punishment" (p. 160), Freud regarded superego resistance as also connected with the death instinct. In this regard, note Freud's comment (1923, p. 53): "[In melancholia] . . . the super-ego is, as it were, a pure culture of the death instinct. . . . "[3]

Although Freud eventually (1940) spoke of these two ostensibly non-ego resistances as having "different origins," he

---

[2]Brenner (1987) has, from a different perspective, developed reasons, with which I agree, for no longer needing the concept of "working through."

[3]Waelder (1937) was moved to counter specifically any inherent and necessary connection between the superego and the death instinct. I believe that the early understanding of that concept as the specific reason for a "working through" process has, through the popularization of that phrase, contributed to maintaining homage to a silent "ghost" of the death instinct.

added: "They may both be embraced under the single name of the 'need to be ill or to suffer' [and] they are of a kindred nature" (p. 179).

Yet, Freud did not entirely give up the hypothesis of superego as an ego function. Kanzer (1972), calling attention to analysts' relative neglect of Freud's last writings, observed that at that time Freud was "becoming increasingly aware that superego analysis constituted a new frontier for psychoanalysis . . . " (p. 262). Referring to the final paragraph of the unfinished "Outline," Kanzer noted that the superego was placed "in a position usually accorded the ego" (p. 262) when Freud (1940, p. 207) had stated that "the super-ego takes up a kind of intermediate position *between the id and the external world"* (italics added). Kanzer added Freud's observation that the severity of the superego "corresponds to the strength of the *defence* used against the temptation of the Oedipus complex" (Freud 1940, p. 206, Kanzer 1972, p. 263, italics added). "Defense" also suggests an ego function.

Thus, I see several consequences of the wide influence of Freud's predominant tendency to characterize the superego as a superordinate, ego-independent structure: (a) It removed superego manifestations from the realm of well-focused scrutiny of conflict by the analyst, an undertaking more often carried out in respect to those defensive ego activities traditionally labeled "mechanisms of defense."[4] (b) It essentially prevented closer examination of the technical use of superego as transference for personal influence, for suggestion, in "overcoming" resistances. (c) It prolonged an implication that the superego's "connection" with the id is one which links it inseparably with instinctual qualities that defy analyzability, at least in the sense that the fears motivating the acknowledged defenses can be analyzed. Only once do I find that Freud, seemingly out of exasperation, approached the solution that specifically making the superego's

---

[4]For a view elaborating the limitations surrounding the concept of "mechanisms of defense," see Brenner (1982a).

processes conscious is analytically therapeutic. This referred to negative therapeutic reactions associated with unconscious guilt, the "severe neurosis" (1940, p. 180): "In warding off this resistance we are obliged to restrict ourselves to making it conscious and attempting to bring about the slow demolition of the hostile super-ego."

Freud's three monumental additions and revisions of theory (1920, 1923, 1926a), had little effect on bringing about a shift away from *using the influence* of a reexternalized and transferred superego, toward *analyzing* the superego as a defense activity. Even after revising the problem of anxiety so that analysis of conflict and resistance became possible, and so that he was impelled to grant "a concession to the ego that it can exert a very extensive influence over processes in the id, and . . . is able to develop such surprising powers" (1926a, pp. 91–92), Freud said (1926b):

> . . . personal influence is our most powerful dynamic weapon. . . . The neurotic sets to work because he has faith in the analyst, and he believes him because he acquires a special emotional attitude towards the figure of the analyst. Children, too, only believe people they are attached to. . . . [We make use] of this particularly large "suggestive" influence. Not for suppressing the symptoms . . . but as a motive force to induce the patient to overcome his resistances. [pp. 224–225]

Freud obviously meant that suggestion is not to be used in the early sense for directly banishing symptoms by post hypnotic suggestion. However, the statement fails to recognize that the patient's superego is rendered transiently less effective by the use of suggestion. *Using suggestion to make a compromise formation less effective is, in fact, a form of symptom suppression.*

Confrontation by a new theory, especially psychoanalytic theory with its built-in difficulties of assimilation, creates ambiguity in comprehending simultaneously two competing ideas. Freud could manage this; ordinary analysts are less able to do so.

In reviewing Sterba's *Reminiscences of a Viennese Psychoanalyst* (1982), Gero (1984) confirmed the presence of the troubled or rejecting reactions to new theory. Sterba gave a useful picture of the analytic atmosphere evoked by the introduction of Freud's newer theoretical perspectives. After years of being educated to be instinct "hunters and detectives," especially for the "task of discovering the culprit libido" (Sterba 1982, p. 75), analysts had not only to add the importance of aggression to their knowledge and to contemplate exposure to the unconscious ego, but also to confront the wrenching significance of the "new theory of the origin of anxiety," which "forced a complete turnabout of . . . theoretical thinking" (p. 77). The new perspective may even have threatened to undermine some of the sublimations that draw analysts to the work, and disturbed those individuals who could sense the implication that such a theory made certain of their hard-earned skills insufficient, maybe even at times counterproductive.

II

Freud's creative flow of ideas, while continuously enlarging his scope, gave relatively modest attention to details of revising his earlier positions. Since then, theorists have largely confined their efforts to bringing clarification and order to this body of psychoanalytic writings, which often appear to contain "everything." Let us turn now to some of the contributors who tried to reduce the ambiguities with which we have been concerned.

Seeking better definition of the superego during the analytic process is intrinsically associated with the problems that have delayed more knowledge of the ego itself. Among Anna Freud's contributions, those central to a better understanding of the ego's defensive activities met a difficult road. The monograph (1936) she courageously introduced met with a cold reception (M. Katan, personal communication).

Anna Freud's concept of the "second kind of transference" (p. 19), the *transference of defense*, is most relevant to the comprehension and analysis of superego vicissitudes during the psychoanalytic process. Formally establishing another kind of transference ran counter to the familiar and still prevalent concept of regarding transference only as a drive cathexis with instinctual gratification as its aim. The idea that objects may also become cathected because they provide "law and order" support for the child's attempts to inhibit conflicted impulses should long have been familiar. Anna Freud appeared aware of the problem of new theory that calls for a major change in analytic technique. In her acknowledgment of the traditional form of interpretation of "the first transference," transference of the id, she noted that, typically, after an analyst has interpreted a disturbing "passionate emotion" being expressed in the present as "belonging" in the past, the patient "is quite willing to cooperate with us in our interpretation [because] we release him from an impulse in the present . . . " (p. 19). Since she knew that resistance is continuous, this description appears as a gentle criticism of prestructural technique, implying that such an interpretation inadvertently provided *a new defense.* She waited for decades (1981) to take credit for the concept of transference of defense. The essence of her progressive idea of transference of resistance is that the compulsion to repeat is a concept that should be extended "equally to former *defensive measures against* the instincts" (1936, p. 19, italics added).

It is precisely Anna Freud's (1936) concept of "transference of defense" that I regard as an early step on the way to analysis of the superego *primarily*[5] as a defensive function of the ego. It represents a further step when she equates the analysis of the defensive manifestations attributed to "the ego of the same in-

[5]By "primarily" I am suggesting that other motives for the formation of such compromise formations, at least *in the analytic situation*, are, from a practical, technical point of view, typically less important.

fantile period in which the id impulse first arose" (p. 21), with the "not very felicitous term 'character analysis' " (p. 22).[6] This observation appears to provide a key to the eventual perception of the superego as an analyzable neurotic activity of the ego.

Among those who sensed the lag in applying newer theory to older practice, Fenichel (1941) lamented that although much was being said about defenses, rarely did anyone speak about how to analyze them. In a rather neglected observation, highly relevant to this paper, he stated:

> In a certain sense it can be said that all defense is "relative defense"; relative to one layer it is defense and at the same time, relative to another layer it is that which is warded off. There exists in the human psyche a particularly impressive example of this: the superego whose demands, *analogous* to instincts, are warded off, *is in essence itself a defense structure.* [p. 62, italics added]

Sterba's introduction of the term and concept "ego split" created "a storm of indignation and rejection" (1982, p. 91). Nevertheless, his recognition that the patient's gradual achievement of a selectively available rational attention goes hand in hand with effective analysis has become a keystone in the entranceway that brings the unconscious conflict-solving ego activities into a usable awareness.

Gillman (1982) suggested that a recent increase in contributions specifically on the superego may reflect a reactive discontent with the state of theory in this area. As far as I know, Brenner (1976c) is the only contemporary contributor to write about the analysis of the superego. Although he did not approach the superego as a hierarchical function of the ego, some of his conclusions come close to my own: "Superego analysis presents

---

[6]In Lester Schwartz's (1971) report on the Kris Study Group on the superego, he said: "The consensus was that superego analysis was an aspect of character analysis and that . . . interpretation of resistances, defenses, and unconscious fantasy was of paramount importance" (p. 189).

a variety of technical problems. . . . In essence they are no different from the problems of defense analysis in general" (p. 106); in *The Mind in Conflict* (1982b), " . . . the superego is both a consequence of psychic conflict and a component of it. . . . *The superego is a compromise formation* . . . " (p. 120); and more recently, " . . . a compromise formation [is] dynamically indistinguishable from a symptom" (1987, p. 106).

Space permits only a sampling of other contemporary contributions. Although not focused directly on superego analysis, they explore relevant incongruities in methodology created by the persistence of superseded earlier phases of Freudian theory. Brenner (1984) has for years challenged a variety of persisting practices and provided reassessments. Schur's (1966) contribution on regulatory principles of mental functioning is most valuable. Although Gill (1963), in his early definition of the id and the ego, chooses to "not deal specifically with the superego" (p. 144), his discussions of hierarchical arrangements of defenses appear not to rule out superego manifestations as functions of the ego. At one point, he refers to the superego "as a primitive system of defence" (p. 144). He also draws attention to a relevant observation of Glover's: "A more elaborate differential of superego structure will, however, involve a closer study of the *relation of different ego systems to consciousness* (Glover 1956, pp. 340–341).

Friedman (1969) specifically confronted "the paradox of having to rely on something in the patient which must be dissolved" (p. 142). Boesky (1983) has demonstrated how "character resistance as a concept is a theoretical and technical anachronism" (p. 24). Spiegel (1978) has shown that clinical manifestations traditionally viewed as "*unconscious* guilt" are more usefully understood as transferences of defense involving *ad hoc* regressions to masochistic solutions. The implications here are far-reaching. I anticipate that further study of details of superego functioning will lead to the identification of "*conscious* guilt" as an *ad hoc* defensive regressive solution to intrapsychic conflict. Collins (1980) provided a searching examination of

Freud's own unending struggle with the issue of suggestion in analysis.

III

It is important to psychoanalytic technique, I believe, that we reduce the ambiguity surrounding superego analysis. While it is true that analysts currently *deal* in various ways with the superego, they also still widely practice the therapeutic *use* of the superego in analysis. In my opinion, "dealing with" the superego is often not analysis of the superego; "therapeutic use" of it is never analysis of it.

By *analysis* of the superego, I mean: systematically making available to consciousness those repetitions of defensive formations in the analytic situation—including pre- and post-internalizations—which were earlier mobilized, especially in connection with the oedipal situation, to the end that the compromised ego function components can be progressively reclaimed, from the beginning of the analysis, by the relatively autonomous ego. In particular, I have in mind the components of self-observing capacities and the conscious executive capacity over the instinctual investments co-opted by the superego, especially that of aggression.

I take the position that optimal analysis of the superego, as of resistance generally, is best achieved by perceiving and interpreting superego manifestations *mobilized during the analytic situation,* primarily as part of the *ego's* defensive activities.

If we reflect on the continuum from the "normal" process of civilizing development to neurotic development, it is easier to grasp how the superego is dynamically like a symptom. Freud's (1926a) description of the ego's strength and weakness in relation to the id, well illustrates the role of symptoms in that relationship. In the following passage from this work, I insert in brackets the word "superego" where I want us to consider how it might fit as well as the word "symptom."

> It does sometimes happen that the defensive struggle against an unwelcome instinctual impulse is brought to an end with the formation of a symptom [superego]. . . . But usually the outcome is different. The initial act of repression is followed by a tedious or interminable sequel in which the struggle against the instinctual impulse is prolonged into a struggle against the symptom [superego]. . . . The ego is an organization. It is based on the maintenance of free intercourse and of the possibility of reciprocal influence between all its parts. Its . . . necessity to synthesize grows stronger in proportion as the strength of the ego increases. It is . . . natural that the ego should try to prevent symptoms [superego] from remaining isolated . . . by using every possible method to . . . incorporate them [the superego] into its organization. . . . As we know, a tendency of this kind is already operative in the very act of forming a symptom [the superego]. . . . The ego now proceeds to behave as though it recognized that the symptom [superego] had come to stay and that the only thing to do was to . . . draw as much advantage from it as possible. It makes an adaptation to the symptom [superego]—to this piece of internal world which is alien to it just as it normally does to the real world. . . . The presence of a symptom [the superego] may entail a certain impairment of capacity, and this can be exploited. . . . In this way the symptom [superego] gradually comes to be the representative of important interests; it is found to be useful in asserting the position of the self and becomes more and more closely merged with the ego and more and more indispensable to it. [pp. 98–99]

That Freud comes specifically to refer to the symptoms of obsessional neurosis, a condition we associate with an intense superego, suggests further conceptual parallels. In speaking of obsessional neuroses he continues:

> [T]he forms which the symptoms [the superego] assume become very valuable to the ego because they obtain for it . . . a narcissistic satisfaction which it would otherwise be without. The systems which the obsessional neurotic constructs flatter

> his self-love by making him feel that he is better than other people because he is specially clean or specially conscientious. . . . When the analyst tries subsequently to help the ego in its struggle against the symptom [superego], he finds that these conciliatory bonds between ego and symptom [superego] operate on the side of the resistances and that they are not easy to loosen. [pp. 99–100]

Precisely this last parallel has placed the superego as a challenging but potentially analyzable factor in approaching the work of the analysis. Understandably, before the new, 1926, view of anxiety and intrapsychic conflict, an exploitation of the influential transference was necessary to ostensibly loosen the "conciliatory bonds" between the ego and the "ego-ideal." The newer view permits analysts to see the dynamics of superego formation as one of the ego's stratified defensive responses (Gero 1951) to the conflicts of the oedipal situation.

Before the ego's compromise formation involving internalization brings about the more definitive resolution of the Oedipus conflicts, other compromise formations have shaped, for the child, the external perceptions of impulse inhibiting authorities. Creating or defensively enhancing those fear-evoking perceptions typically involves projection of aggressive impulses. With the dramatic process of internalization of those inhibiting images,[7] the more familiar superego formations are established. In the analytic situation, as in many other relationships, the transferential repetition of the pre-internalized superego perceptions takes place steadily and usually rapidly. Just as the pre-internalized view of the judging parental authorities was necessary for instinctual control, so the patient now needs to distort the otherwise disturbingly unauthoritarian reality of the neutrality and permissiveness (only action is restrained) the ana-

[7]The similarity between the compromise formations in this process and the symptomatic process in dramatically rapid religious "conversions" is of interest, a similarity which may be inferred from Freud's "Group Psychology and the Analysis of the Ego" (1921).

lyst provides. This is an example, *par excellence*, of transference as resistance (Freud 1912), although that phrase is traditionally regarded as referring to *id* transferences. Again, these transferences of images of childhood authority obviously are alternatively the technically exploitable source for the power of suggestion.

In previous papers (Gray 1973, 1982), I have outlined in more detail technique for the analysis of unconscious conflict within the immediate analytic process. My approach to technique led me to increasing awareness of the extent to which the phenomena observed and just described include transferential repetitions of the ego's pre-internalized defensive attempts at protection from fear of instinctual impulses. It follows that the methodology I have already described in those papers is applicable in analyzing superego vicissitudes. In keeping with my undertaking here as "introduction," I shall only briefly describe the process through an excerpt from Chapter 3 of this volume.

> The more clearly we analysts can conceptualize for *ourselves* the detail of the analytic work of observing we may wish to have patients undertake, the greater the likelihood that we can facilitate *their* learning to do so. Let us look closer at the autonomous ego functions analysands need in order to observe the conflict-motivated defensive activities of their egos. As analysands are interrupted by the sound of the analyst's voice, they must draw back from the more spontaneous and less rational mode and must now take up objective capacities. In this new and more rational alliance . . . they may sequentially undertake the following: (1) rationally attend to what the analyst is saying; (2) recognize that the interpretive intervention implies an invitation to turn objective attention back over the reconstructed or recounted sequence of material the analyst has offered as evidence of a conflict the patient encountered during the attempted spontaneity and to which the patient's mind automatically responded with a protective, defensive solution; (3) comprehend that the motivation for the conflict

> solution *was due in part (and this part will be explored) to the fact that while the analysand was revealing thoughts and feelings to the other person in the room, some fantasied risk of doing so arose*; (4) analyze that irrational risk (a bit more each time) and through understanding it gradually reduce the automatic need for the patient to inhibit, by the specific means identified, those particular elements that had shortly before come into conflict; and (5) return attention to the essential task, permitting a more spontaneous access to the inner self, in particular, allowing greater freedom to let emerge those conflicted elements, the inhibition of which had just been explored. [italics added]

In this simplified description of technical intent, (1) and (2) show something of the process of regaining, in its original uncompromised form,[8] the patient's observing ego that had been pre-empted by other ego functions, namely, those infantile defensive measures designated as the superego. It is, of course, (3) and (4) that hold the crucial potential for gradually making fully conscious the transference of the previously externally perceived, images of authority used by the child for restraint.

Just as in the child's early and later development, the internalization process does not eliminate the ego's "uses" of external authority for auxiliary control, so also the internalization is not so stable structurally that its reprojection cannot regularly recur in varying degrees. Transferences of external authority are as ubiquitous as the transferences of id objects (Brenner 1976c). That this occurs in the analytic situation, with its explicit aim of avowing the disavowed, is inevitable. This technical approach aims at providing an opportunity for a *maximum* of new, conscious ego solutions to conflict and a *minimum* of solutions involving new internalizations. This does not detract from the

---

[8]Dale Meers called my attention to Waelder's (1937) proposal that "the power to objectify the self and to achieve detachment from it" constituted an early acquired ego capacity which provided an "imaginary standpoint from which we confront the rest of our personality" (p. 435). Waelder (1936, p. 93) compared it with the "fixed point" of Archimedes.

fact that internalizing forms of solution to conflict are capable of providing therapeutic action for many analytic patients. There is an inherent universal tendency toward solutions to conflict using a superego-like internalizing process as an outcome of growth experience. For some patients, it is unavoidable; their analytic process will "demand" such a therapeutic action. There are, however, avenues for mental growth through analytic experience other than those brought about through internalizations that are compromise formations and symptom-like in nature. For those patients who, I believe, have a greater capacity for non-internalizing solutions, let us return to the discussion at hand.

Usually, in the course of the analysis, a hierarchy of transferred, inhibiting fantasies is uncovered, beginning with more recent versions of expected reactions from authority and working gradually toward earlier and more vivid defense-motivating infantile dangers—"calamities" (Brenner 1982b, p. 55).

In the approach I am advocating, the potential for genetic and reconstructive interpretations is completely open quantitatively. The essential characteristic lies in the strong emphasis on analysis of resistance, which is the central point of superego *analysis*. Therefore, the genetic and reconstructive work points less toward establishing that there *were* infantile objects of the emerging instinctual drives. (The existence and nature of the transferred fantasy objects of id impulses becomes inexorably clear as impulse aims are freed from resistance.) Instead, the emphasis is on learning about the infantile context in which perceptions of danger opposing these impulses were so frightening that, for safety, the child cathected inhibiting, not gratifying objects (Sandler 1983), now repeated as "armamentarium of the past," involuntarily and unnecessarily as resistance to the analytic task. The shift of genetic interest might be expressed in the following way: from "How and why, as a child, did you wish to destroy someone" to "What was it, as a child, that made you need to stop knowing that you could hate some individuals enough to want to destroy them, and how did you manage to stop knowing?"

Obviously, the origins of both defense and that which is defended against are inseparably interrelated, but if the analysis tilts or appears to tilt toward a search for instinctual impulses as if they "belonged to the past," rather than being alive within us all, then a sense of "closures" may evolve. Versions of "narrative persuasion" (Spence 1983) may become operative. On the other hand, consistent attention to the persistent evidence of conflict and resistant conflict solutions, though diminishing in frequency and intensity, *keeps the process open* to further analysis of the anxiety-producing fantasies of danger from additional increments of pressing id strivings. The fantasies of danger are the bases of the conflicts and motivation for the defenses we observe as resistance.

In practice, when one observes and interprets superego activities as chronically maintained or repetitively activated ego processes, primarily mobilized for defensive purposes, one's attention is drawn, in particular, to the extent to which this process inhibits *derivatives of aggression*. The defensive meanings of the diversion of aggressive drives onto the self, a fundamental and familiar aspect of superego development, then assume a more conspicuous role in comprehending mental functioning. Conflict solutions during the analytic process that involve a version of redirecting an aggressive aim from an object to the subject, including varieties of subtle or sadistic self-accusation or self-directed aggression via projections onto the analyst, all bear the stamp of an ego activity which, in the "normal" course of events, would represent superego manifestations. In general, *superego analysis is possible only to the extent that aggressive drive derivatives are truly returnable to the ego's voluntary executive powers*. The patients who can make best use of this particular technical opportunity are largely, but by no means entirely, at the other end of the clinical spectrum from those in the "wider scope" category.

Finally, as a stimulus for further exploration of the subject,

I cite one of those provocatively enigmatic observations of Freud's (1933a): " . . . *we are all too ready to regard as . . . normal* [the situation] where the external restraint [parental influence, love, threatening punishments which are feared on their own account, realistic anxiety] is internalized and the super-ego takes the place of the parental agency . . . " (p. 62, italics added).

6

THE ANALYSIS OF THE EGO'S PERMISSIVE SUPEREGO

INTRODUCTION

Analysts widely and wisely hold the view that to be most effective, psychoanalytic work should result in structural alterations in those psychological functions that are commonly referred to as the superego. In my prior paper on this subject (Gray 1987 [Chapter 5, this volume]) I maintained that analysis becomes more effective if, during the analytic process, the analyst approaches the defensive uses of the "conscience," just as one approaches any other of the ego's functions that are mobilized in the service of resistance; the more extensive the ego analysis—in the context of intrapsychic conflict resolution—the more thorough will be the analysis of the ego's superego activities. I stressed that it is essential to recognize the patient's use, in the analytic situation, of the re-externalization—a transference manifestation—of the images of authority he or she used as a prelatency child in their *external* version, for relief from painful instinctual conflict. Whenever an individual faces the task of psychoanalysis, such transferences of authority typically occur promptly. In my 1987 essay I encouraged recognizing their influence on conflict manifestation in the verbal flow from the earliest moments in the analysis. Not only is this a part of the analysis of resistance, but it also progressively engages the patient's capacity for observing otherwise unconscious defensive activities. By contrast, I showed how technique in the early decades of psychoanalytic practice—and often continuing today—compromised precise conflict analysis by *using* the transferred superego authoritarian power in order to crucially *persuade* the patient to respond to interpretation. I dealt then with those transferred images of authority concerned with *censoring* and *restraining* the child from discharge of instinctual drives.[1]

In this essay I shall cover the following. First, I shall explore another kind of transferential re-externalization of images of authority the ego uses to protect against anxiety, this time by providing a defensive illusion of safety through *fantasies of affectionate approval*. I shall then examine how important theoreticians and practitioners of wider-scope analytic methods, rather than regarding it as a resistance, have made therapeutic use of this second form of transference, often enhancing its influence by fulfilling certain of the patients' infantile needs for safety. I shall

---

[1]In that introductory essay I might well have included reference to Sandler's (1960) suggestion that under continued theoretical scrutiny "much of what might be called superego territory has been yielded up to the ego" (p. 143). "In a sense the superego has thus lost some of its theoretical identity . . . " (p. 144). He suggested further that clinical analysis itself also reflects such a "*conceptual dissolution*," as the "object relationships and conflicts which entered into superego formation have unfolded themselves onto the person of the analyst . . . and . . . the . . . processes which have contributed so much to superego genesis *have been seen as defensive or adaptive ego mechanisms* which were called into play during critical phases of oedipal and preoedipal development" (p. 144. italics added). Following a presentation of my 1987 essay, my attention was called to Esman's (1972) contribution on values and adolescence, in which he was "inclined to the view that the superego is best understood as a specialized group of identifications within the ego itself . . . " and, further, he regarded the "*executive* functions—self-criticism, self-punishment, etc.— . . . as residing within the ego" (p. 90).

explore the argument that these trends, although sometimes clinically necessary with certain patients, both reflect and support professional inhibitions against improving our methodology for *essential* structural psychoanalysis. I shall offer some clinical examples of how to avoid using the nonanalytic influence of this particular transference for purposes of resistance. In conclusion, I predict that improved conceptualization of the methods of analyzing the ego's superego activities will help to unify now divergent theories.

TRANSFERENTIAL FANTASY OF AFFECTIONATE APPROVAL AS RESISTANCE

I examined previously (Gray 1987) how childhood perceptions of authority figures as *inhibitors* are, in the analysis, re-externalized and transferred to the analyst for purposes of resistance. In prelatency childhood they were first used defensively in their external form and then internalized as the ego's superego solution to conflict. A second category of re-externalized images of authority confronts us with a more troublesome conceptual and a more demanding technical task in superego analysis than the previous one. In contrast to the transferences of the restraining, inhibiting images of the authorities of childhood, these are the transferences used to resist conflict-anxiety through a fantasy of the analyst as an *affectionate, approving, and protective authority*. These repetitions bring about relief from conflict by providing a fantasy of safety from criticism, punishment, and loss of love, not because *as analysands* the patients are entitled to an uncriticizing professional, but because they feel as though they are in the presence of an affectionate parental attitude.

These images—like the images of critical authority—are selectively available for transference in the service of defense and resistance against the conflict-anxiety mobilized by attempting free association. By avoiding anxiety (via the transference fantasy of affectionate approval) over the exposure of certain instinctual derivatives, patients effectively bypass their egos' unconscious threat of censorship. This false sense of safety provides effective "resistance to uncovering resistance" by blocking other, "normal," manifestations of resistance that would otherwise occur through the effects of the *inhibiting, censoring images of authority* that have been replaced by the affectionate one.

The greater difficulty in analyzing transferences of affectionate safety lies especially in the degree to which they blend in with the analyst's wish to be regarded as noncritical. One is often reluctant to recognize that the analysand's ability to acquire a viable sense of *objective safety* in allowing inner spontaneity and its disclosure is an incremental process through analysis of the inhibiting fantasies of danger. It takes a long time for most patients to risk emotionally (and often intellectually) accepting the analyst as *analyst* and as actually working with a *morally neutral* attitude. It is often safer for the patient to choose between the fantasy of a critically restraining image or an affectionately forgiving one.

We are naturally reluctant to examine the supportive elements of transference. Beyond their virtually ubiquitous use for psychotherapeutic relief of human suffering, these aspects of transference contribute to the matrix of congenial relatedness among people generally. As *transference fantasy*, their presence is often difficult to demonstrate even in a consistently neutral analytic situation, virtually impossible in a non-neutral one. *Acts* of kindness, of humaneness, and the provision of empathic communication or consolations about life outside the analytic situation may render the experience too similar to the fantasy to demonstrate transference convincingly.

The advantages of analyzing ostensibly benign, supportive elements rather than using them for purposes of "alliance" in the analytic situation are stressed in the work of Curtis (1979) and Stein (1981). Brenner (1979) captured the essence of the matter: "It is as important to understand why a patient is closely 'allied' with his analyst in the analytic work as it is to understand why there seems to be no 'alliance' at all" (p. 150). The structural theory and the revision of the problem of anxiety have not only made it possible to analyze these elements but also have shown the analytic necessity for doing so. It remains, however, an idea whose wide acceptance in practice is lagging.

The history of Freud's reluctance to abandon parts of his pre-1926 theory and practice is particularly clear in this area of technique. Let us review some of it. Freud's (1913) need for suggestive influence was clear: "It remains the first aim of the treatment to attach [effective transference] to it and to the person of the doctor. . . . [to] link up the doctor with one of the imagos of the people by whom he was accustomed to be treated with *affection*" (pp. 139–140, italics added). Further (1914), "If the patient starts his treatment under the auspices of a mild and unpronounced positive transference it makes it possible at first for him to unearth his memories *just as he would under hypnosis* . . . " (p. 151, italics added).

Although Freud's (1926a) revision of the theory of anxiety would render obsolete—*in theory*—the necessity for technical *dependence* on transference influence to overcome resistance, his own technical discussions led analysts for decades to continue it in practice; the most explicit evidence is found in the concept of the not-to-be-disturbed "unobjectionable" (Freud 1912, p. 105) part of the transference. Freud credited Ferenczi (1909) with the discovery that there are two kinds of hypnotism: " . . . one *coaxing and soothing* . . . modelled on the mother, and another *threatening*, which is derived from the father" (Freud 1921, p. 127, italics added). Near the end of his life, Freud (1940) was still encouraging suggestion, now in structural terms: " . . . transference brings with it . . . advantages. If the patient puts the analyst in the place of the father (or mother), he is also *giving him the power which his super-ego exercises over his ego, since his parents were, as we know, the origin of his super-ego*" (p. 175, italics added). Hearkening back to Ferenczi, Freud said more about the "advantage": "With the mention of resistance we have reached the . . . more important part of our task. . . . we desire . . . that the ego . . . shall dare to take the offensive in order to reconquer what has been lost. . . . The ego draws back in alarm from such undertakings, which seem dangerous and threaten unpleasure; *it must be constantly encouraged and soothed* if it is not to fail us" (p. 178, italics added). Here Freud clearly illustrated exploiting the *use* of transferential re-externalization rather than analyzing it.

The influential transference images, although they may free the patient from some anxiety and resistances, are nevertheless clearly incompatible with an analytically earned, rational view of the analyst as neutral. *Whenever these transference images are allowed to remain influential, an important part of the patient's ego's superego activity and potential for neurosis remains unanalyzed.*

Stein (1981, p. 881), questioning the unobjectionable part of the transference, drew upon Lewin's (1955) comparison of the speaking analyst to one who awakens a dreamer, and observed, "Inevitably [the analyst] becomes the transference representative of . . . the conscience." Stein continued: "I would venture that the loving, conscious, unobjectionable part of the transference is directed toward the analyst as the one who *soothes*, who induces sleep and *allows the patient to feel less frightened* . . . " (italics added).[2]

From the above, it should be apparent that the "coaxing and soothing" images (often of the non-disciplining parent or sometimes only another view of the same parent) are mobilized to create an illusion not unlike that of an all-accepting mother or of an especially benevolent, forgiving father-confessor. The patient is (transferentially) convinced that: "My listener has such positive, personal feelings for me that it is *safe* to reveal a *certain number* of secret things about myself." As I have described, this contrasts with the use of transferred images of a stern authority to provoke inhibiting defenses, experienced as: "My listener is a potentially wrathful one, so I will try even harder to remain good and not think of or speak of forbidden things."

Transferentially encouraging, anxiety-relieving images are,

---

[2]See also Schafer's (1960) germane contribution on the "loving and beloved" superego.

of course, capable of enormous influence. They, alternatively with the inhibiting images, are the essential backbone of the vast majority of psychotherapies. Fundamentalist religious ideologies are an example, par excellence, of the ubiquitous phenomenon of projecting early loving parental images *in the service of reducing anxiety and guilt*. The portrayal of a loving, forgiving "savior" can frequently produce tranquility and compliance in an ego plagued by conflict anxiety. Obviously the fundamentalist example contains, alternatively, a re-externalized threat of punishment.

Although we have been considering anxiety-relieving transferences that may, during the analysis, exert their significant influence rather subtly, there are clinical moments that draw our attention more conspicuously to the existence of an influencing authority who is an *uninhibiting* figure in the transference. This occurs when the affectionate, approving, indulging image becomes exaggeratedly encouraging, as in the case of transference of the image of a parent who has vicariously acted out by chronically (compared to acutely traumatic) and seductively promoting the child's sexual or aggressive development. In the analysis the result may initially be a lowering of resistance to emerging instinctual elements, but such conditions may rapidly become too stimulating, too permissive, and the resulting conflict may lead the patient to reach for a different transference image, one of an inhibiting authority. Here, the patient may be caught between two equally disturbing alternatives and will have to avoid the analyst out of fear of either overstimulation or excessive harshness. At such times it becomes clear that his or her belief in the possibility of a neutral, objective listener is indeed remote, and the analysis of the resistance is indeed challenging. In such cases, unless the analyst can demonstrate the re-creation of these erstwhile internalized superego influences of the ego and how they work in their transferential versions, the patient may perceive no recourse but to try new adjustments with some fresh influences of a newly internalized illusion of authority. The patient may "insist" on *converting* to a safer equilibrium.

TRANSFERENCE OF AFFECTIONATELY PERMISSIVE AUTHORITY, AND WIDER-SCOPE ANALYSIS

I shall briefly examine some of the implications and inadvertent effects the treatment of wider-scope patients has had on progress in the area of analyzing how patients use transference and re-externalization of affectionate authority for purposes of resistance.

Recent access to letters of Freud and Ferenczi provide us with more than data for gossip. I am grateful to Ilse Grubrich-Simitis (1986) for her elaboration on six previously unavailable letters of Freud and Ferenczi. Her inclusions from the Ferenczi-Rank literature are also relevant to my topic and may help us to avoid repeating what we do not remember. She reminds us that Ferenczi was, without doubt, "the first systematic investigator of severe ego-pathologies and their treatment . . . " (p. 276). His clinical encounters and personal skills in his work with the wider scope of patients convinced him of a need for stressing flexibility in the analyst's responsiveness, and he illustrated this well in his writings. Certain ad hominem anecdotes concerning Ferenczi's deviations or innovations have only obscured our recognition that in our field, trends toward nurturance and care-taking are inevitable; although they may well be emphasized because of individual needs of some therapists, they need not depend on personal idiosyncracies.

Analysts, at times, take a variety of necessary, parent-like, authoritative roles in their analytic work with children, often with adolescents, and sometimes with those adults whom Freud (1940) characterized as having "remained so infantile that in analysis too they can only be treated as children" (p. 175). In simple terms, these authoritative roles include selective disciplinary and certain permissive attitudes, often confined to the treatment setting. What these therapeutic positions have in common is that they provide auxiliary superego roles, on the therapist's assumption that ego immaturity or distortion exists to such a degree that the patient would be harmed or unable to mobilize any therapeutic momentum without such supports. In a limited way, we can usefully characterize as *paternalistic* and/or *maternalistic* those early and persisting forms of analytic technique that use transferentially influencing auxiliary measures. In the probably more familiar and time-honored transference images of paternalistic forms, the patient, pressed by a "fundamental *rule*," is subservient to a feared authority whose presence, *inner* and *outer*, stimulates superego forces to overcome, not analyze, resistance.

The attitudes of analysts dealing with wider-scope patients are central to our *second* kind of transferential non-analytic influence on resistance; they are predominantly *maternalistic* in nature. The transference images involved are likely to be affectionately tender and caring, tolerant, permissive and/or soothing of fears (distinct from but not exclusive of libidinally gratifying elements). Ferenczi (1931) spoke of a need for technique "in peculiarly difficult cases" (p. 128) "rather like that of an affectionate mother . . . " (p. 137); elsewhere (1929) he said, "*What such neurotics need is really to be adopted and to partake for the first time in their lives of the advantages of a normal nursery*" (p. 124). Rank eventually carried his interests in providing patients with infant-like conditions for his "analytic" explorations to the point of a planned, limited, nine-month (i.e., gestational) period for the treatment.

As the data are reviewed, it becomes apparent that Ferenczi, in collaboration with Rank (1924), stressed interpersonal techniques (intended for real and/or ostensibly primitive needs) that considerably *excluded* mature ego participation by the patient. A methodological trend of psychoanalytic practice evolved rapidly and regressively, and was made explicit and embraced. Ferenczi and Rank declared, "This possibility of *reviving hypnosis*, or other suggestive techniques, in analytic therapy would then perhaps represent the *culmination of a development which inclines—in our view correctly—towards a simplification of analytic technique*" (p. 62, italics added). Concerning training, they wrote: "Reducing the method to more simple elements . . . would have, in time, inestimable practical consequences; on the one hand the acquisition of psychoanalytic knowledge by doctors in general (and not just by psychotherapists) would be much easier and on the other, the nature and length of treatment would undergo an essential simplification. Given this level of practical accomplishment, the splendid isolation which was indispensable for the creation and elaboration of psychoanalysis, would no longer need to be maintained so strictly" (p. 63). So much for training standards.

Grubrich-Simitis (1986) reminds us that "it was Michael Balint alone who, *expressis verbis*, carried on his teacher's legacy, citing [Ferenczi's] concepts over and over . . . " (p. 275). Balint repeatedly brought his ideas to groups of physicians in the United States.[3]

Some of the inheritors of Ferenczi's and Balint's creative interests in intensive applications of aspects of psychoanalytic thinking for the wider range of patients have at some point acknowledged that what they are attempting would not be applicable to the traditional scope of analytic patients. These acknowledgments are often blurred by time and disciples. Yet, it is unrealistic to expect analytic innovators to be protective of existing areas of theory and practice; that is not part of creativity.

It should be obvious that many wider-scope patients are beset with deeper, often intractable resistance against developing a capacity for relative autonomy and acceptance of reality. The egos of such patients require protective measures *that preclude some of the aims of essential psychoanalytic methodology.* These aims include full consciousness of the detailed existence of and motivations for defensive contributions against instinctual derivatives, in particular the ego's superego activities. Of course, the resistances I speak of are, in varying degrees, ubiquitous. What follows from this is that whenever new analytical methods are

[3]In response to Ferenczi and Rank's book, Freud wrote to Ferenczi in 1924 of his impression "that the path opened up here could lead away from psychoanalysis, that it promises to become a path for travelling salesmen" (see Grubrich-Simitis 1986, p. 267).

developed for working with more vulnerable patients, analysts find such approaches often (secondarily) appealing for more general use. The practitioner is relieved of the significant challenge of having to analyze all the restraints of neurotic fear, or the anxiety-relieving, affectionately permissive maternal-like fantasies. Instead, by letting the patient retain important degrees of *unconscious* internalized superego defense, the analyst exposes the patient *and himself or herself* to fewer manifestations of live primitive impulses.

Schlesinger (1988), recognizing the influence of Ferenczi and Rank on psychoanalytic psychotherapy, notes the resulting shift of emphases in modes of theory and practice. He states: "For many theorists the affective aspects of the process came to be seen as having less to do with the energic components of a repressed idea and more to do with the affective climate in which the treatment takes place. The therapeutic relationship began to be seen as the 'message' as well as the 'medium.' The empathic bond was seen as equally important to the effectiveness of interpretation as the ideational content. In this way, 'suggestion,' implying the power of the relationship, which officially had been excluded from among the therapeutic factors relied upon by psychoanalysis, returned and was reembraced, though under a series of different names" (p. 16). Schlesinger refers to this "reembraced" suggestion as a "bonding" (*ibid.*) and suggests that the new forms of the "unobjectionable positive transference" include Alexander and French's (1946) "corrective emotional experience" and Weiss and Sampson's (1986) "passing the patient's test." Schlesinger appears uneasy about separating the therapeutic actions of psychoanalytic psychotherapy from those of psychoanalysis proper. He regards "analyzing . . . any suggestive element in the treatment situation, including the transference" (1988, p. 13), as—contrary to my own view—a "fastidious goal" (*ibid.*).

The supportive, therapeutic *uses* of transference, widely true for object-relations practitioners, draw especially on preoedipal elements of maternal relatedness. Modell exemplifies this in his recent continued elaboration of Winnicott's (1965) "holding environment." Here, Modell (1988) includes a dedication to Balint (p. 590). He recognizes his affinity with Schlesinger's characterizations of the "medium" as the "message" (p. 584). He intends for the patient to experience what he describes as a "dependent/containing transference" as part of the "psychoanalytic setting" (p. 577), an unanalyzed aspect of the "medium." In Modell's opinion, this transferential safety net *needs* to remain in place for those patients whose vulnerability is characterized by *"any threat to the integrity of the self"* (p. 591).

If Modell were to confine his theory and methodological recommendations to the clinical area of narcissistic pathology which he is primarily addressing, I believe his characterization of the *dependent/containing transference* might contribute to a unifying spectrum of analytic theory and practice; it could provide a better theoretical avenue for clarifying choices of analytic technique based on clinical differences in patients. The familiar and inevitable problem arising from most wider-scope schools is illustrated when Modell states that "we . . . learn that . . . *this* fear regarding the integrity of the self may be *universal*"; he believes "that *all* patients seek to establish certain conditions of safety in order *to protect the self*" (p. 592, italics added).

To the extent that wider-scope theorists successfully teach analysts that there is a ubiquitous clinical *need to preserve* safety-seeking aspects of transferences of defense, they inadvertently detract from the possibility of effective analysis of the ego and superego activities for many patients who demonstrably do not need such limitations.

If, and whenever, Modell's description of self-vulnerability portrays accurately the psychopathology of the patients primarily in question, I suggest that it occurs in individuals with egos trying to cope with very primitive aggressive potential by means of very primitive internalized fantasies of authority. Such archaic presuperego intrapsychic components may defy conflict analysis and only "modify" through auxilliary internalization. Such patients cannot risk trusting the analyst, *unless* they can project protective pregenital maternal fantasies, dynamically quite akin to religious faith, for which "dependent/containing" is a reasonable label. Patients who do not need such supportive maintenance of certain defense transferences have an ego maturation that transfers images of less primitive parental caretakers, and does so to secure safety against anxiety related to the more familiar dangers, not to prevent loss of integrity of the self.

In both instances a major therapeutic aim and action will be progressive *modification* of the form and intensity of the superego activities. In the case of therapeutic actions dependent on an "object-relations" approach, change would depend on fresh reinternalizations of a fantasy of relatedness to authority, still unconscious but more benign than the primitive pathological versions—which, as in any analysis, will continue to exist in the patient as a *potential* regression. The effectiveness of the new internalization will depend on the *continued existence* of a fantasy of object relatedness with the analyst. That bonding fantasy is involved in the various versions of the "unobjectionable transference," whatever it may be named.

For patients with less primitive superego pathology, it is possible to approach analytically the re-externalized transferential repetitions of protective fantasies, either the inhibiting, controlling images or the anxiety-relieving, affectionately permissive images we have been examining. Such analyzing brings into consciousness vital aspects of the ego's defensive patterns of superego activity that the analytic aims and tasks strongly mobilized as resistance from the beginning of the analysis.

Regarding the therapeutic claims of these two analytic methodologies, I think there is much to be said for each. With highly narcissistically vulnerable analysands, *as long as the continuing unanalyzed influence of an internalized bonding fantasy of the object-relations approach Modell recommends remains undisturbed*, I could envision general symptomatic relief comparable to a standard structural approach. On the other hand, what may be gained if such safety-seeking fantasies can be analyzed instead of used as a silent part of the therapeutic "medium" is achievement of a greater measure of capacity for exercising ego autonomy from unconsciously motivated superego activities. Though it may not be as important in many other aspects of life, this added measure of capacity for autonomy is essential for practicing analysts, for they must be able to achieve the degree of selected, transient, moral neutrality that is so advantageous in analyzing the superego activities of the egos of other individuals.

In summary: I am arguing that unless the point is made that methodologies dealing with wider-scope patients represent alternatives required only by analysands who are unanalyzable by more conventional conflict- and resistance-oriented analytic technique, their use may discourage or preclude a much wider potential for the analysis of the ego's superego functionings.

ON DIMINISHING THE UNANALYTIC EFFECTS OF SUPPORTIVE TRANSFERENCE

Having argued against relying on transference of superego elements for overcoming resistance in the analysis of those patients who are potentially able to gain more from essential psychoanalysis, I shall consider some ways of minimizing such measures. Some inroads into this subject were part of my introductory paper (Gray 1987, Chapter 5 in this volume). In the case of the second form of reexternalized affectionate, possibly more maternally based transferences, the task, for reasons I have touched on, is more challenging for the analyst, but rewarding for the patient.

First, let us consider some transference *messages* the *medium* might convey and how to substitute for them the messages the analyst relays: the ideas intended to further patients' conscious, rational, and usable insight into how their mind works, so that they may gain greater autonomous control over it (as contrasted with interpersonal fantasy). Kohut left us with a useful description of a part of the mother *as medium* that has a self-esteem building ("affirming") effect for the small child: "the gleam in the mother's eye." In a workshop at the International Congress in

Vienna, I asked him how much "gleam" he felt should be conveyed in the analyst's comments to the patient. His quick reply was, "You cannot do analysis with a computer!" I believe that answer avoids the point. Actually, there is a considerable range of analytically effective non-gleam, non-affirming attitudes the analyst can impart without beginning to resemble an impersonal computer.

What the analyst chooses to convey stems, optimally, from an ad hoc clinical decision. I am aware that the distortions of unanalyzed transference weigh heavily on what attitude the patient hears in any communication of the analyst. A professional man with considerable narcissistic character disturbance, with whom I chose to speak at one point in a particularly thoughtful, gentle voice, shook his head from side to side as though wishing to shut out my voice, and cried out, "Why are you shouting at me?" He was not being facetious; he heard it that way. Nevertheless, what the analyst manifestly conveys, the patient in most instances eventually perceives either as though the analyst is one who wishes to make an idea intellectually clear, or as though the analyst is willing, instead, to be supportive by being an "understanding" person.

It is dismaying the way many of the attitudinal components of wider-scope methodologies have spilled over into analytic contexts where such attitudes are unnecessary and contraindicated. I have "sat in" at classes in "standard" technique where the instructor gave advice about the *manner of speaking* to analysands. One recommendation was that the analyst always "share empathy" by speaking movingly and sympathetically when referring to a patient's painful affect. A different setting yielded a suggestion that the analyst speak softly and tenderly, as a lover might share an intimate thought. Another group was instructed that to "like" the patient would be an especially important factor in the success of an analysis—there seemed only a choice between liking and disliking, no mention of tactful objectivity. The therapeutic anxiety-relieving effects of emotionally charged comments, when well timed, can, of course, be profound. I would suggest, however, that the structure of the superego activities of the patient's ego would be merely bypassed and would remain basically unchanged. My contention is that with patients not strikingly narcissistically vulnerable, one can, with tact and experience, verbally engage the patient's observing capacities without inviting the transferential influence of an affectionate, sympathetic, re-externalized parental image.

The second approach to minimizing the anxiety-relieving uses of maternal-like transferences (I recognize that the transferred figure need not be a woman) is by *analyzing the way the patient uses such repetitions of resistance*. That such uses may secondarily also be gratifying is taken for granted, but in an essential analytic situation, there is technical advantage in giving priority to the defensive aspect.

The sound of the analyst's voice might also be viewed as part of the setting, the medium; it is easily used by the analyst to convey a "gleam" or by the patient's transference fantasy to imagine a "gleam." Here is an example of not letting the patient settle for using the medium as the message, having to do with the analyst's voice. A woman analysand had for some time gained the freedom to permit and describe the experience of allowing the sound of my voice—manifestly conversationally objective—to flow over her in a gratifying way, linked by association to certain bathing experiences. Eventually, it became clearer that precisely at moments when I was conveying some insight about an inhibition of her own self-observing capacity, she would successfully avoid "grasping" the content of what I was saying. As we analyzed the danger of revealing her observing and intellectual skill in my presence, she eventually reached the freedom, as she put it, "to go either way; I can let it flow over me, or I can take the ideas and use them." As Schlesinger (1985) has pointed out, what remains inhibited is often the capacity for taking positive "action" with insights. I emphasize (and this may be Schlesinger's emphasis as well) that the neglected "action" is to exercise the capacity for furthering one's analytic progress in the analytic situation, and so to gain individual, as contrasted with primarily interpersonally dependent, self-observing, and self-analyzing ability.

Transferences as part of the "medium" are not essentially different from any other transferences. They involve fantasies based on previous experience that in the analytic situation attach themselves to the analyst or the analyst's environment, primarily to provide resistance against anxiety.

A woman musician, early in analysis, had overcome, *for a while*, her inhibition of using her talent. It became clear eventually that her "relief" while performing was connected with a transference fantasy of "finally" finding someone who listened with warmly approving pleasure when she spoke about her musical and sensual interests. In the often unappreciative atmosphere of her early childhood, only a governess had for several years warmly encouraged her early musical interests. Now, much later in the analysis, she was again, this time through insight, overcoming her inhibition. She spoke of how, after a recent, more confident performance, she had received two recalls to the stage for applause and had become aware of the exciting thought that "I finally even outdid my sister." She paused, and added, "If you had been there, you would have been proud of me." Shortly after the analyst noted this, she could see how she had just taken refuge in the familiar transferential relationship of a little girl with an affectionate, encouraging authority, in order to deny having just confessed to pleasure in the competitive use of her adult skills. She then commented, "Actually, it now occurs to me if you'd been there, what you'd have felt would've probably been admiration . . . [*a pause*] or even envy that I'm that good." The evidence here of conflicted phallic-oedipal issues did not now "develop" in the analysis after a deficit had been filled; they were there all along, but she had resisted them with pregenital defenses.

A young man in his early twenties, with many adolescent qualities, had previously been in therapy, which he characterized as not helpful. Early in analysis—and for the first time in any treatment—he spoke rather freely of many personal experiences that obviously conflicted sharply with his current ideals. He indicated so often what a great relief it was to unburden himself of these things at last to someone he "knew" liked him that I eventually inquired tactfully about the nature of that view of me as "liking" him. With a sudden anxious insistence, he said, "Don't you *ever* question that feeling of mine . . . [*pause, quieter*] . . . at least for a couple of years." It is not surprising that his sense of time, which he needed in order to cling to such a defense transference fantasy, referred to his regressive infantile distortions of his ego needs, rather than to some actual ego deficit requiring replacement. He would begin to explore the anxiety-relieving fantasy long before his estimated time. As the fantasy of the affectionately permissive figure—in this instance a favorite uncle—became analyzed and was not protecting him any longer, he was gradually able to take on the experience and analysis of the anxiety he was resisting. The resistance use of the transference for purposes of safety was quite separate from the eventually accessible id transference of homosexual impulses.

DISCUSSION

By now it should be clear that I believe that analysis of the ego's superego activities is central to the analysis of resistance. The extent to which superego analysis is possible or desirable can provide a very practical dividing line or zone, dividing those patients who are clinically suitable for essential psychoanalysis from those who are not, or are less so, and who instead need to be permitted transferentially supportive elements, a concession that *naturally compromises resistance analysis.*

In the realm of intensive exploratory therapies, we really cannot expect any general agreement about which "schools" are practicing *psychoanalysis* and which are practicing something else. The title has become so valued that it virtually sticks to any or all of the variations. Be that as it may, I argue that we need some kind of designation as to the kind of psychoanalysis being practiced, in order to keep alive the issue that qualitative differences are involved; a merely quantitative continuum obscures much that is clinically crucial.

I propose that *essential psychoanalysis* refer to an essentially uncompromised, resistance analysis and that *wider-scope psychoanalysis,* including "object relations" analysis, refer to methods that need to preserve certain transferences of defense in order to achieve their goals. Further, I feel that there is an important key to some unifying concepts between, on the one hand, methodologies with analytic theories based on object relations concepts and, on the other, those oriented toward the object aspects of Freudian structural theory (Lussier 1988, Spruiell 1988), emphasizing analysis of defense/resistance arising out of conflict. This key lies in better comprehension of the analysis of the ego's superego activities. By unifying, I do not mean seeing a continuum that minimizes differences, but instead a qualitative highlighting of the differences in methodology and clinical application within the framework of a single theory—the structural and instinctual drive theory.

7

MEMORY AS RESISTANCE, AND THE TELLING OF A DREAM

In this essay, I want to share with the reader some of my recent thoughts on possibly the most demanding of our analytic tasks, that of increasing patients' autonomous access to their ego's unconscious activity at the very point where and when it opposes instinctual derivatives.

Our knowledge in this area has lagged partly—as Anna Freud reminded us—owing to a displacement of interest toward the widening scope of analysis. Necessary and valuable as it may be, attention to broader applications of analysis inevitably results in theoretical and technical modifications that become applied indiscriminately. Perhaps the explanation is that some modifications reduce the goals and ostensibly the complexity of the tasks involved, making them easier to use than treatment based on theories of structure and instinctual drives. This haphazard application frequently results in short-changing those analysands actually equipped to gain more from analysis. So I invite your attention to the analytic process in patients of the somewhat *narrower* clinical scope, aiming to extend our skills in this area—and beyond. I have tried to select a manageable portion of the extensive and complex technical task we confront. My goal is to stimulate us to conceptual clarification.

I examine in more detail than before, the familiar defense in which the patient displaces the context of time and place away from the analytic situation, in particular when his ego uses its function of memory for this purpose. Resistance to insight into ego activity, that is, resistance to uncovering resistance, makes a wide use of this defense. I then discuss a particular use of such resistance, when the patient recalls and relates the memory of a dream, and I shall suggest a technical response to that. This response to the telling of a dream differs from what we often do with dreams, and represents a realignment of our technical and theoretical priorities to better correspond with the changes Freud set in motion when in 1926 he revised the theory of anxiety. I begin with some theoretical and practical observations in the more general context of making the unconscious ego conscious, and include some facilitating technical suggestions.

Those of us who regard the structural theory, including the theory of instinctual drives, as the major foundation for our methodology find that, for the most part, it continues to resonate well with our clinical tasks. It is true that in some areas of our work we have been rather slow to expand its applications beyond what the topographic theory previously covered. Not long after Freud discovered that the part of the patient's ego crucial to resistance was also unconscious, he ungraciously abandoned his colleagues to work out for themselves much of the methodology for making that unconscious ego conscious. Since then complacency has tended to obscure the need to bring conscious ego not only to the id, but also to those unfamiliar ego activities that, in spite of being near at hand, have remained estranged from the patient ever since oedipal childhood.

Certainly we have not been totally without progress in making the unconscious ego conscious, but in our struggle we had to depend more on perspiration than on an inspiring methodology. We have every right to expect it to be difficult to attain technical competence in this area. Freud (1933c) was not jesting when he said to the phantom audience of his *New Introductory Lectures* that if they found the id difficult, wait until they confronted the complexity of the ego. He left us not only with the task of developing *methodology* for making the unconscious ego conscious, but even with the elaboration of much of the *theoretical bases* for the task. We understand that there is "resistance to the uncovering of resistance," but viewing this opposition only as we viewed opposition to id impulses does not provide us with a useful conceptual picture of the process.

Only near the very end of his life did Freud imply that analysis might offer ways of rehabilitating the defensive alterations in ego functioning. Meanwhile, most of the technical tools at hand provided ways only for either bypassing those alterations or *influencing* them in ways favorable to the analysis, the latter depending mostly on the undeniable power of transference. Such measures do a great deal for bringing id derivatives into consciousness, but without allowing them to move forward naturally, as they would if the analyst brought to life and made palpable the ego's specific, incessant responses silently bent on resistance.

In order better to appreciate the complexity of the ego's maneuvers to change the context of analytic attention by displacement of time and place—quite different from displacement of object—let us consider the immediate scene of intrapsychic activity so that we may enhance our focus. For the intrapsychic realm we are observing, I shall use the imperfect but familiar metaphor of "the stage" of consciousness or interchangeably, considering our interest in conflict, "the arena" of consciousness. As analysts we use that theater stage in various ways, asking the patient to try both to "occupy" it, that is to be *on it* experientially, and also to observe it. Freud's (1913) instruction to the patient to describe what is in his mind as if he were telling the analyst what he sees through the window of a moving train, has been useful over the years. Yet the fact that this model was conceived long before the role and complexity of the ego's activity were recognized limits its value. Freud devised the train window narrative at a time when it was not yet important for either the analyst or the patient to learn how dynamics of conflict and resolution are enacted *within* that moving landscape.

Access to previously unconscious *ego* depends on insights developed *in consciousness*. Patients have to learn through demonstrations of the dynamic activities within their manifest productions what it is they are trying to observe and to understand. Patients learn to become concerned with *how* they are or are not able to think during the analytic hour before gaining insight into *why* they think that way. In an earlier paper (Gray 1986, Chapter 3 in this volume) I explored some techniques that help analysands to observe their elusive ego activities.

Rather than stressing analytic alertness to drive derivatives *not yet admitted to consciousness,* I emphasize the technical value of shifting the focus of attention even further "upward" than usual. Banal though it is, one can apply the metaphor of moving the focus of a microscope upward and discovering that one has been looking through layers that are actually closer to the observer. The emphasis is on bringing into focus any instinctualized elements that have to some degree *succeeded in becoming conscious*. Then, as the intensity of that particular affect or ideational content increases, the growing conflict results in one or more of the mind's versatile measures proceeding to move that drive derivative dynamically off the stage of consciousness. After such defensive action, the elements that had briefly gained consciousness before succumbing to the ego's objections are usually not deeply repressed, and with appropriate analysis of the conflict, can reenter consciousness more freely. This way the analyst can share with the patient detailed observations of activity in the arena of consciousness more convincingly than if the derivative and the defense were both *not yet* conscious. Then, when the patient observes the process, he has first to consider it with rational attention, even though increasing amounts of tolerated *irrational affect* are the direct or ultimate result of his or her insight.

Warming to the heart of my subject, I shall now turn to the special case of resistance by displacement, when it occurs through the ego's selective use of the functions of *memory*. We know that the ego may use memory as a defense in a variety of ways. I shall focus on the frequent defensive use of the *avoidance of the sense of the immediate present.* A sense of the immediate present is an ego orientation that the analyst and the patient need in order to experience and observe phenomena occurring on the stage of consciousness. Here, I am taking a more detailed look at a subject I first approached some time ago (Gray 1973, Chapter 1 in this volume).

Memory, of course, is an ego activity that, like any ego activity, can be used as defense. Our effectiveness in making the unconscious area of the ego more accessible will grow as we become more familiar with the complex of functions that we frequently lump together under the label of *memory*. We often confine ourselves narrowly to the familiar side of the subject, the *recovering of memories*. However, as we listen to our patients, we deal continually with manifestations of the function of memory in a variety of contexts or forms, to which we do not always attend. Success in communicating our observations to the patient depends a great deal on *how* the patient makes use of his function of *recall*.

One of the complex of functions we group under the title of *memory* is the capacity to transform something first thought of as referring to another time and place—the *past*—into awareness that it exists as internal imagery in the *present*. We are more familiar with the reverse of this shift in tense: a patient saying "I'm thinking of a scene—I do not know if it is a memory. . . . [*later*] "It *is* a memory, at that time I *was* doing. . . . " It has become historical, the *past* tense. By contrast, shifting from perceiving a memory as in the past, to sensing it as now located on the immediate stage of consciousness involves a change in the sense of tense, or place of contemplation, that can be carried out with every memory—if the patient is not afraid to do so, and to acknowledge it to the analyst.

It is not too dramatic to say that in that arena/on that stage, if the patient chooses (and depending on the state of the resistance) he can transiently suspend *time sense*. This is not a regression; it is a self-observing function. We may demonstrate to the patient the ego's use or avoidance of this capacity in the analytic situation even better than the familiar concept, "willing suspension of disbelief" conveys. Obviously, there is a wide range of uses the mind makes of the context for the sense of "present."

Normally, people do see memories as past context—it is a part of life and helps us to orient ourselves within our history. Let us now put on our hat as analysands at a moment when we need to *restrict* the contemplation of a memory to something in the past context. For instance we may do so *defensively* in order to have it appear to the analyst, and to ourselves, that the images, affects or impulses to which the memory referred could not be part of our living present. When we say: "I *used to* think . . . ," it enables us to be unaware—to deny—that in saying it we must be thinking that thought consciously, just now. A context in the *past* removes us to a safer distance from the stage where anxiety occurs. The sense of relief that so often accompanies the shift of content away from the current stage of the mind is a familiar and often valuable therapeutic action, but it is a psychotherapeutic, not a psychoanalytic, action.

It is not that we are unfamiliar with the capacity to adjust our sense of time and place and contemplate memory as a present-tense event on the stage of our mind. When dealing with something that is *not* conflicted, we indulge in permitting immediacy more freely; we call it *reminiscence*. Freud saw hysterics as suffering from reminiscences. Had he reappraised this idea, after his revision of the theory of anxiety and elaboration of the concept of intrapsychic conflict, he might instead have said that hysterics suffer from *inhibition* of the *ego capacity for reminiscence*. If individuals become *able* to reminisce about their past, they do not have hysterical symptoms.

There is an old Spanish sentiment sometimes spoken at a moment of parting: "To remember is to live again." To reminisce is a pleasurable function that can certainly become conflicted and inhibited; reminiscence can also serve as a defensive use of recollections during the analytic process; it can reduce the motivation for insight. What it has in common with the capacity for awareness of and reflection on things as *present* during the analytic hour is its use of the sense of immediacy. The patient is usually eager to escape into the familiar way of experiencing memory with its safe context of another time and place, allowing him to avoid experiencing and observing life on the immediate stage of consciousness.

How is this relevant to the relation of insight to consciousness? Analysts often avoid this area by entertaining the incongruous concept of *unconscious insight*. In speaking of insight, it is more useful clinically to mean possession of something *now*, to *have* immediate knowledge of it. When patients say, "I know that is so," they are closer to accepting the stage of consciousness as being something alive than when they say, "I guess I knew that." It is the essence of Descartes' "I think, therefore I am." Patients who only feel alive when they experience suffering, violence, or physical pain, probably are suffering from severe pathology of the ego function of the sense of immediacy.

We understand the role of memory in the psychoanalytic situation very differently from the way it is regarded outside our field, as in popular psychology, fiction, the movies, or the cartoons of the *New Yorker*. Certainly, *during the analytic hour*, the mind crafts *all* memory, *ad hoc*, through the screen of the ego's defense activities. We are easily distracted from refining our technique in relation to the function of memory if we become too preoccupied with analyzing memory in relation to historical or narrative "truth." What is most important to us in the analytic process is the degree to which our analysands acquire, with our help, the capacity for a *true* observation of the contents and dynamic changes *in consciousness* that determine whether or not they are avoiding some wish, emotion, or impulse. For patients to appreciate that they may be using familiar, "normal" memory to avoid exposing the truths on the immediate stage of their minds, they must first become transiently familiar with the discomforts they feel when they observe and reveal what *is* present in that arena.

Let us turn now to one of the many analytic moments that lend themselves admirably to the resistance use of *the context of the past, as it displaces the analytic focus to some other time and place.* This occurs when the patient is *telling the analyst a dream.* Though I shall be presenting what may be a rather wrenchingly unfamiliar point of view, in sharing my convictions about it, I shall try not to strain my rapport with the reader.

Two plausible ideas that analysts resist are, first, that there is no such thing as *the* manifest dream; rather, there is a memory of something dreamed that is being *continually* reshaped; second, that ever since we have had the structural theory, it is not really necessary to have a "royal road" to the unconscious. These two concepts, however resistant some of us may be to them, are essential to my thesis. Brenner (1969, 1976a), of course, gave us an unequivocal view of these ideas, but I shall not burden him with any responsibility for where I am about to take them.

So that my personal preference for a particular technique of listening and responding to the recitation of a dream is clear, I shall provide as much theoretical basis as possible. I shall also stress again that the clinical context for this preference is generally, but not always, directed toward the "narrower scope" of analysis. With some analysands of the wider scope, and with certain of my patients in analytically oriented psychotherapy, I may still approach dreams much in the classical manner I acquired early in my training.

Why do we often hesitate to apply more of our evolving analytic theory to the *telling* of the dream itself? Perhaps it is because virtually all of the perspectives on and uses of the dream were deeply grooved into habit years before the structural theory and conflict analysis were available. Also, typically when we were candidates, we often tended, because of the nature of our curriculum, to internalize and repeat much of the historical development of psychoanalysis learned before we arrived at Freud's later theories and their potentialities. It is true, we do sometimes take immediate, noncontent aspects of the dream-telling into consideration, for example, the "glossing" comments made about the dream, and excessively long dream recitations. However, this is not the same as following the patterns of change just before and within the flow of the dream narration, the conflict and compromise activity in its relevance to the process *at the moment of telling.*

We know that a dream has essentially the structure of a symptom. By and large we tend not to analyze symptoms; they reveal their nature as part of the overall analytic work. Yet, out of habit, we typically approach the dream as once we regularly approached symptoms. Parenthetically, just as I acknowledged using traditional measures with dreams in *some* clinical situations, so too I sometimes "analyze" symptoms. Clinical possibilities and limitations should influence our choice of therapeutic action.

No recollection nor telling of a dream during an analytic hour escapes the ego's remarkable shaping influence, except possibly if the dream is read, and such dreams are not yet for analyzing. What *is* for analyzing in that instance is the need to resist freer communication by reading the dream. Analysts often treat the telling of a dream as if it were in a frame, not quite etched in stone, but certainly not a living mixture of some exposure of drive derivative and much defense against it, even as the patient describes it.

In a clinically suitable analytic situation, when a patient tells a dream, the method I am suggesting is, first, to note the place of the narration in relation to what the patient was saying or experiencing just before verbalizing the dream. I do not say before the dream "came to mind" (although that also may be true), because the patient may have had the memory of the dream in awareness and had only spoken of it eventually, depending on the state of the resistance; second, to observe and learn from the panorama of fluctuations within the sequence of the words, ideas, and images *as the patient portrays them while telling the dream.*

If, in contrast, we attend to conflict solutions that ostensibly confronted the patient when the patient dreamed the dream, we enter a realm of speculation fraught with many more variables than are involved when we choose to analyze the patient's actual mental processes as they take place within the hour where one can observe them. What is available for immediate observation is the verbal material that *is* the recitation of the dream. We can work with the narration that makes up the patient's description of the dream in much the same way as with any other sequence that might come up during an hour. The place in the hour when reference to the dream entered the material is as important as the place in an hour when the patient tries to escape intrapsychic observation by falling silent, or falling asleep. Incidentally some patients, no longer needing the defense of falling asleep, recall and report memories of dreams at moments of conflict when previously they would have fallen asleep. Let us examine a brief illustrative clinical excerpt.

A young lawyer initially sought analysis for anxiety attacks in anticipation of doing courtroom litigation. Later, sexual inhibitions and writing blocks proved to be more basically motivating for his treatment. Throughout much of his childhood, his mother, who suffered a chronic obsessional illness, sometimes of psychotic proportions, often grotesquely restricted him and his two siblings in a variety of ways, for example, by threats that any rebellion on their part would be the cause of her death. Psychiatric treatment for her, and her death during his teens eventually brought the patient manifest relief and permitted a superficially satisfying social adjustment. After a brief stint in a divinity school, his interest in religion subsided and he entered law school.

In the course of the analysis so far, the patient had gained an increasing capacity to recognize, when they were pointed out to him, patterns of defense that often occurred when he ventured into conflicted material.

Our example is from an hour occurring about a year into the analysis. The patient has been exploring briefly, sometimes hesitantly, certain memories of his childhood. As he described how for almost a year his mother made his little brother wash his bedsheets every morning, because of only *one* episode of soiling, a perceptible degree of anger and disgust with his mother began to creep into his voice, and then suddenly he became quieter, almost inaudible. He stopped and then said, now quite audibly:

Yesterday I forgot to tell you a dream I had over the weekend. I think I was in a large room with a multitude of people. [By now in the analysis I was not surprised by his use of the word "multitude."] I had on a black robe, like a judge. I guess it was a courtroom. They were listening to me. Then, it's funny, I realized that actually I was in white . . . I was embarrassed, 'cause I hadn't shaved. The crowd got restless, muttering . . . grumbling at me . . . I don't know what . . . my mother was in the crowd . . . It looked as though she might be crushed . . . I couldn't help her . . . I was upset . . . I woke up.

Analyst: In your description of the dream you seem to pick up on the problem you were up against just before you told me the dream.

Patient: [He appeared to be thinking for a moment.] It was something about my mother . . . the sheets.

Analyst: You sounded as if you were hesitating to speak critically about your mother, and then the memory of the dream interrupted.

Patient: Yes, I remember.

Analyst: Maybe it got unsafe to show me critical feeling toward your mother.

Patient: I don't want you to think I'm being unfair to her.

Analyst: In your memory of the dream you first pictured yourself as a judge, and then you took that away by making a white-robed, unshaven figure out of yourself.

Patient: It was like several days' growth . . . but the white robe was very clean.

Analyst: You spoke of becoming a white-robed figure . . . speaking to a crowd . . . a "multitude," who then grumbled at you.

Patient: Yeah . . . is it that Christ thing again? [In earlier hours, rather frequent remarks of, "Oh Christ," although a mixture of resentment and despair, had led to information about adolescent martyr fantasies in identification with Christ. He had been exposed to intensive Sunday school lessons throughout his childhood.]

Analyst: I guess it suddenly got safer for you to have me see you as sort of Christlike and on the receiving end of someone *else's* resentment, rather than my hearing *your* resentment toward your mother.

Patient: Well, I know you won't be critical of me.

Analyst: What I have in mind is the moment when you didn't want me to think of you as unfair to your mother. [Here I was interested in learning about the transference image of authority, which was actively motivating him to be cautious.]

Patient: Well, I guess I expect you to be like other people. [Here I was aware that in the past the patient and I had noted that sometimes he lapses into a general comment to relieve some conflict about being more specific. He often hesitated to explore evidence of some fantasied danger from me—in this instance a particular kind of criticism—because, as with most patients, the reexternalized image of restraining authority effectively motivated caution, and the patient did not want to uncover transference images that supported resistance.]

Analyst: Could "other people" be one of the generalizations that's a safer way of putting it?

Patient: Well, everyone at home . . . I guess I mean my father [now a freely angry tone] *He never let up . . . Christ! . . . He was always yelling I was being unfair to my brother . . . If he had only been as tough on my mother!* [I noted to myself that after exploring the form and motivation of his resistance, he was freer to expose his anger even though it was now displaced to his father, who instead of the patient may now appear as potentially aggressive to the mother.]

Let us reflect on the material. As we might suspect, the patient has been especially careful to avoid aggression toward his analyst. Some of his thoughts and feelings displaced toward other objects hint at what was eventually to become manifest in the id transference. I did not overlook that the angry accusation that his father "never let up" appeared soon after I pressed him a bit about my transference role as an inhibiting authority. Nevertheless I could not yet show him evidence, in that hour, that he had found it safe and then conflicted to be aware of even a bit of criticism of me. In keeping with my emphasis, as long as the patient manifested conflict and defense *while speaking about the objects of displacement themselves*, I noted *that* occurrence as the closest *demonstrable* conflict and ego solution, and I gave it priority.

As a patient *consciously* displays the conflicted tip of the iceberg of his instinctual drives, that tip, through insight, becomes less burdensome and allows more of the stratified mass of the *not yet conscious* fantasies and potential impulses to edge up into view.

After the material just recounted, as the patient learned more about his fear of feeling and speaking aggressively and unfairly about his mother, in the presence of the analyst, namely, about the fact that he feared I, like his father, would be harshly critical, he could allow increasing disappointment and anger with me to surface. As the patient first briefly permitted critical moments about me and then restrained or repressed them with familiar ego activities, I could again closely demonstrate these conflicts and their ego solutions without having to make speculative interpretations about what still remained unconscious.

Because our ears are trained to resonate hungrily with id material, it is tempting to be distracted by much that I do not take up with the patient. It is not difficult to notice in the material a number of highly plausible issues, unconscious to the patient, which we can reasonably detect and hypothesize about. For example, in the patient's conflict over aggression toward his mother in the dream description, and in the approaching cruel "manhandling" of his mother by the crowd, we could suspect a regressive version of oedipal, primal-scene conflict. But I stress that the conflict I can demonstrate is over aggression that is not yet oedipal. As the patient's anger at his father for not controlling his mother's cruelty finally appeared (where he said, "If only he had been as tough on my mother!") a hint of an underlying oedipal complaint appears. While it is not difficult to be sensitive to such deeper constellations, it is the nearer conflicts and solutions that are the stuff of systematic resistance analysis. At another moment, his breakthrough of anger toward his father reveals a sidelight, an admission that, as a child, the patient picked on his brother. We could now speculate that his upset at watching his mother's cruelty to that brother probably involves a reaction formation—maybe even against a masturbatory beating fantasy. That would be interesting, and possibly correct, but it would be a distraction from the activity at hand.

I might have directly interpreted such issues to advantage in an analysis with a patient of limited capacity for extended, consistent resistance analysis, or where severe pathology would not even gradually permit superego-free self-observation and I might fall back on greater use of suggestion to overcome resistance. In a less intensive, analytically oriented therapy where systematic conflict analysis would be technically impractical, I might do the same. In those instances the resistance to plausible, not yet consciously conflicted derivatives is often transiently overcome by the familiar technique of interpreting them directly, making use of the considerable authoritative influence. By contrast, in the technical approach I am illustrating here, the total emphasis on analysis of resistance includes early and consistent analyzing of that transferential authoritative influence, not leaving it in place for purposes of suggestion.

To return to my illustration, what did the patient and I learn from observing the words he chose in telling the dream? When he was beginning to experience conflict in the hour, the memory provided some relief through displacement to a context of conflict in the past, the night of the dream, when he had survived by awakening from a risk associated with a discomfort like that in the hour. We are familiar with a similar principle in one of the meanings of examination dreams (Freud 1900), but in our current instance it is the *memory* of the dream that recreated a momentary scenario safer than what he had just been approaching.

Attention to the details of the dream description in the context of the hour showed the analyst and the patient several things. It served to remove the patient from the role of judge, the role he had risked taking in the hour a few moments before remembering and telling the dream, when he was revealing himself to the analyst as a critical judge of his mother. It became apparent that by *remembering* the dream in the form and sequence in which he remembered it, he was, in effect, repeating the martyr solution as he faced an immediate situation of conflict. By thus remobilizing in the hour defensive aspects of his adolescent religious fantasies, he could momentarily reestablish a reaction formation to protect himself from sounding "unfair." Surely these dynamics were also relevant when he first had the dream, but relevant to something more remote and less alive than the analyzing of what it means that the memory of the dream is suddenly being told at that moment in the analytic hour.

Not only did the patient use the memory of the dream defensively, but he also allowed into consciousness briefly, albeit with the advantage of the displaced context, a previously forbidden degree of drive derivative: *someone other than himself* being crushed. Thus, at that phase of the analysis, presumably not only when the dream occurred, but at that very point in the hour, he could for a moment risk *picturing to himself and, most important, risk revealing the picture to the analyst*—something violent about to happen to his mother. Even though the defense is the important focus here, it was the first time in the analysis such a picture could reach and be acknowledged in consciousness, and was evidence of further analytic progress.

It was also possible to share with him the observation that in his thoughts the crowd turning from respect for his authority to a muttering disapproval represented repetition of a pattern of defense, frequently noted in his analysis, the turning of feared aggression or authority on himself. It provided one of the ways by which he avoided making judging, critical observations of his analyst or others, such as in a courtroom, by reestablishing through a sometimes masochistic transference the conditions of *being judged.* In that way he could reexternalize an inhibiting, restraining view of his father, which he had since childhood internalized for his ego's superego purposes. Our trained sensitivity to deeper id derivatives could lure us in a distracting way to note the potential for negative oedipal, passive homosexual elements, but we know it is an issue that will become clear later on—if we do not skip the conflicted material nearer the surface.

I recapitulate why I did not try to reconstruct reasons for his having the dream *in the first place.* I gave precedence to the search for reasons why he returned to the dream at that moment in the hour. I give authority to meanings that show the analyst and patient as much as possible of the activity on the immediate stage of consciousness *while the patient is resisting the emerging drive derivatives.* The aim is to make that insight regularly accessible to awareness, and so to increase the patient's autonomy.

If we doubt that the reason the patient surfaced the dream, or that *how* the patient remembered and told the dream, is intimately related to whatever else was taking place at that instant in the analysis, we are indeed selling short our theory of how the mind functions during the analytic process. When the analyst can resist the patient's familiar habit of "bracketing" a dream into a "frame" from another time and place, a more dynamic perspective becomes available. We may more readily follow the *immediate* analytic process if, to a very real degree, we regard the place of the dream in the material of the hour *as if the patient were, at that moment, redreaming the dream and narrating it.*

CONCLUSION

While proposing an alternative method of working with the telling of a dream, I am aware that analysts vary in the degree to which they feel the need or clinical possibility for making all elements of structure conscious. My argument is that if one *is* interested in bringing into stable accessibility the ego's unconscious patterns of resistance to unconscious conflict, then it is of ultimate value that greater attention be given to the immediate mental area where those defensive activities can be observed and demonstrated. We can attend to the telling of a dream with that immediacy.

If we can acknowledge the computerlike speed with which the versatile ego, threatened by anxiety, can process its defensive needs, we can motivate ourselves to step up demands on our own observing skills accordingly, and pay more effective attention to the moment-to-moment activity within the patient's productions.

I have presented a paradigm for attention to memories in analytic material, elaborating in particular the example of memories of dreams. My aim is a consistent approach to *all* of the patient's words, with priority given to what is going on with and within those productions as they make their appearance, not with attempts to theorize about what was in mind at some other time and place. Although my emphasis on closer attention to the patient's words aims for continuing search for the life of the elusive ego, the executor of resistance, I must note another advantage this emphasis may gain for us. Abend (1989) has observed: "The further one departs from verbal material, the more one relies on one's emotional responses to nonverbal dimensions of the interaction with patients, the more difficult the challenge of verification seems to become" (p. 394).

By giving more emphasis to observing the ego *while it is in action*, not only are the defensive uses of memory laid bare, but also a more autonomous access to vivid affects is possible during recollection. If we can expand the experience of remembering to include greater awareness of such experience as an immediate, active phenomenon, not a mere recalling of something past, the inner life of the patient is enriched. A new dimension is added to "past" and "present." When we analyze rather than merely overcome the multiple forms of resistance, and when the conscious mind uses its full potential, it can tolerate a greater range of intrapsychic freedom than it ever permits in dreams. Dreams are regressive phenomena that *always* include defensive control of what "comes to mind," if only to protect sleep. An ego that has had an analytic chance to function with mature freedom can allow an infinite scope of imagination. In its quiet complexity, the ego, whose nearby activities are often treated as if transparent and not observable, deserves even more scrutiny than dreams. The most profitable "roads" to the unconscious exist on the stage of the patient's consciousness, just a few feet away from us.

Freud's (1933c) own late revisions of dream theory convey a seeming reluctance to bring the definition of the dream fully into line with his own revisions of the theory of anxiety and intrapsychic conflict. Even today, analysts are tempted by tradition to enshrine the brilliant but long-surpassed landmark, known as "a dream is the *fulfillment* of a wish." Freud's eventual view of the role of anxiety in the solution of intrapsychic conflict leads us inexorably to a new definition of the dream: *A dream is the ego's response that thwarts the id's attempt to gratify a conflicted wish.*

I am urging that we give increased attention to the ways in which the resourceful ego often uses memory for instant compromise formation and displacement, away from the immediate stage where the living issues are being enacted. This attention is in contrast with and augments our rich tradition surrounding the many ways in which memory is subject to repressing forces. For those who may be unfamiliar with it, if I have succeeded in stimulating your interest in this way of analytic listening, I hope that you will submit my convictions to serious clinical testing. I acknowledge that nothing I have offered makes our job easier. In fact, I have asked us to add more work of learning and practice on top of an already challenging task.

PART II

TEACHING AND SUPERVISORY GUIDELINES

8

A GUIDE TO ANALYSIS OF THE EGO IN CONFLICT

Although candidates readily grasp the theoretical concept of the ego's central role in the management of conflict that characterizes the neurotic process, I believe that the most difficult aspect of teaching candidates the clinical skills of psychoanalysis lies in helping them to pay closer attention to observing and analyzing the actual manifested process of the ego's responses to conflict during the immediate analytic material. I have found the following brief conceptual guideline significantly helpful when shared with my students and supervisees.

CONFLICT AND DEFENSE ANALYSIS: A SUMMARY OF MODES OF OBSERVATION OF IMMEDIATE, MANIFEST MATERIAL AND SOME GUIDELINES FOR USEFUL ANALYTIC INTERVENTION

I shall briefly describe a basic analytic methodology for consistently providing analysands with a greater than traditional degree of participation in observing, grasping, and using their acquired insights into the nature and motivations of their ego's defenses as they are remobilized in the face of conflict over progressive consciousness of instinctual derivatives. Phase 1 describes the *focus of the analyst's attention* on points of change in the flow of material in order to identify the conflict and its involuntary resolution in the immediate context. Phase 2 explains how to *demonstrate to the patient* the defensive manifestations against specific drive derivatives, in a manner that allows the patient to attend to those processes in preparation for exploring the motivations for such defensiveness. Phase 3 describes analyzing the seminal role of the ego's defensive use of transferences of authority.

Phase 1: Focus of Attention; Surface and Context

Although analysands provide many indirect sources of information about the mind's activities, there are advantages in giving virtually exclusive attention to the verbal material. For verbal material is the data we have asked patients to provide us with and it is their verbalizations that we can best use to document and share our observations. In listening, we give priority to maintaining a close and even focus on the audible flow of words and affects for manifestations of instinctual derivatives emerging into consciousness. Once a derivative appears, the analyst continues to listen to the *subsequent sequence* of material for changes (alterations in context, content, etc.) that indicate, by their content, that the ego has initiated a defense in order to stem a rising or anticipated discomfort (anxiety, sense of risk) because of conflict over exposing a specific part of the material containing some drive derivatives.[1]

[1]Although it is true that all painful affects (unpleasures) may evoke defensive action of the ego (especially anxiety), I regard it in general of equal or more importance that all painful affects lend themselves admirably as *defensive alternatives* to experiencing, *and revealing*, instinctual derivatives accompanied by pleasurable–exciting affect. Of course the latter can be drawn on for purposes of defense as well.

Note that in this approach to analysis of conflict and defense, analysts do not need to make use of their own "unconscious" in order to understand the material. The drive-invested materials (drive derivatives), at the moment the ego senses too much conflict and acts to inhibit them, are all directly observable. When appropriate, the analyst can demonstrate them to the patient, in anticipation of moving toward bringing into awareness the nature of the fantasy (reexternalized transference of authority) motivating such defense (see phase 3). It is important to resist changing one's focus away from the immediacy of the material, that is, not to get caught up in the external context of the content and be distracted from listening as carefully as possible to the process occurring while the patient is speaking (Gray 1973, Chapter 1 in this volume). That patients move naturally to think in a context of past or future (a displacement from the present) should not divert the analyst's attention from noting the sequence and qualities of the material as immediate orchestrations under the ego's guarded attention. We know that once patients grasp the analytic task of attempting to verbalize to the analyst whatever appears on the stage of consciousness, their egos become *continuously* alert to the danger of "too much" exposure. Therefore, the analyst may regard the flow of material (associations) as containing drive derivatives striving for consciousness, but now influenced by the ever available transferences of inhibiting fantasies of authority (or fantasies of affectionate permissiveness). In analyzing the defense-resistance, the analyst does not have to search below or beyond the conflict-ridden manifest surface (verbalizations in consciousness) for crucially relevant data. The instinctually derived material will incrementally move more freely into consciousness as the surface-accessible conflict and the ego's defensive solutions are analyzed.

Phase 2: Demonstrating the Defensive Manifestation to the Patient

In this phase, the analyst communicates to the patient the observed manifest data that reveals a degree of drive derivative had been *expressed*, encountered conflict, and had thereby prompted the ego to either revise it or remove it from consciousness.

We must remind ourselves that to the extent that patients actually attempt the primary task of spontaneous verbalization, some degree of defensive regression burdens the ego. When indicated and possible, our task is, in effect, to invite the patient to suspend that attempt for a moment and, in a more rational mode, listen to a description of what the analyst has been observing. If we want the patient to gain insight into the ego's activity, our comments must be clearly understood and *bearable.*

The degree to which analysts succeed in this phase depends on their sensitivity to patients' receptivity at the moment of interpretive intervention, with a view toward engaging patients' capacity to observe with rational attention. Clearly, in addition to attentive listening, the analyst's language and conceptual skills are crucial to this effort. To apply these skills appropriately and successfully the analyst must develop a reasonably accurate sense of what knowledge the patient already has (from the analyst or elsewhere) about *why* the analyst is conveying these observations and ideas. It should not surprise us that, at times, the patient's actual knowledge of what the analyst is attempting and the *availability* of that knowledge may vary as the neurotic manifestations of inhibiting transference transiently assert themselves.

The word *bearable* pertains to the fact that since the analyst is communicating a conceptual sequence or "package" that includes references to the manner in which, and to the place where, the ego's protective activity responded to an identified drive derivative, the analyst is asking the patient to allow into consciousness once again awareness of the very recent point of conflict. The analyst's task is to clearly include the essentials of the "package" of defense and what it interfered with, without overloading the patient's ego as the patient attempts to think back and recontact a sustainable degree of the drive derivative, all the while coming to sense that because there was, and is, conflict over revealing it, the ego initiated protective reaction (resistance).

It is here, in providing a bearable, that is, sufficiently ego-syntonic intervention, that the analyst's clarity of conceptualization and communicative language are very important. Granted that suggestion-free communication is only an idealized goal (sought in psychoanalysis, not usually in psychotherapy), it is the skills under discussion here that can bring us closer to that ideal.

Typically, we wish to formulate our intervention in such a way that the patient realizes that we are less concerned with persuading him or her to "reveal more" of the conflicted, usually drive derivative–invested material, than we are in coming to learn what expectation the patient came up against at the relevant moment, that motivated him to draw back from revealing it (phase 3). To repeat, as our theory and practice teaches us, if the fantasied risk can be analyzed, the next time the conflicted material tries to reach consciousness, it will not encounter the same degree of conflict, and will thus incrementally reveal itself more and more successfully.

Clinical Examples

Here I shall use convenient source material by noting some moments recorded and transcribed for process study (Dahl et al. 1988). First, we shall consider only the matter of observing the flow of material, listening for moments that best reveal the ego in its responses to conflicted material that it has briefly allowed into consciousness, only to sense, at some point, that it cannot permit any further exposure. At the end of phase 3 we shall look at the matter of intervening to convey our observations to the patient.

It is very early in the analysis, but already some characteristic modes of defense are manifest, including conflicts over exposing derivatives of aggression. Now comes a moment which illustrates this: " . . . *I am annoyed by that kind of person, but some of it's got nothing to do with her* . . . " (p. 16, emphasis added).[2]

[2]In a current close process study group, all ten analysts cited this passage as an example of the ego's defensive response to a drive-derivative conflict.

Following the revealing of annoyance, beginning with "but," the patient's ego responded defensively.

Somewhat later the patient reveals, rather closely together, two more occasions of conflict and defense: "*She's very boisterous and kind of, well, coarse is too strong a word, but*" (and again) "*well, loud and I think in a way unfeeling, although she can be very kind and with boys she's quite sensitive to them and, and has a real sense of them as individuals* . . . " (pp. 16 17, emphasis added). Revealing critical feelings, the patient runs into conflict over the possibility of referring to the woman as "coarse," and the ego moves to retract or diminish the criticism, but then the reduction itself, "loud and . . . unfeeling," becomes unsafe to show, and the ego reacts again by turning attention to positive or complimentary observations, a brief moment of reaction formation.

Here the intent of any interventions is to demonstrate what just took place in a manner that allows the listening patient to grasp the potential insight because it is clear and plausible, and to provide an opportunity for the ego to deal with the revisited conflict at a newly conscious level. Optimally, the analyst's remarks are not to be suggestively persuasive; the timing, the content, and even the sequence of the comments can go far in assuring that aim. Reference to the drive-derivative material should be accurate, but not so blatantly characterized that the ego cannot take on the conflicted material and tolerate sensing the discomfort that may accompany more intense exposure; that is, "your resentment" rather than "your hatred."

In the interpretive intervention, it is not necessary to make observations regarding evidence of any hidden drive-derivative elements within any newly formed compromise formation that may characterize the state of affairs after the ego has made its defensive move. Instead, what the analyst must conceptualize for the patient is the primary function of the defense that the newly observable ego solution served, that is, precisely where it developed and why it became necessary. That defense provided some relief from a discomfort the patient experienced or nearly experienced and was mobilized by a background perception, often not in the patient's attended awareness, of transference-created images of the analyst listener. Often the analyst can plausibly surmise unconscious id elements in the compromise formation, but "naming" of not yet conscious drive derivatives is an approach that continues to persist from the times of predefense analysis. As described, the emphasis instead should be on drive derivatives that were briefly fully in consciousness, and on what happened as they encountered conflict. "Direct" interpretation of unconscious id elements, although it may set off a historically useful therapeutic action by furthering the patient's access to drive derivatives, treats the aspect of the structural theory dealing with modern ego defense as if it were something merely added on to previous methodology, rather than an "entirely new" theoretical perspective (Kris [1938] commenting on Anna Freud's [1936] monograph *The Ego and the Mechanisms of Defense*) allowing for a new technique. In this phase, when the patient intermittently pays relatively rational attention to the analyst's syntonically offered observations (Apfelbaum and Gill 1989), a greater degree of stability is possible than when, a few moments earlier, the patient was trying to set aside rationality in the service of spontaneous, "free" association and thus was more vulnerable to defensive regression. This method of interaction optimally gives the patient's ego another chance to manage the conflict tension, again, at a conscious level.

The patient is more capable of bearing the burden of returning to the point of conflict, provided that the analyst has intervened in a systematic manner (Gray 1986, Chapter 3 in this volume), including such measures as speaking of the defensive position or material *before* documenting, in the immediately following comments, what drive derivative had become conflicted and was diminished or removed from consciousness by the defense. Obviously, this is a close process application of the familiar precept "defense before drive." It is often a challenging task to draw patients' attention to the fact that whether or not they move their conscious focus of attention to the past or future, the *immediate* simultaneously resisted context inherent with the *telling* (Gray 1992, Chapter 7 in this volume) continues to exist. This brings us to the next phase, since it is primarily in this immediate context of the patient's verbal expressions, in the presence of the analyst, who from the onset is endowed with transference of authority, that the motivations for the ego's defensive activity occur and are accessible.

Phase 3: Analyzing the Defense Transferences of Authority, Reexternalized from the Ego's Superego

Once analysands, in response to the analyst's interventions (phase 2), are able to look at the places and the discomforts that, in the course of verbalizing to the analyst, have evoked specific defensive solutions, they are in a position to look at what was the immediate source of conflict encountered by certain of their disclosures to the analyst. This area of intervention is crucial to the analysis of the ego's defensive uses of its superego activities. At this point the analyst invites patients to undertake the effort of attending to the presence of the influencing transference of authority that they have reexternalized upon the analyst. They are to bring into focus the background fantasy of assumptions about the analyst as judgmental, or reactive in ways that made it difficult to risk showing more of what was coming to mind. These transferences have been the time-honored sources of the "unobjectionable" (Freud 1912a, p. 105) transference *influence* (Curtis 1979, Gray 1991, Chapter 6 in this volume, Schlesinger 1988, Stein 1981) in the analytic situation, originating in the prestructural, topographic, era. Prior to the revision of the theory of anxiety, the "remnant of the hypnotic method" (Freud 1913) was essential for overcoming the "mechanisms" of defense, that defined the resistances. After 1926 (Freud 1926a), the opportunity to analyze, rather than therapeutically manipulate, the allowable transferences became theoretically both possible and essential. Except for the limited approaches of pointing out, "labeling," certain material as defense (or resistance), the search for a coherent methodology for *analyzing* defensive solutions has been an uphill inquiry. There has not been a pronounced incentive for moving further into the ego's complexity. It should not come as a surprise that patients show considerable reluctance to recognize and analyze that aspect of transference the ego finds so effective for restraining *disclosure*. Once children have made *self-civilizing* use of a perception of a parent as an auxiliary guardian of their morals, of their struggle against their dangerous instinctual drives ("my mother/father would *never* let me do, or say, that"), they do not want to believe that the authoritative figures are, in fact, usually less inhibiting than illusion would have them believe. Further, they do not want to face their God-equivalents, to see them too clearly, they only want them to always "be there" serving that controlling role.

The most valuable interventions directed toward analyzing the ego's defensive uses of transference of authority will be those leading patients to their own exploration of the experience, close to the appearance of the *non-neutral* figure whose transference presence they try to maintain for safety against anxiety. The ego may use these transferred images to maintain inhibiting caution or alternatively to contribute to safety in speaking of some things more freely, based on fantasies of affectionate approval (Gray 1991, Chapter 6 in this volume). The most effective "superego" analysis occurs when the repetitive details of the imagined figure before whom analysands are at risk can become so vividly portrayed by them that the discrepancy with the actuality of the experience of having a neutral listener, the analyst, becomes convincingly apparent, and the patient's own role in remobilizing those inhibiting or affectionately supporting fantasy images becomes clearer.

We know that components of the patient's conflict and stimuli for the ego's activity of defensive resistance occur regularly away from the analytic setting. Patients at times make use of their awareness of that fact to avoid analysis of the accessible, ubiquitous, manifest experience of the conflict in the analytic situation; that is, "But I'm reluctant to speak of these things with anybody . . . I can't even think them easily." This implies: "It has nothing to do with you." The patient often reluctantly recognizes that, even if those nonanalytic, "conscience" experiences are real, it is precisely because they repeat themselves when speaking with the analyst that renders such occasions a close, immediate source of valuable insights. Defenses (resistance) against acknowledging the presence of influencing imagery transferred onto the analyst usually yield only gradually. After all, the idea of a context in which one actually is allowed, and expected, to think, feel, and say anything is for a long time frightening.

Clinical Example (for additional examples, see Gray [1986], Chapter 3, this volume)

In formulating interventions relevant to the ego and conflict, it is the principles involved that are of importance, not the use of specific words. The principle here, again, is that the analyst, illustrating the ego's defensive activity against a definite drive derivative that has appeared briefly in consciousness, speaks in a manner *chosen* to convey to that particular patient at that particular time, ideas clearly conceptualized to help the patient gain insight into how and why the mind functioned in the face of conflict.

In choosing how to verbalize the interventions, the analyst makes use of an ongoing sensitivity about the patient's receptivity. One may use *empathy*, or rely on skilled rational observation of phenomenological data (Shapiro 1981). It is important here to define the intended use for such perceptions. Any "empathy" in this case is not the message; it is not intended to create a therapeutic action. In fact, the manifestation of the sensitivity or empathy can be so subtle that the patient can take for granted that the purpose of the analyst's comments is only to discuss the phenomena that have just occurred; they are not to supply the patient with a supportive sense of "being understood."

How then, as one of many possible wordings, might one intervene in the case of the first example [phase 2] where the analyst has observed conflict and defense? The patient is interrupted at the end of, or quite near to, the material cited.

> *Analyst*: I'm aware that you're now thinking of how some things that set off your feelings toward X (the person spoken of) had nothing to do with X, but in addition can we notice how, as you bring this last view to mind, you've moved yourself away from . . . sort of diminished, having expressed annoyance with X. Is this one of the moments in which when you tell me of a critical thought about someone other than yourself, you then react as if, unless you took it back or modified it, there would be some problem created right here? Maybe, again, we could learn something more about what that risk might be.

If this intervention is successful, the patient's attention has been drawn to what has occurred. The analyst directed the first of the comments to the part of the material being experienced as safer, from the side of the defense, and captured the patient's attention in a way that did not at once confront the patient with the conflicted drive derivative. By the time the analyst mentions the "forbidden" feeling, or word, enough ego is engaged that the conflict is bearable without a new surge of defense. The patient is not to experience the intervention as an exercise in intellectualization, but intelligence. By calling attention to the drive derivative the analyst has, optimally, evoked in the patient a sense of conflict remobilized, or revisited and accompanied by a present degree of conflict and associated discomfort that is, at least transiently, being engaged in awareness. This contrasts with the form of destabilization of the equilibrium of mental forces (Arlow and Brenner 1990) accompanying direct interpretations of unconscious derivatives that have not yet been able to penetrate to consciousness (in the analytic situation), a technical measure often characteristic for interpretations of compromise formations, and depending on a different therapeutic action for its effectiveness from the therapeutic action sought here.

The analyst's inquiry about the inhibiting transference moves the process in the direction of gradual elaboration of the ego's use of the reexternalized transference of authority, in order to show eventually that by this means patients try to assure safety by opposing revelation to the analyst of the unconscious life and its potential taboos. Ultimately the analyst can clearly demonstrate how the presuperego perceptions of parental authorities, eventually internalized and resurrected in the analytic situation (and elsewhere), include, and contain, due to projection, the instinctual wishes and impulses that the child needed to control.

I am much aware of the additional burden on the analyst who is asked to consider the ego's activities in such detail. Whether *analysis* of defense, rather than *interpretation* of defense, finds its place as an inevitable extension of Freud's discoveries remains to be seen. Only in the future shall we find the measure of our resistance to greater knowledge of how the mind works, relative to the ego's potential for mature growth.

ON CONSTRUCTIVE ORIENTATION OF POTENTIAL ANALYSANDS

Candidates, and recent graduates, all too often experience uncertainty and inhibition when they need to orient those patients for whom analysis appears to be the treatment of choice, to the nature of the analytic task and the patient's participation in it. These analysts frequently become discouraged over ever holding a largely analytic practice when they lose potentially analyzable patients because the analysts' insufficient therapeutic methods have failed to protect the patients' original degree of motivation. The methods of teaching candidates to cope more effectively when making introductions to analysis are often inadequate when dealing with this problem. Although this can be a tough area for students to grasp, the difficulty probably lies more in certain ambiguities within the curriculum, or in supervisory guidance.

Although analysts have always instructed patients in what they expected of them during the analysis, what was said varied with the theory prevalent at the time. In early decades, theory provided simpler concepts that justified simpler instructions. In addition, the ubiquitous role of suggestion in *overcoming* resistance (Freud 1917a, p. 451) discouraged early analysts from engaging the patient's intellect beyond bare necessity lest intellectualization interfere with the treatment. Two reasons point to the need for significantly greater attention to orienting prospective analysands today. The first has evolved from today's greater knowledge of the ego's complex role in the nature of neurosis; the second arises from the, probably fortuitous, coincidence of the contemporary and not unreasonable emphasis on taking patients into nonemergency treatment only if they are prepared to give informed consent. This is fortuitous, because it stimulates analysts to formulate clearly what analysis consists of in terms of contemporary theory. Not only can analysts more often assist patients in making an informed consent in this way, but even more important, they can provide patients with information enabling them to participate more effectively in the analysis. The latter has particular value if the analyst accepts as a contemporary treatment aim the providing of greater knowledge of and access to a more autonomous, mature ego, an acceptance that, in practice, has not kept pace with our theory. If we take this last perspective seriously, then we need to prepare our analysands accordingly with useful ways of conceptualizing and coping with the greater burden and complexity of the analytic work ahead.

To help with this dilemma, I offer the following pedagogical contribution; it has proven helpful when shared with students and especially with supervisees.

SOME GUIDELINES FOR PRELIMINARY INSTRUCTIONS TO ORIENT A POTENTIAL ANALYSAND TO THE TASK OF A BASIC PSYCHOANALYSIS

Before an analytic situation begins, the analyst's "influence," based on a positive-enough relationship (transference), usually works to sustain motivation and helps the patient to overcome any sudden increase in resistance. This supporting, influencing attitude is usually necessary to oppose the mounting resistance that often moves in when the patient contemplates beginning an analysis. Once the analyst has reached the decision that analysis is the treatment of choice, such an active approach is desirable because the situation, not yet being analytic, usually does not yet allow for *analyzing* resistance. If the analyst's influence is sufficient to gain the patient's cooperation in setting up the administrative details of the analysis (arrangements for hours, fees, "second opinion" for control cases, etc.), it is advisable to have those plans in place *before* telling the patient about the nature of the analytic work itself. This rule of thumb is based on the recognition that the ego typically responds with more defense-resistance, once the implication is clear to the patient that the expected effort toward a verbalized spontaneity ("free association") inevitably threatens to reveal "everything." If the resistance proves too severe to move ahead with arrangements for an analysis, particularly in the case of disappointments or traumas in previous treatment, the analyst may help reduce such resistance by letting the patient air those experiences sufficiently. In certain cases where the "mystery" of analysis, or consciously disturbing fantasies about analysis, mobilize too much fear, some selective sharing by the analyst of the treatment rationale in more detail is a piece of reality that, when added to positive, motivating transference influences, may reduce the inhibiting fantasy of danger. As fearful expectations return during the analysis, the context will make them more amenable to analytic exploration. Note that judicious use of positive transference while initiating arrangements for analysis is not the same as accepting an "unobjectionable" (Freud 1912a, p. 105) positive transference (Curtis 1979, Gray 1991, Chapter 6 in this volume, Schlesinger 1988, Stein 1981) during the analysis itself. It is making a practical and often necessary use of an unavoidable-inadvertent opportunity, which, if sacrificed to a too passive attitude on the part of the analyst, may lead to the flight of the patient, literally, or into an unyielding resistance.

Ideally, the analyst should orient the patient to the analytic tasks as early as the patient can understand the ideas. Obviously, receptivity varies. Some patients can grasp such orientation quite early. In others, resistances may for some time handicap receptivity to guidelines and rationale. Even if the analyst can impart only one step at a time, there must develop somewhere in the patient's mind, early in the analysis, a concept of the work and process that the ego is trying both to allow and also to avoid.

Here is an example of the sort of information the analyst might convey to a patient, depending on rapport and receptivity.

> When we first met, we spoke of how the problems that brought you here might be the result of some current events or circumstances and that, if we could discover and examine them in detail, we might bring about a favorable change. We also considered, on the other hand, that the problems might be due to characteristics that in one form or another have been a part of you for much of your life, and now have become attached to certain contemporary events or relationships. We considered how in that case, although briefer therapy might allow you to feel better for a while, the problems probably, as in the past, would come back. I said then, that if the longer history of problems were the case, psychoanalysis would be the treatment of choice because, to bring about more lasting change, you would have to come to understand how and why your mind fails to serve your best interests. Now it's clear that your problems do have a long history; that they become aggravated from time to time; that they repeat themselves; and that psychoanalysis *is* the treatment of choice.
>
> In order to reach the things in your mind that contribute to your problems, things that are not otherwise accessible, we go about it in a rather simple, though not necessarily easy, way. The aim is to understand the ways you have been able to keep these parts of yourself out of awareness, and why that has been necessary. As a result, you'll come to have better access to them and, if you wish, may *choose* some different solutions than the involuntary ones that trouble you now.

This may well be a place to consolidate plans for analysis and take up arrangements (hours, responsibility for absences, etc.). Once these are established, then, as I indicated earlier, the orientation might continue with more specifics. This takes into account that once the implications of the extent of exposure that is soon to begin are clearer to the patient, the defenses typically become stimulated. Hence, it is often better to have commitments in place.

> Part of your task, when we start, will be to try to let thoughts spontaneously come to mind, observe what is there and, to the extent that you can, *put all of those things into words so that we may gradually study them.* Typically, it will sometimes be difficult to show me your mind in that way, and my listening and commenting on what I observe is intended to help you to understand the obstacles that get in the way. You can do it more successfully by lying on the couch.
>
> The problems that brought you here, as you know, are repetitive experiences [or behavior, symptoms, situations, etc.] over which you haven't had much control or choice. Basically, they're solutions to conflicts you were up against as a child. There was a time when they were the best solutions you could work out, and they may have been successful for what you needed *then.* As you've learned, now these solutions don't always fit in with what you want in your life today. How will it help to study all of your thoughts and feelings, as you gradually make them available here? Because, in the process of working to reveal these things here, you'll encounter versions—close-ups—of the very problems you've described in your life outside of this room.

Here, in order to illustrate what you mean, it may be helpful to share with the patient examples of conflict and automatic solutions based on clinical data obtained earlier from the patient, for instance:

> You'll probably encounter here, as you have earlier in life, impulses to solve something by running away from it ["moving, 'arranging' to go elsewhere etc."]. [Or:] Just as you reach

> places in your professional work [etc.] where you lose your interest and motivation [or "block" in your work or writing etc.; become anxious, depressed, etc.] we'll be able to see versions of those things develop here as automatic, involuntary solutions to difficulties in making all of your thoughts and feelings available to us.

An alternative way of presenting some of the rationale for the work might be:

> Reasonably, you know, or will come to know, that it is safe here to undertake this task of showing me—in words and feeling—all of the things that enter your mind. But many of your past life experiences will automatically caution you to oppose undertaking the job. It is to *study these involuntary, inhibiting reactions based on repeated versions of previously conflicted and obstructing experiences, that will be our primary task*. As we work at this, you will gradually make available for us—for yourself in particular—the part of your mind that has remained largely out of your reach and has thereby, in a sense, robbed you of being whole. Your familiarity with this manner of observing the conflicts and the involuntary, symptomatic ways that your mind has used to deal with them is not only essential in allowing you to gain control over these involuntary solutions—held onto from childhood—but will give you knowledge and skill you may take with you and use by yourself to keep these restored mental activities available.

If the patient remains significantly receptive, or becomes again receptive, communicating the following about observing tasks is analytically useful; the earlier the better, *if one is to bring alive the patient's unconscious ego, and its ways of rendering selected drive derivatives unconscious.*

> In our work you'll learn to use several different kinds of observing. The first has to do with observing what is on your mind, so that you can put it into words. On the other hand,

when I interrupt to tell you about something I've noticed taking place within what you have been saying or feeling, you'll need to suspend telling me the spontaneous flow of your thoughts, so that you may reflect back over what I've noticed while listening to you; we'll do a sort of instant replay. That is probably a more reasoning kind of observation than you were using just moments before. It's intended to familiarize us with what your mind, without your always being fully aware of it, may have been doing, in a sort of self-protective way, just as you were speaking to me.

In this way, as you learn about these self-protective measures that your mind has been taking right in the midst of what you were saying, you have an opportunity to return to that place in your thoughts where that protective diversion automatically took place, and by being there again, you're able to sense more clearly the form of discomfort which was arising as you began to get into that particular thought or feeling. When you can do that, it will allow us, each time, to learn more about what was the anticipated risk, possibly in the background, that caused you to interrupt speaking what you had in mind and draw away; we can also notice the manner in which you did this. By actively using this insight you can gradually gain useful access to parts of yourself which your problems are keeping from you.

This way of observing the activity within your thinking may be entirely new to you. Often it takes some practice. Basically, it involves being able to shift from regarding your expressed ideas and feeling only in the familiar contexts of the past (recent or distant) or future (that is, before or beyond the present analytic hour itself), and to turn to learning how you experience and influence those same thoughts and feelings *as you reveal them aloud here*.

9

BRIEF PSYCHOTHERAPY, DYNAMIC PSYCHOTHERAPY, AND PSYCHOANALYSIS

The noted physiologist Anton J. Carlson steered generations of students toward good scientific attitudes by responding—in his Scandinavian accent—to their stating so-called "facts," with "Vat iss da effidence?" His urologist colleague Charles B. Huggins captivated medical students with a somewhat different approach: "There are only five facts you need to learn from my course." As a researcher he went on to win the Nobel Prize. In order to respond to a request for a "brief communication" about therapeutic actions, I will take a lesson from Huggins's approach. In order to be relevant to the work of practitioners who do not confine themselves to one mode of treatment, I shall make brief, rather dogmatic remarks about some therapeutic situations. I shall address three categories of psychological treatment: brief psychotherapy, dynamic psychotherapy, and essential psychoanalysis. Rather than elaborate many technical details, my aim is to point up the contrasts by making some generalizations that may help orientation for the therapeutic tasks.

A. BRIEF PSYCHOTHERAPY

Propose a limited number of consultations. The therapeutic situation is intended primarily to use *suggestion* as the therapeutic action, not to strive for genuine[1] insight. The patient needs rapid, positive, respectful rapport. Don't examine transference. Sensitively focus dialogue repeatedly on symptoms or problems. One therapeutic aim is, through a moderate, *conflict-stimulating* attention, to mobilize a shift from the patient's current defense solutions (symptoms, character traits) to defenses with less pain, and, if the patient's superego will tolerate it, more gratification. If they are not too near the "mark," sympathetically given "wild analytic" interpretive comments (theoretically plausible genetically, but speculative), may loosen the defense structure by providing new, helpful "explanations," and so, via *approved (ego–superego syntonic) displacements*, take some of the load off the conflicts caused by the ego's superego vigilance. Both explicit and implicit auxiliary ego and superego provisions, via the therapist taking a helping authoritative role, can be highly useful. When ending the work, leave the way open for further contact, in order to facilitate the *necessary continuance* of the transference fantasy that has supported the patient's relief from conflict. The insights valuable in brief psychotherapy are supported insights; they might be regarded as revised personal myths, or even facsimiles. Their utility, for what they are intended, should not be underestimated nor demeaned.

B. DYNAMIC PSYCHOTHERAPY

Since all psychological therapies are conceptualized in terms that are directly derivative of some aspect of Freudian psychoanalytic

[1]Genuine insight refers, here, *to observable psychological phenomena* that can be reperceived voluntarily, *without transference support* (hypnosis, suggestion, "conversion to," etc.). It is *owned knowledge*, because it has been fully earned by learning through "stark" therapeutic experience. It is stable knowledge, subject to change through further learning; it is not held on faith.

theories, both A and B could each be called "analytically oriented," an ambiguous phrase I am avoiding. Also, any therapeutic work done by an analytically trained individual presumably has *some* analytically informed perspective. The widespread practice of using disorganized, watered-down versions of an ostensible psychoanalytic model, and referring to it as "analytically oriented therapy," has led, in the field of therapy, to the almost impossible task of knowing who is doing what to whom. In order to further the differentiation from psychoanalysis proper, I use the time-honored phrase "dynamic psychotherapy."

Patients in this category may be approached with the orienting advice, "The more you can tell me *about yourself*, the more I will be able to help you." This promotes "free communication" (what the patient chooses to talk about) *not* "free association." In fact, given the widespread ignorance among patients as to "what is going to happen," it can help with some patients if you make the distinction between these two concepts explicit. That puts the patient on notice that many of the defenses *will not* be approached and, as a result, less regression is stimulated, and the patient is often able to cooperate with the treatment more fully.

Once the therapist can comfortably accept the idea that if there is no analytic situation, analysis is not going to take place, then it becomes possible to relax certain analytic modes and make optimum use of a number of other therapeutic actions.

As in most psychological therapies, the therapeutic aim is to bring about useful modification of those defensive activities of the ego that we usually conceptualize as superego manifestations. To do this non-analytically, it is important to rely on a positive but not overly stimulating transference, for a relief from the defensive conflicts; this means to rely on suggestion, and to strive not to pull the rug out from under the necessary, *and continuing*, supporting transference fantasy, conscious or unconscious. The nature of the supporting transference fantasy and its helpful mobilization depend on the existence in the patient's past of at least one reliable figure. Occasional uses of plausible, genetic speculations (speculative, since in this setting, *systematic analysis of resistance against memory is not possible*) are often of therapeutic value. Frequently such "interpretations" give relieving displacement away from conflicts in the immediate environment, and by providing the superego with less trying conflicts (often including a sense of absolution), help keep potentially disturbing attention to the therapist at a minimum. A popular form of "family therapy" makes use of this principle, with an institutionalized displacement technique that focuses on "genealogy." The typical, useful outcome in such therapies is some form of "flight into health" (usually not as rapid as was the original implication of the phrase). Obviously, this occurs in order to protect against mobilized areas of conflict (transference and otherwise), which the treatment situation is often ill prepared to deal with constructively. Here again, although need for "room," in the form of interruptions or discontinuations of treatment, is important; equally important is an implied or explicit opportunity to return for "further work." The open-ended attitude helps extend the necessary supportive transference. The problem (perhaps ethical) of when such measures, if long extended, tend to delay the possibility for analytic treatment, if such care is in fact feasible and necessary for actual resolution of continued troubling pathology, is beyond the scope of this essay.

C. ESSENTIAL/BASIC PSYCHOANALYSIS

Our aim is to put into practice methodology beyond the limitations imposed by theories developed during the original topographic orientation. Let us look at a therapeutic action context made possible by Freud's later structural and anxiety theory. Here we choose the opportunity of *analyzing* resistance, instead of *overcoming* it. *Conflict analysis* does not require patients to be motivated on a rack of their superego by imposition of a "fundamental rule" of "free association." Offering a *fundamental task* for the patient may be a useful alternative, since we seek active use of the patient's ego, not its traditional circumvention. We should have confidence that the thrust of the drive derivatives (our allies) will persist without our having to reach for them—if we will only *analyze the resistance.*

In dynamic psychotherapy it is not uncommon to orient the patient to the work ahead, to suggest: "The more you can tell me about yourself, the more I can be of help to you." In contrast, it is more to the point of a basic analytic situation, and as soon and as explicitly as possible, to indicate the following: that the patient's symptoms or character traits are ways of keeping certain long-buried thoughts, feelings, or impulses from coming to mind so that they may be able to deal with them in terms of *current* realities, rather than having to hide from them as was necessary in earlier times. In order for analyst and patient to come to learn how the mind isolates one from a part of oneself, and for what reasons—the details vary with each individual—the patient has to *work at a particular task; namely, trying to put into words whatever spontaneously comes to mind.* When this is *attempted,* the analyst has an opportunity to observe *how* the patient's mind becomes conflicted over, and opposes *speaking of,* certain kinds of thoughts or feelings. These observations can be *shared* with the patient and the two can gradually learn how and for what reason the patient's involuntary mental activities oppose this "opening up" of the mind. As such knowledge accumulates, automatic "solutions" for conflict (symptoms or character problems) over troubling ideas, feelings, or impulses no longer are necessary, and other *voluntary* choices become possible and may be preferable.

This greater degree of sharing in the orientation regarding the treatment considers the need for a greater degree of involvement of the patient's ego. This must take place in order to achieve the slowly evolving goal of bringing the unconscious ego, with its major role in processing of resistance (defense in the analytic situation) into a useful consciousness. Sharing with the patient a schematic view of how to go about the work has, from the beginnings of psychoanalysis, always been part of the initiation. This sharing was briefer, in the beginning, only because knowledge of the work itself was less complex than our current views. Sometimes explanation may also have been deliberately vague out of a recognition that the role of suggestion, then necessarily heavier than is now needed for *analyzing* resistance, was thereby facilitated.

For the patient to gain insight into the methodology of the analysis is not to be confused with *intellectualization*; that is a specific form of defense which misuses the *intellect*. We do not avoid it by avoiding the patient's intellect. As Freud (1900) indicated, ways of observing one's mind may be entirely unfamiliar and difficult even before resistance adds to the picture; they deserve careful description from the analyst to the patient. It is possible to experience what appears in the mind from the point of view of the *past*, the *future*, or as representations on the *immediate stage of consciousness*. These are all distinct ego experiences, and understanding them is important to the task, if consistent defense/resistance analysis is to occur. Early identification of, and continued attention to, these ego functions through their conceptualization by the analyst, shared with the patient, is essential.

10

THE EGO'S PREDICTABLE RESPONSE TO THE UNFAMILIAR ANALYTIC SITUATION

Recognizing the ego's special burden in analytic situations—in contrast to most psychotherapeutic situations and "life" generally—helps us to understand better the orientation of conflict-and-defense analysis that works by using the data of direct observation.

As we know, beginning at age 5 or so our egos depend on superego devices to adapt to, or defend us against, too-strong instinctual drive derivatives, thus keeping us more "civilized." We call such phenomena our "conscience," and most of the affects that it mobilizes to help regulate us are versions of guilt or signals of anxiety. Although some conflicted appetites, wishes, remain too forbidden to approach consciousness, in general, living provides relatively conflict-free moments of private awareness of "forbidden" thoughts, daydreams, and culturally tolerated prejudices. Possible exceptions may be individuals who function within very tightly constructed adaptations that maintain virtually inflexible control over even private contemplations; some in certain cloistered religious orders may qualify here, but ordinarily they, wisely, do not encounter analytic situations.

In an analytic situation, there is a constant threat that the *inner* measures will not provide a sufficient sense of "safety." This is because analysands are deliberately placed into circumstances that promote—through intrapsychic stimulations and external conditions enhancing a form of permissiveness—a continual atmosphere of potential risk; the risk that they may experience and reveal to another individual conflicted ("uncivilized") wishes or impulses. This unusual, unremitting condition exists owing to the accepted *task* (not "rule") that they *verbalize* for the analyst's attention everything coming into consciousness.

Faced with this unfamiliar ominous situation, the analysands' egos regressively reactivate, via reexternalizing transferences, the illusory "presences" of authorities much as they experienced them before they internalized the perceptions of them. Characteristically these are images either of intimidating, restraining figures, or images of figures who were affectionately permissive (conditionally so). Incidentally, such regressions revive, also primarily for purposes of defense (safety), important aspects of the oedipal constellation. In traditional methodology, such phenomena—that is, transferences of authority—have, for the most part, been "left in place" and *used* as residuals of hypnosis for purposes of authoritatively influencing analysands to "overcome" resistances, and to follow a "rule" to reveal all the thoughts. In more recent times, whenever there is emphasis on consistent *analysis* of conflict and defense, with attention primarily to directly observable data within the verbalizations, the method is modified to take into increasing consideration Freud's eventual concepts regarding the ego's more sophisticated role in the neuroses. Here, attention is directed in particular to analyzing those defenses mobilized against conflicted elements that have briefly *gained consciousness*. These defensively intended ego activities are often just out of the analysand's focus of attention, but since they are in consciousness, they are potentially demonstrable to the analysand—analyzing them is essential to the work. Equally essential, and pertinent to the ego's handling of this unique task, is the analyst's attention to bringing into awareness the transferences of defense manifested by the rapidly mobilized "presences" of the reexternalized authorities. The analysand's ego is, thereby, permitted incrementally to gain sufficient insight and strength to continue to take on additional degrees of conflicted derivatives *without* immediately having to stimulate new defense (resistance).

11

REFLECTIONS ON SUPERVISION

Dr. Rowntree has asked for personal observations or reflections about supervision from those who were for some years on the earlier COPE (Committee on Psychoanalytic Education) Study Group on Supervision. Although I would consider us all within the "mainstream," we had a fairly wide spread in our group on certain issues. I was on that end of the spectrum which regarded supervision primarily as a *teaching opportunity*. I differed from the often traditional position of "helping the supervisee develop his own style." With my supervisees I assume, and I make it explicit, that they will have many years after graduation to develop their own "style." Meanwhile I opt for their trying to learn broadly Freudian methods from several supervisors so that, having gained from each of them, they can eventually choose what methods they like. I consider it my supervisory obligation to be the best supervising teacher of my own views than I can be. Obviously this is always based on being sensitive to the individual learning capacities of the supervisees.

Once an analytic supervision is about to begin, the supervisor can spell out in advance certain assumptions about the work. My approach to supervision includes preliminary time making sure that my supervisee has a reasonable grasp of "where I am coming from." This was true in our COPE group, too, where I was encouraged to spend as much time as I felt necessary accounting for applications of theory in my own analytic work, before getting to illustrations from a particular supervision. Hence, any brief communication of mine on the practice of supervision may risk sounding more like lectures on theory and technique (and theory of technique) than informal observations about "supervision."

Our manner of requiring a series of supervisions from different supervisors typically places an inordinate task of learning on the candidate. But I know of no better alternative. To be subject, in an overlapping way, to a variety of supervisors' predilections, to contain a growing body of knowledge, and yet maintain an ability for independent openness to personal appraisal, is having to experience the tasks of an "impossible profession" at an early time. But that is precisely what supervisees need to learn. The supervisor must make certain that the candidate clearly grasps the supervisor's conceptual approach and its applications and yet does not endorse it alone over other approaches. Discussions between the two of details about the supervisory method itself are useful. For example, both the supervisee and I know that, short of taping the analytic hours and listening to the transcription (I have not yet had such an opportunity in actual supervision), process notes differ in varying degrees from what actually transpired. Nevertheless, for our purposes, we essentially regard the sequence of the material *as if* that were the way it happened. This is useful for facilitating a consistent manner of listening to material; the emphasis is on attention to the immediacy of the material—the content *as it is verbally revealed in the context of the analytic situation.*

I try to understand what the supervisee had in mind in making or not making particular interventions, and to conceptualize and support in theory ways we might be viewing it alike or differently. Awareness of the possibility of transference influence on learning in such a setting encourages discussing many aspects of the work, as rapport between supervisee and supervisor permits, sharing uncertainties militates against idealization. Keeping alive a spirit of inquiry and gratification in the work is important. An example of this is alertness on the part of the supervisor to interesting examples of patients' responses to the work that supervisees can earmark, so that some time in their own teaching (most are involved, or will be soon, in some teaching experiences) they can take pleasure in using them. I would expect all supervisees to develop, from the beginning, professional skill in managing process notes *and their reporting to the supervisor* so as to fully preserve the patients' anonymity.

When an institute's arrangements allow it, I believe there is advantage in the supervisor working with beginning candidates *before* they have started a first analytic case. A psychotherapy case provides an excellent opportunity for teaching toward a capacity to listen and respond to a patient *not* in an analytic situation in ways that can offer more therapeutic advantage than the widespread habit of analysts-to-be, or "analytically oriented" non-analysts, of attempting a sort of watered-down version of their understanding of analysis. Such therapy typically takes place in a setting that offers no opportunity for analytic progress and in which a number of psychological advantages are being neglected merely because they are seen as avoided in analysis. This usually causes the therapist to work more frequently, longer, and in a sense, harder than necessary. Since candidates-in-training meanwhile acquire increasing knowledge of analytic theory, they are often gratified to learn and observe that the reality of transference in the psychotherapeutic setting, while providing little practical opportunity for "interpretation," provides the therapist with remarkable power for skilled therapeutic influence. Growing familiarity with valuable uses of analytic theory in non-analytic situations is an excellent experience in anticipation of applying that same knowledge of theory quite differently in psychoanalysis. Once analytic supervision begins, the supervisor can continue to remind the candidate of such contrasts.

Time and space do not allow for elaboration of methodological emphases characteristic for me. In any pre-analytic supervisory sessions I would explain these theoretical biases. I shall mention one predilection in terms of *focus*. I am especially interested in diminishing our lag in applying the profound technical changes made possible by Freud's newer concepts of the ego in conflict and the corrected role for anxiety. I give priority to observations of and demonstrations of the ego's defensive management of conflict *over the verbal exposures* of drive derivatives that the analytic situation necessarily sets in motion. Furthering the supervisee's capacity for observation of these many repetitive phenomena requires ongoing, close attention to the *manifestations in consciousness* of the ego's defensive responses to having revealed "too much" while attempting to be candid and spontaneous. In psychotherapy such demonstrable evidence of a patient's "defensiveness" over certain revelations may lead to helpful insight. Positive transference can provide much support for modifying such "unreasonable demands" by a harsh superego. But the most significant lessening of the "lag" can, in an *analytic situation*, come about by teaching the supervisee from the beginning to develop the skills to gradually demonstrate and analyze the reexternalized (defense) transference of the influential authorities—a ubiquitous manifestation and aspect of the "dissolution" (Sandler 1960) of the ego's superego in the analytic situation.

In this way, the supervisee can usually observe that the analysis of the transference of authority has allowed the patient to manage the defenses on the basis of insight rather than through the influence of suggestion. How this contrasts with other therapeutic settings, where an *unanalyzed* defense transference of authority may provide valuable therapeutic action, through its capacity for *influence*, can be usefully discussed with supervisees.

12

ELEMENTS OF SUPERVISION

A WORKING THEORETICAL CONTEXT

The analysis of the ego's *consciously* accessible neurotic solutions (i.e., defensive patterns/operations originating in childhood) to intrapsychic conflict *during the psychoanalytic situation* is sufficient to bring about Freud's most developed aim for analysis, that is "to secure the best possible psychological conditions for the functions of the ego." (Freud 1937a, p. 250).

A BRIEF HISTORICAL BACKGROUND FOR THIS CONTEXT

Not only did the prestructural period of analytic methodology *bypass* neurotically compromised aspects of the ego, but some measures for *overcoming the resistances* rather than *analyzing* the defensive activity of the ego persisted even after the development of the structural theory. With the newer understanding of the role of anxiety in the formation of neurosis, defense analysis should and could have progressed without any longer bypassing the ego aspects in analytic technique; it usually did not. Instead, there is commonly a neglect of important, defensively used ego activities ordinarily attributed to the "superego." The major hurdle in bringing about this natural progress in methodology is the task of bringing the patient's (and the analyst's) *consciousness* into a full participation in an analytic situation, as well as bringing about a recognition that the particular aspect of the ego, consciousness, is itself an object of observation in the analytic process.

For reasons of considerable eventual interest, it is a relatively recent development for analysts to become aware and make analytic use of the extent to which the ego *regularly* experiences intrusions of drive derivatives into *consciousness*, where they frequently stimulate the ego to respond defensively to growing conflict *over their verbal exposure with the analyst.* These phenomena take place before the listening analyst, who can observe and demonstrate them to the analysand. To analyze these intrusions amounts to an analysis of the ego in the analytic situation. Application of consistent, close attention to defensive activity against specific, demonstrable derivatives that have transiently reached consciousness *makes "interpretations" about still unconscious derivatives, wishes, impulses, and fantasies redundant, as well as often counterproductive to thorough defense analysis.* In Fenichel, we can find early anticipation of this shift away from the technique of Freud's traditional interpretations of the Repressed Unconscious (the "two records" [Freud 1940, p. 160], or the "bi-phasic process" [Stone 1973, p. 47]) to the technique of confining interpretive interventions to the *accessible consciousness.* Fenichel (1941, p. 18) observed that an interpretation should be only of a derivative "which can be recognized as such by the patient merely by *turning his attention to it*" (italics added). The trend I emphasize for a "focus of *attention*" (A. Freud 1936, p. 20) continues to move explicitly away from that used in traditional interpretations, including those directed at the ostensible unconscious drive-gratifying aspects of "compromise formations." Freud developed the conceptual framework for this post-traditional, structural methodology and Anna Freud (1936) made its application to technique accessible.

SUPERVISORY HOUR GUIDELINES

1. There should be a previous understanding that all notes and reported material must maintain the patient's privacy by omitting or disguising anything that might reveal identity, *including to the supervisor.* This provides opportunity for supervisees to develop their "creative" skills regarding all notes and reports.

2. Through reporting their notes, supervisees revisit the process and have a second, more leisurely opportunity to hone their close-process attention skills. Here they may experience how much of ego activity they can perceive through *direct observation*, and without resorting to the use of intuition or empathy as a source of information on drive-derivative, conflict, and defense management. They can also leisurely reevaluate their use of sensitivity (empathy or intuition) in sensing, and communicating accordingly, the patient's capacity to be receptive to the analyst's comments.

3. What the supervisee observes, considers, and reports should ideally pertain to what the patient reveals *during the the analytic hours.* Exceptions will largely concern extraclinical behavior with which the supervisee may need to deal in non-analytic ways in order to preserve the analytic situation from being lastingly interrupted.

4. It is helpful for the supervisee to comment briefly on any evidence of freer drive derivatives noted since the previous supervisory hour.

5. Part of such a summation might include newly revealed history, past or current, without indicating *at this point* what defensive functions each memory served as it came into the flow of the process.

6. A reminder may be needed that the above memories are *not sought as ends in themselves*. They serve primarily as a kind of measure of analytic progress through lowering a need for defense. They are also data for eventual reconstructions of the genetic origins of neurotically retained defensive phenomena.

7. A review of a current sampling of close-process notes should include, as the supervisee's pace and knowledge come to permit comfortably, the following areas:

> (a) If possible, include examples, in passing, of *demonstrating* to the patient the conscious, but probably unnoticed—*not repressed*—moments of conflict encountered, of a *brief disequilibrium,* and then the ego's reaction in order to rapidly reestablish a more stable equilibrium. Note whether the selection was well judged in terms of the patient's tolerance for self-observation, and whether the analyst's comments facilitated the patient's relatively syntonic—that is, bearable—understanding. Further, note whether the *patient takes on the experience* and sustains, without rapid or instant defense, some degree of *now conscious disequilibrium* (discomfort over conflict). Meanwhile, during the reconfronting of the stream of material (via the reported process notes), the supervisor and supervisee can note evidence of conflict and defense solutions that did not, when noticed, warrant demonstration. In time, note whether at any point the patient shows evidence of capacity to observe the defensive activity against conflicted material in a self-analytic way; note whether the patient uses self-observation for purposes of defensive self-criticism or for progress.
>
> (b) Note the degree to which the patient shows progress or readiness to turn back and to recognize the main point, namely, that the interest is in what in the hour motivated the need for defense against the spontaneous verbalizations, that is, how much or whether he or she can allow awareness of the transferences of authority. If the patient chooses the route of compliance in a "confessional"

mode and ignores the search for defense motivation, note whether an intervention by the analyst was in order to call attention, in a syntonic way, to that avoidance.

(c) If the patient can tolerate the awareness of the transference of defense (transference of authority), note whether the supervisee eventually communicated concepts that leave the patient with some insight into how that transference phenomenon includes a form of turning on the self. Such insight can eventually lead to the patient's understanding that the original, genetic perceptions of the parent versions of inhibiting authority must have been distorted *by projection* in order to defend against inner conflict over the patient's own aggression.

13

A CONVERSATION WITH PAUL GRAY

Marianne Goldberger interviewed Paul Gray before he gave his plenary address, "Memory as Resistance and the Telling of a Dream," at the 79th annual meeting in New York of the American Psychoanalytic Association.

MG: Would you tell me something about how your ideas about analytic technique evolved?

PG: At some point in my analytic training I became aware of what seemed to me a puzzling discrepancy: In teaching, analysts emphasized the importance of following the events in the patient's mind; but in clinical conferences, continuing case presentations, and supervision, they frequently showed interest in the patient's behavior outside the analytic situation, an interest I had come to associate with psychotherapy. My attempts to resolve this discrepancy were greatly facilitated when I found support for my own views in the contributions of Anna Freud and Fenichel. Continuing their efforts, I've tried to develop a technique of defense analysis that would attain the most effective access to drive derivatives and in that way facilitate analytic progress. I believe that focusing attention consistently on what happens "inside" the analytic hour helps patients become aware of the many unconscious activities they use to resolve conflict *at the time they're using them*. This focus provides patients with a vivid demonstration of their defenses in action. Opportunities for analyzing defenses in this way arise in many forms, including the defensive use of memories.

I have found support also in the writings of Ernst Kris and Richard Sterba, as well as in the confident words of Rangell and Brenner. In more recent years, several papers were, of course, important—among them Lawrence Friedman's seminal paper on the tasks of a theory of the mind.

Although theory informs practice, it is also true that theory arises out of clinical observation. For me, this has been increasingly true over the past 15 years. I do a fair amount of supervision, and that enriches my interest in technique and how to teach the gathering of data from what the analyst *observes*, rather than from what he *feels*. I believe that in psychotherapy (which I also teach and which I find very interesting) there is plenty of room for resonating sources of knowledge between the patient and the therapist. But in analysis, if you want to take the patient's ego along for the whole journey, it's better to use data that both patient and analyst can corroborate.

MG: Does your emphasis on observing the "immediate present in the analytic hour" mean that you think only transference is important?

PG: No. Although one can more easily observe and demonstrate transference in that context, the crucial issue is that in analysis the intrapsychic necessity for resistance is continual. So the best opportunity for effective insights is in observing and demonstrating the phenomena of conflicts and their defensive solutions by the ego *as they occur* in the material of the analytic process. Calling attention to these phenomena at the very moment they arise in the analytic hour provides the most convincing illustration of them for the patient (and for the analyst, too). Gaining access to the live "theater" of consciousness is advantageous for productive analytic work, especially for helping the patient to become capable of self-analysis. It's probably true that I give priority to transference of defense, as compared with transference of the id. The reason is that so-called id transferences will more easily reach their conscious manifestations if the transferences of defense are well analyzed first, and that's why I set my priorities as I do.

MG: Does your approach eliminate suggestion?

PG: Hardly. I've explicitly indicated that suggestion can never be eliminated. The spectrum of possible degrees of suggestion is, however, considerable—from hypnosis at one extreme all the way to skilled efforts to engage the patient's rational attention and observation at the other—and I favor staying as close as possible to the latter end of the spectrum. The systematic analysis of the transferences of authority, as manifested in the reexternalizations of the ego's superego function, will make analysands less susceptible to the power of suggestion and allow them to perceive external and internal reality more accurately. In fact, analyzing the transferences of authority will reduce the patient's susceptibility not only to suggestion, but also to other irrational influences. That's why I feel it's so important to develop technical approaches that diminish the use of suggestion. Of course, you would not agree if you believed that it's all right to bypass the rational ego, which is what suggestion does, or that it's even advantageous to do so (as is often true in psychotherapy). After all, even hypnotherapy has its serious adherents, and practitioners in that area are much more sophisticated today than in Freud's time.

MG: Some people object to your preference for analyzing the superego as a defensive measure of the ego, since patients often defend against the manifestation of superego activity. How do you respond to that?

PG: I don't see any problem there. The ego can regularly defend against any painful affect—that's the nature of the "unpleasure principle"—even when the ego itself has initiated the pain out of some previous defensive or resistance need.

MG: But you're not addressing the issue of unconscious guilt.

PG: First of all, I think it's practical to regard the affect of guilt as something the ego does to reinforce restraint of conflicted drive derivatives. I'm referring here to conscious affect: the idea of unconscious affect is not very convincing to me. The concept of an "unconscious need for punishment" may be useful to account for the behavior of everyday life, but in the analytic process "punishing" affects are evidence of the ego's efforts to reinforce the resistance against the emergence of drive derivatives.

I think the same is very likely true for all painful affects in the analytic process. If the patient is feeling guilty about something during the analytic hour, the primary purpose of that painful affect is not to punish for an act in the past, but to provide immediate reinforcement against any repetition. Such reinforcement frequently includes measures of "turning against the self." The painful affect heads off any instinctual gratification that manifested itself previously and now in the analytic moment is threatening to emerge again.

To push this idea still further: In everyday life, the labels guilt, shame, embarrassment, and humiliation are all usefully applied to phenomena that assure more civil behavior, but in the analytic situation, civility is not a requirement of behavior. Likewise, the purpose of rational or "appropriate" communication in the analytic situation is not to enhance civility, but to enhance the effectiveness of the communication. I have no disagreement with thinking of all the ego's "moral" responses as compromise formations. My point is that the special requirements confronting a patient in the analytic situation tilt patient's ego function of balancing drive against defense clearly to the side of the defense. From the moment the analysand understands the goal of exposing "everything," resistance becomes the ego's highest priority and it stays there throughout the analysis.

MG: Is the claim that you tend to neglect dreaming an unfair one?

PG: Maybe all's fair in questioning someone else's—and one's own—ideas. I have no problem with our theory of dream formation: it involves compromise formation, just as symptom formation does. I emphasize paying attention to the patient's *telling* of a dream, to the dynamic implications within its content, and to where it occurs in the hour. My stress, in the analytic situation (though not necessarily in analytically oriented psychotherapy), is observation of the intrapsychic reality of the moment in the hour, as compared with external realities.

MG: Doesn't your technique limit what you perceive in the material?

PG: I hope it does. In every variation of listening to or perceiving analytic material, the analyst must choose some perspective on the material, usually on the basis of his conceptual orientation for analyzing the data. I'm aware that some practitioners claim to approach patients without any theory or technique—I have in mind some of the self psychology proponents, who say "just listen and learn."

I'm also aware that an early description of analytic listening used the term "free-floating attention," by which Freud meant to emphasize the possibility of contact between the patient's unconscious and the analyst's unconscious. Even though one can achieve such resonance with free-floating attention, some things are left out—the unconscious operations of the ego, for example. The idea of free-floating attention was formulated by Freud long before he grasped the structural concept of the ego and its implications for the role of anxiety. Making all the mind's unconscious structures conscious was a goal that could not be conceptualized at that time.

The particular perspective on analytic material that I write about is merely a more specific version of Anna Freud's recommendation that in order to include the analysis of the ego it is necessary to have "a change of focus." Such a change of focus certainly does not exclude uninterrupted attention to id derivatives in the material, an essential hallmark of analytic listening. But observing conflict in close process is a more demanding task than the essential one of merely noting drive derivatives. I see acute sensitivity to id derivatives as the prerequisite for noticing where in the flow of the material these derivatives encounter conflict and where the ego then deals with them in a variety of ways in order to relieve the edge of anxiety or other painful affect that signals an approaching danger.

My emphasis is on derivatives that have intruded slightly into the patient's conscious material. And I choose those derivatives solely because the ego's subsequent resistances to them can be demonstrated to the patient. In making this choice one can hardly avoid being aware of underlying levels of instinctual elements. The id is unquestionably fascinating (for both the patient and the analyst), but one must not become so intrigued with id manifestations that one cannot work with what is taking place nearer the surface. You could claim that that is "limiting what is perceived," but I prefer to characterize it as choosing to keep the microscope focused at a level of action that can more likely be shared with the patient's observing ego.

MG: Some analysts have said that when they apply your technique patients feel they are being nagged.

PG: I assume that those analysts are not referring to patients who regard *any* comment of the analysts as "nagging," but if that's not the explanation, then I would look into how the technique is being applied. For example, the patient may feel nagged if the analyst's observations about conflict and defense make the patient feel responsible for having "gone and done that again." Defense-oriented interpretations that start with "But you didn't say anything about . . ." often sound to the patient like nagging. In any case, such interventions are not helpful because they show the patient nothing about the when and the why of the defense.

The analyst must pay careful attention to the tone and wording of defense interpretations so as to engage the patient's curiosity, and this can be done only when the patient does not feel wounded. For example, any repetition of a familiar observation may be perceived by the patient as nagging unless it is offered with sensitivity and with appropriate variations in the precise wording. In fact, the analyst needs to develop an appropriate repertoire for applying the technique I've suggested—a repertoire free from judgmental words and tones. But if a patient feels criticized even when analytic observations have been expressed with these qualifications in mind, one need not conclude that something is lacking in the technique. A more likely explanation is that some important character trait of the patient is responsible. And, of course, the character trait itself becomes a subject for analysis.

MG: Some of those analysts also say that such close observation of the moment-to-moment events in the analytic hour lends itself to joint obsessional thinking.

PG: The purpose of focusing attention on the moment-to-moment events in the hour is to hold the analytic process close to what the patient is actually experiencing. If that leads to *increased* unconscious defense ("obsessional thinking"), then the method is being misused. *Any* analytic technique can lend itself to intellectualization if the analyst is so inclined. The whole point of focusing on the immediate moment is to help the patient know how, when, and why he uses defenses. In this way, the patient can eventually choose whether or not he still will use these (formerly unconscious) means to ward off affect-laden mental contents.

MG: In summary, would you say how your approach differs from that of so-called classical analysis?

PG: There are two different emphases in strategy. First, I pay particular attention to those drive elements that intrude into the conscious field and encounter conflict, with the result that the ego's defenses remove those elements from consciousness. These are psychic events demonstrable to the patient and subject to analysis. You can see how this approach differs from the "classical" one, in which deduced evidences of *not-yet*-conscious drive derivatives are the subject of interpretation.

The second difference in strategy concerns reconstructions of the initial circumstances in the patient's childhood that required the use of ego defenses. Whereas the emphasis of classical reconstructions is to pinpoint the existence of specific infantile instinctual interests, the aim of my reconstructions is primarily to identify *how* and *why* the ego brought defenses into play against those specific interests.

In addition, there are two tactical differences. First, this approach pays significantly closer attention to the moment-to-moment, sequential flow of associations than does the classical method. This tactic requires a form of attention more complex and demanding than "free-floating" attention alone. Second, I assume that right from the beginning of an analysis, the patient invests the transference with the reexternalization of the internalized images of authority. Because these images have a history of helping to reduce the dangers of conflicted instinctual derivatives, they reappear in the transference to facilitate resistance. I stress the importance of analyzing these transferred superego functions of the ego, whereas the classical method leaves them largely in place to empower the analyst to help the patient to *overcome* resistances.

I want to emphasize that I apply these techniques only with patients whose psychological potential permits a consistent and extensive focus on the analysis of resistance. For patients who are unable to allow increasing ego participation, even though given an extended opportunity to do so, I recommend reverting to a more traditional interpretive approach or using dynamically oriented psychotherapy.

References

Abend, S. (1981). Psychic conflict and the concept of defense. *Psychoanalytic Quarterly* 50:67–76.

_____ (1989). Countertransference and psychoanalytic technique. *Psychoanalytic Quarterly* 58:374–395.

Abrams, S. (1980). Therapeutic action and ways of knowing. *Journal of the American Psychoanalytic Association* 28:291–308.

Alexander, F., and French, T. M. (1946). *Psychoanalytic Therapy: Principles and Applications*. New York: Ronald Press.

Apfelbaum, B., and Gill, M. M. (1989). Ego analysis and the relativity of defense: technical implications of the structural theory. *Journal of the American Psychoanalytic Association* 37:1071–1096.

Arlow, J. A., and Brenner, C. (1964). *Psychoanalytic Concepts and the Structural Theory*. New York: International Universities Press.

_____ (1990). The psychoanalytic process. *Psychoanalytic Quarterly* 59:678–692.

Bibring, E. (1954). Psychoanalysis and the dynamic psychotherapies. *Journal of the American Psychoanalytic Association* 2:745–770.

Blatt, S. J., and Behrends, R. S. (1987). Internalization, separation-individuation, and the nature of therapeutic action. *International Journal of Psycho-Analysis* 68:279–298.

Boesky, D. (1983). Resistance and character theory: a reconsideration of the concept of character resistance. *Journal of the American Psychoanalytic Association* 31 (Suppl.): 227–246.

Brenner, C. (1959). The masochistic character: genesis and treatment. *Journal of the American Psychoanalytic Association* 7:197–226.

_____ (1966). The mechanism of repression. In *Psychoanalysis—A General Psychology*, ed. R. M. Loewenstein, L. Newman, M. Schur, and A. Solnit, pp. 390–399. New York: International Universities Press.

_____ (1969). Some comments on technical precepts in psychoanalysis. *Journal of the American Psychoanalytic Association* 17:333–352.

_____ (1976a). Analysis of dreams, symptoms, fantasies, and similar phenomena. In *Psychoanalytic Technique and Psychic Conflict*, pp. 133–166. New York: International Universities Press.

_____ (1976b). Defense analysis. In *Psychoanalytic Technique and Psychic Conflict*, pp. 59–78. New York: International Universities Press.

_____ (1976c). *Psychoanalytic Technique and Psychic Conflict*. New York: International Universities Press.

_____ (1979). Working alliance, therapeutic alliance, and transference. *Journal of the American Psychoanalytic Association* 27 (Suppl.): 137–157.

_____ (1982a). The concept of the superego: a reformulation. *Psychoanalytic Quarterly* 51:501–525.

_____ (1982b). *The Mind in Conflict*. New York: International Universities Press.

_____ (1982c). Defense. In *The Mind in Conflict*, pp. 72–92. New York: International Universities Press.

_____ (1984). Bibliography of Charles Brenner (1937–1982). *Psychoanalytic Quarterly* 53:5–12.

_____ (1987). Working through: 1914–1984. *Psychoanalytic Quarterly* 56:88–108.

Collins, S. (1980). Freud and "the riddle of suggestion." *International Review of Psycho-Analysis* 7:429–437.

Curtis, H. C. (1979). The concept of therapeutic alliance: implications for the "widening scope." *Journal of the American Psychoanalytic Association* 27 (Suppl.): 159–192.

Dahl, H., Kachele, H., and Thoma, H., eds. (1988). The specimen hour. In *Psychoanalytic Process Research Strategies*, pp. 15–28. New York: Springer Verlag.

Eissler, K. (1963). Unpublished minutes of the Scientific Faculty Meeting of the New York Psychoanalytic Institute, October 4.

Esman, A. H. (1972). Adolescence and the consolidation of values. In *Moral Values and the Superego Concept in Psychoanalysis*, ed. S. C. Post, p. 87–100. New York: International Universities Press.

Fenichel, O. (1937). Symposium on the theory of therapeutic results of psychoanalysis. In *The Collected Papers of Otto Fenichel*, Second Series. New York: Norton, 1954.

_____ (1938). Problems of psychoanalytic technique. *Psychoanalytic Quarterly* 7:421–442.

_____ (1941). *Problems of Psychoanalytic Technique*. New York: Psychoanalytic Quarterly.

Ferenczi, S. (1909). Introjection and transference. In *First Contributions to Psycho-Analysis*, pp. 35–93. New York: Brunner/Mazel, 1980.

_____ (1929). The principle of relaxation and catharsis. In *Final Contributions to the Problems and Methods of Psycho-Analysis*, pp. 108–125. New York: Brunner/Mazel, 1980.

_____ (1931). Child analysis in the analysis of adults. In *Final Contributions to the Problems and Methods of Psycho-Analysis*, pp. 126–142. New York: Brunner/Mazel, 1980.

Ferenczi, S., and Rank, O. (1924). *Entwicklungsziel der Psychoanalyse: Zur Wechselbeziehung von Theorie und Technik.* Leipzig: Internationaler Psychoanalytischer Verlag.

Fleming, J. (1971). Freud's concept of self-analysis: its relevance for psychoanalytic training. In *Currents in Psychoanalysis*, ed. I. M. Marcus, pp. 14–47. New York: International Universities Press.

Freud, A. (1936). *The Ego and the Mechanisms of Defense*. New York: International Universities Press.

_____ (1969). *Difficulties in the Path of Psychoanalysis. A Confrontation of Past with Present Viewpoints*. New York: International Universities Press.

_____ (1981). The application of analytic technique to the study of the psychic institutions. In *Discussions in the Hampstead Index on The Ego and the Mechanisms of Defence. Bulletin of the Hampstead Clinic* 4:5–30.

Freud, S. (1896). Further remarks on the neuropsychoses of defense. *Standard Edition* 3.

_____ (1899). Screen memories. *Standard Edition* 3.

_____ (1900). The interpretation of dreams. *Standard Edition* 4 and 5.

_____ (1909). Analysis of a phobia in a five-year-old boy. *Standard Edition* 10.

_____ (1910). Five lectures on psycho-analysis. *Standard Edition* 11.

_____ (1912a). The dynamics of transference. *Standard Edition* 12:98–108.

_____ (1912b). Recommendations on analytic technique. *Standard Edition* 12:111–120.

_____ (1913). On beginning the treatment (further recommendations on the technique of psycho-analysis I). *Standard Edition* 12.

_____ (1914). Remembering, repeating and working-through. (Further recommendations on the technique of psycho-analysis II). *Standard Edition* 12.

_____ (1915). The unconscious. *Standard Edition* 14.

_____ (1917a). Introductory lectures on psycho-analysis. *Standard Edition* 15 and 16.

_____ (1917b). General theory of the neuroses. *Standard Edition* 16.

_____ (1919). Lines of advance in psycho-analytic therapy. *Standard Edition* 17.

_____ (1920). Beyond the pleasure principle. *Standard Edition* 18.

_____ (1921). Group psychology and the analysis of the ego. *Standard Edition* 18.

_____ (1923). The ego and the id. *Standard Edition* 19.

_____ (1925). An autobiographical study. *Standard Edition* 20.

_____ (1926a). Inhibitions, symptoms and anxiety. *Standard Edition* 20.

_____ (1926b). The question of lay analysis. *Standard Edition* 20.

_____ (1926c). Psycho-analysis. *Standard Edition* 20.

_____ (1927). Humour. *Standard Edition* 21.

_____ (1930). Civilization and its discontents. *Standard Edition* 21.

_____ (1933a). The dissection of the psychical personality. *Standard Edition* 22.

_____ (1933b). New introductory lectures on psychoanalysis. *Standard Edition* 22.

_____ (1933c). Revision of the theory of dreams. *Standard Edition* 22.

_____ (1935). Postscript to an autobiographical study. *Standard Edition* 22.

_____ (1936). A disturbance of memory on the Acropolis. *Standard Edition* 22.

_____ (1937a). Analysis terminable and interminable. *Standard Edition* 23.

_____ (1937b). Constructions in analysis. *Standard Edition* 23.

_____ (1940). An outline of psycho-analysis. *Standard Edition* 23.

_____ (1987). Letter 75. In *The Origins of Psychoanalysis. Letters to Wilhelm Fliess, Drafts and Notes: 1887–1902*, pp. 229–235. New York: Basic Books, 1954.

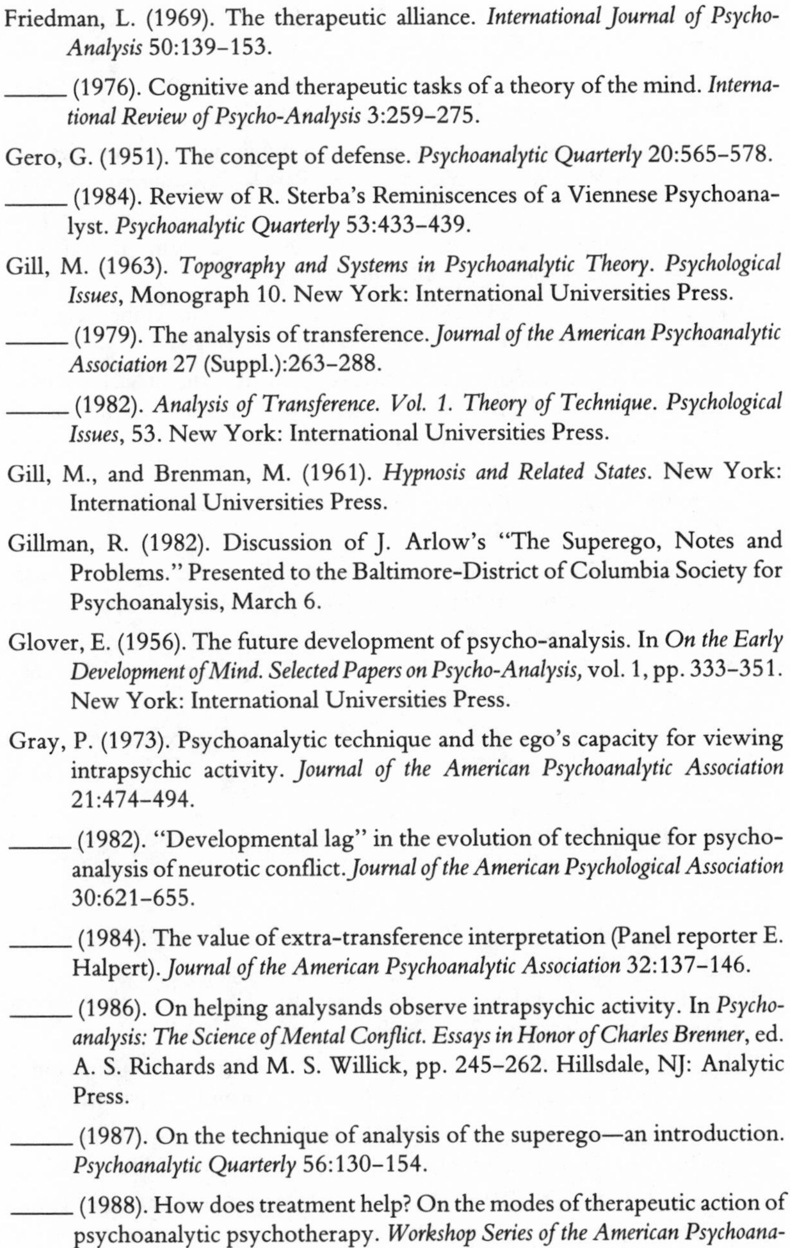

Friedman, L. (1969). The therapeutic alliance. *International Journal of Psycho-Analysis* 50:139–153.

_____ (1976). Cognitive and therapeutic tasks of a theory of the mind. *International Review of Psycho-Analysis* 3:259–275.

Gero, G. (1951). The concept of defense. *Psychoanalytic Quarterly* 20:565–578.

_____ (1984). Review of R. Sterba's Reminiscences of a Viennese Psychoanalyst. *Psychoanalytic Quarterly* 53:433–439.

Gill, M. (1963). *Topography and Systems in Psychoanalytic Theory. Psychological Issues*, Monograph 10. New York: International Universities Press.

_____ (1979). The analysis of transference. *Journal of the American Psychoanalytic Association* 27 (Suppl.):263–288.

_____ (1982). *Analysis of Transference. Vol. 1. Theory of Technique. Psychological Issues*, 53. New York: International Universities Press.

Gill, M., and Brenman, M. (1961). *Hypnosis and Related States*. New York: International Universities Press.

Gillman, R. (1982). Discussion of J. Arlow's "The Superego, Notes and Problems." Presented to the Baltimore-District of Columbia Society for Psychoanalysis, March 6.

Glover, E. (1956). The future development of psycho-analysis. In *On the Early Development of Mind. Selected Papers on Psycho-Analysis,* vol. 1, pp. 333–351. New York: International Universities Press.

Gray, P. (1973). Psychoanalytic technique and the ego's capacity for viewing intrapsychic activity. *Journal of the American Psychoanalytic Association* 21:474–494.

_____ (1982). "Developmental lag" in the evolution of technique for psychoanalysis of neurotic conflict. *Journal of the American Psychological Association* 30:621–655.

_____ (1984). The value of extra-transference interpretation (Panel reporter E. Halpert). *Journal of the American Psychoanalytic Association* 32:137–146.

_____ (1986). On helping analysands observe intrapsychic activity. In *Psychoanalysis: The Science of Mental Conflict. Essays in Honor of Charles Brenner*, ed. A. S. Richards and M. S. Willick, pp. 245–262. Hillsdale, NJ: Analytic Press.

_____ (1987). On the technique of analysis of the superego—an introduction. *Psychoanalytic Quarterly* 56:130–154.

_____ (1988). How does treatment help? On the modes of therapeutic action of psychoanalytic psychotherapy. *Workshop Series of the American Psychoana-*

lytic Association, monograph 4. Madison, CT: International Universities Press.

——— (1990). The nature of therapeutic action in psychoanalysis. *Journal of the American Psychoanalytic Association* 38:1083–1097.

——— (1991). On transferred permissive or approving superego fantasies: the analysis of the ego's superego activities. Part II. *Psychoanalytic Quarterly* 60:1–21.

——— (1992). Memory as resistance, and the telling of a dream. *Journal of the American Psychoanalytic Association* 40:307–326.

Greenacre, P. (1959). Certain technical problems in the transference relationship. *Journal of the American Psychoanalytic Association* 7:484–502.

——— (1966). Problems of overidealization of the analyst and of analysis: their manifestations in the transference and countertransference relationship. In *Emotional Growth*, vol. II, pp. 743–761. New York: International Universities Press.

Greenson, R. (1967). *The Technique and Practice of Psychoanalysis.* New York: International Universities Press.

Grubrich-Simitis, E. (1986). Six letters of Sigmund Freud and Sandor Ferenczi on the interrelationship of psychoanalytic theory and technique. *International Review of Psycho-Analysis* 13:259–277.

Grunberger, B. (1971). *Narcissism. Psychoanalytic Essays.* New York: International Universities Press, 1979.

Gutheil, T. G., and Havens, L. (1979). The therapeutic alliance: contemporary meanings and confusions. *International Review of Psycho-Analysis* 6:467–481.

Hartmann, H. (1951). Technical implications of ego psychology. In *Essays on Ego Psychology*, pp. 142–254. New York: International Universities Press, 1964.

——— (1960). *Psychoanalysis and Moral Values.* New York: International Universities Press.

Hatcher, R. L. (1973). Insight and self-observation. *Journal of the American Psychoanalytic Association* 21:377–398.

Isakower, O. (1957). Problems of supervision. Report to the Curriculum Committee of The New York Psychoanalytic Institute. Unpublished.

Jacobson, P. B., and Steele, R. S. (1979). From present to past: Freudian archeology. *International Review of Psycho-Analysis* 6:349–361.

Jones, E. (1957). *The Life and Work of Sigmund Freud. Vol. 3. The Last Phase, 1919–1939.* New York: Basic Books.

Joseph, E. D. (1979). Comments on the therapeutic action of psychoanalysis. *Journal of the American Psychoanalytic Association* 27 (Suppl.):71–80.

Kanzer, M. (1952). The transference neurosis of the Rat Man. *Psychoanalytic Quarterly* 21:181–189.

_____ (1972). Superego aspects of free association and the fundamental rule. *Journal of the American Psychoanalytic Association* 20:246–266.

Klein, M. (1946–1963). *Envy and Gratitude and Other Works, 1946–1963*. London: Hogarth, 1975.

Kohut, H. (1968a). The psychoanalytic treatment of narcissistic personality disorders. *Psychoanalytic Study of the Child* 23:86–113. New York: International Universities Press.

_____ (1968b). The evaluation of applicants for psychoanalytic training. *International Journal of Psycho-Analysis* 49:548–554.

_____ (1971). *The Analysis of the Self.* New York: International Universities Press.

_____ (1984). *How Does Analysis Cure?* Chicago: University of Chicago Press.

Kramer, M. (1959). On the continuation of the analytic process after psychoanalysis (a self-observation). *International Journal of Psycho-Analysis* 40:17–25.

Kris, E. (1938). Review of *The Ego and the Mechanisms of Defense* by Anna Freud. *International Journal of Psycho-Analysis* 19:136–146.

_____ (1956). The recovery of childhood memories in psychoanalysis. *Psychoanalytic Study of the Child* 11:54–88. New York: International Universities Press.

_____ (1975). Some vicissitudes of insight. In *Selected Papers of Ernst Kris*. New Haven: Yale University Press.

Kuhn, T. S. (1970). *The Structure of Scientific Revolutions.* Chicago: University of Chicago Press.

Lewin, B. D. (1955). Dream psychology and the analytic situation. *Psychoanalytic Quarterly* 24:169–199.

Lichtenstein, H. (1935). Some considerations regarding the phenomenology of the repetition compulsion and the death instinct. *The Annual of Psychoanalysis*, 1975, 2:63–84.

Loewald, H. (1960). On the therapeutic action of psychoanalysis. *International Journal of Psycho-Analysis* 41:16–33.

Loewenstein, R. (1982). Ego autonomy and psychoanalytic technique. In *Practice and Precept in Psychoanalytic Technique: Selected Papers of Rudolph Loewenstein*. New Haven: Yale University Press.

Lussier, A. (1988). The limitations of the object relations model. *Psychoanalytic Quarterly* 57:528–546.

Lustman, S. L. (1968). The economic point of view and defense. *Psychoanalytic Study of the Child* 23:189–203. New York: International Universities Press.

Meissner, W. W. (1973). Identification and learning. *Journal of the American Psychoanalytic Association* 21:788–816.

Modell, A. H. (1976). "The holding environment" and therapeutic action of psychoanalysis. *Journal of the American Psychoanalytic Association* 24: 285–308.

——— (1988). The centrality of the psychoanalytic setting and the changing aims of treatment. A perspective from a theory of object relations. *Psychoanalytic Quarterly* 57:577–596.

Namnum, A. (1972). Time in psychoanalytic technique. *Journal of the American Psychoanalytic Association* 20:736–750.

Novey, S. (1962). The principle of "working through" in psychoanalysis. *Journal of the American Psychoanalytic Association* 10:658–676.

Nunberg, H. (1937). Theory of the therapeutic results of psychoanalysis. In *Practice and Theory of Psychoanalysis*, vol. 1, pp. 165–173. New York: International Universities Press, 1948.

——— (1956). *Principles of Psychoanalysis. Their Application to the Neuroses*. New York: International Universities Press.

Orgel, S. (1974a). Sylvia Plath: fusion with the victim and suicide. *Psychoanalytic Quarterly* 43:262–287.

——— (1974b). Fusion with the victim and suicide. *International Journal of Psycho-Analysis* 55:531–538.

Ostow, M. (1958). The death instincts—a contribution to the study of instincts. *International Journal of Psycho-Analysis* 39:5–16.

Panel (1965). Limitations of psychoanalysis. P. Gray, reporter. *Journal of the American Psychoanalytic Association* 13:181–190.

——— (1967). Defense organization of the ego and psychoanalytic technique. E. Pumpian-Mindlin, reporter. *Journal of the American Psychoanalytic Association* 15:150–165.

——— (1979). Conceptualizing therapeutic action of psychoanalysis. M. Scharfman, reporter. *Journal of the American Psychoanalytic Association* 27:627–642.

Pfeffer, A. (1959). A preliminary report of a procedure for the evaluation of the results of analysis. *Journal of the American Psychoanalytic Association* 7:418–444.

_____ (1961). A follow-up study of a satisfactory analysis. *Journal of the American Psychoanalytic Association* 9:698—718.

Rangell, S. (1983). Defense and resistance in psychoanalysis and life. In *Defense and Resistance: Historical Perspectives and Current Concepts. Journal of the American Psychoanalytic Association* 31 (Suppl.):147–174.

Rapaport, D. (1951). *Organization and Pathology of Thought*. New York: Columbia University Press.

Reich, W. (1928). On character analysis. In *The Psychoanalytic Reader*, vol. 1, pp. 129–147. New York: International Universities Press.

Reik, T. (1948). *Listening with the Third Ear*. New York: Farrar, Straus.

Salk, J. (1973). *Survival of the Wisest*. New York: Harper & Row.

Sandler, J. (1983). Reflections on some relations between psychoanalytic concepts and psychoanalytic practice. *International Journal of Psycho-Analysis* 64:35–45.

Sandler, R. (1960). On the concept of the superego. *Psychoanalytic Study of the Child* 15:128–162. New York: International Universities Press.

Schafer, R. (1960). The loving and beloved superego in Freud's structural theory. *Psychoanalytic Study of the Child* 15:163–188. New York: International Universities Press.

_____ (1968). The mechanisms of defense. *International Journal of Psycho-Analysis* 49:49–62.

_____ (1973). The idea of resistance. In *A New Language for Psychoanalysis*, pp. 212–263. New Haven: Yale University Press.

Schimek, J. G. (1975). The interpretations of the past. *Journal of the American Psychoanalytic Association* 23:845–865.

Schlesinger, H. J. (1985). Some "ingredients" of effective interpretation. Presented to the meeting of the American Psychoanalytic Association, December.

_____ (1988). Historical overview of the mode of therapeutic action of psychoanalytic psychotherapy. In *How Does Treatment Help? On the Modes of Therapeutic Action of Psychoanalytic Psychotherapy*, ed. A. Rothstein, pp. 7–27. Madison, CT: International Universities Press.

Schur, M. (1966). *The Id and the Regulatory Principles of Mental Functioning*. New York: International Universities Press.

_____ (1972). *Freud: Living and Dying*. New York: International Universities Press.

Schwartz, L., Reporter (1971). Superego analysis. Report of Charles Brenner's section of the Ernst Kris Study Group. Meeting of the New York

Psychoanalytic Society, September 30, 1969. *Psychoanalytic Quarterly* 40:189–190.

Scott, W. C. A. (1976). M. Nina Searl's *The Psychology of Screaming. Journal of the Philadelphia Association of Psychoanalysis* 17:117–119.

Searl, M. N. (1936). Some queries on principles of technique. *International Journal of Psycho-Analysis* 17:471–493.

Shapiro, T. (1981). Empathy: a critical reevaluation. *Psychoanalytic Inquiry* 1:423–448.

Spence, D. (1983). Narrative persuasion. *Psychoanalysis and Contemporary Thought* 6:457–481.

Spiegel, L. A. (1978). Moral masochism. *Psychoanalytic Quarterly* 47:209–336.

Spruiell, V. (1988). The indivisibility of Freudian object relations and drive theories. *Psychoanalytic Quarterly* 57:597–625.

Stein, M. H. (1966). Self observation, reality, and the superego. In *Psychoanalysis—A General Psychology*, ed. R. M. Loewenstein, L. Newman, M. Schur, and A. Solnit, pp. 275–297. New York: International Universities Press.

——— (1981). The unobjectionable part of the transference. *Journal of the American Psychoanalytic Association* 29:869–892.

Sterba, R. (1934). The fate of the ego in analytic theory. *International Journal of Psycho-Analysis* 15:117–126.

——— (1940). The dynamics of the dissolution of the transference resistance. *Psychoanalytic Quarterly* 9:363–379.

——— (1941). The abuse of interpretation. *Psychiatry* 4:9–12.

——— (1953). Clinical and therapeutic aspects of character resistance. *Psychoanalytic Quarterly* 22:1–20.

——— (1978). Discussions of Sigmund Freud. *Psychoanalytic Quarterly* 47:173–191.

——— (1982). *Reminiscences of a Viennese Psychoanalyst.* Detroit: Wayne State University Press.

Sternbach, O. (1975). Aggression, the death drive and the problem of sadomasochism. A reinterpretation of Freud's second drive theory. *International Journal of Psycho-Analysis* 56:321–333.

Stone, L. (1973). On resistance to the psychoanalytic process. *Psychoanalysis and Contemporary Science* 2:42–73.

Strachey, J. (1934). The nature of the therapeutic action of psychoanalysis. *International Journal of Psycho-Analysis* 50:275–292.

——— (1961). Editor's introduction. Civilization and its discontents. *Standard Edition* 21.

_____ (1964). Editor's note. Analysis terminable and interminable. *Standard Edition* 23.

Ticho, G. (1967). On self-analysis. *International Journal of Psycho-Analysis* 48:308–318.

Waelder, R. (1936). The problem of freedom in psycho-analysis and the problem of reality-testing. *International Journal of Psycho-Analysis* 17: 89–108.

_____ (1937). The problem of the genesis of psychical conflict in earliest infancy. Remarks on a paper by Joan Rivière. *International Journal of Psycho-Analysis* 18:406–473.

_____ (1956). Introduction to the discussion on problems of transference. *International Journal of Psycho-Analysis* 37:367–368.

_____ (1967). Inhibitions, symptoms and anxiety: forty years later. In *Psychoanalysis: Observation, Theory, Application*, ed. S. A. Guttman, pp. 338–360. New York: International Universities Press.

Wallerstein, R. (1983). Defenses, defense mechanisms, and the structure of the mind. In *Defense and Resistance: Historical Perspectives and Current Concepts. Journal of the American Psychoanalytic Association* 31 (Suppl.):201–225.

Weiss, J., and Sampson, H. (1986). *The Psychoanalytic Process. Theory, Clinical Observations and Empirical Research*. New York: Guilford.

Winnicott, D. W. (1965). *The Maturational Process and the Facilitating Environment. Studies in the Theory of Emotional Development*. New York: International Universities Press.

Credits

The author gratefully acknowledges permission to reproduce material from the following sources:

From the *Journal of the American Psychoanalytic Association*:

"The Capacity for Viewing Intrapsychic Activity," originally entitled "Psychoanalytic Technique and the Ego's Capacity for Viewing Intrapsychic Activity," 1973, 21 (3):474–494. Copyright © 1973 by International Universities Press and reprinted by permission.

" 'Developmental Lag' in the Evolution of Technique," originally entitled "Developmental Lag in the Evolution of Technique for Psychoanalysis of Neurotic Conflict," 1982, 30:621–655. Copyright © 1982 by International Universities Press and reprinted by permission.

"The Nature of Therapeutic Action in Psychoanalysis," 1990, 38:1083–1097. Copyright © 1990 by International Universities Press and reprinted by permission.

"Memory as Resistance, and the Telling of a Dream," 1992,

40:307–326. Copyright © 1992 by International Universities Press and reprinted by permission.

From the *Journal of Clinical Psychoanalysis*:

"A Guide to Analysis of the Ego in Conflict," originally entitled "A Brief Didactic Guide to Analysis of the Ego in Conflict," and "On Constructive Orientation of Potential Analysands," 1993, 2(3):325–334. Copyright © 1993 by International Universities Press and reprinted by permission.

From *Psychoanalysis: The Science of Mental Conflict—Essays in Honor of Charles Brenner*, edited by A. D. Richards and M. S. Willick:

"On Helping Analysands Observe Intrapsychic Activity," by Paul Gray, pp. 245–261. Copyright © 1986 by Analytic Press and reprinted by permission.

From the *Psychoanalytic Quarterly*:

"The Analysis of the Ego's Inhibiting Superego Activities," originally entitled "On the Technique of Analysis of the Superego—An Introduction," 1987, 56:130–154. Copyright © 1987 by the *Psychoanalytic Quarterly* and reprinted by permission.

"The Analysis of the Ego's Permissive Superego," originally entitled "On Transferred Permissive or Approving Superego Functions: The Analysis of the Ego's Superego Activities, Part II," 1991, 60:1–21. Copyright © 1991 by the *Psychoanalytic Quarterly* and reprinted by permission.

From the *Newsletter of the Baltimore-Washington Institute for Psychoanalysis*:

"Brief Psychotherapy, Dynamic Psychotherapy and Psychoanalysis," originally published as "Notes on Therapeutic Situations: A Brief Communication,: 1992. Copyright © 1992 by the Baltimore-Washington Society for Psychoanalysis and reprinted by permission.

From *NewsfromCOPE*:

"Reflections on Supervision," 1993, 9(1):8. Copyright © 1993 by COPE and reprinted with permission.

From the *American Psychoanalyst*:

"A Conversation with Paul Gray," (interviewed by Marianne Goldberger), 1991, 24(4):10–11, 18. Copyright © 1991 by the American Psychoanalytic Association and reprinted with permission.

From *The Standard Edition of the Complete Psychological Works of Sigmund Freud,* translated and edited by James Strachey:

Reprinted with permission of Sigmund Freud Copyrights, The Institute of Psycho-Analysis, and The Hogarth Press.

From *Inhibitions, Symptoms and Anxiety* by Sigmund Freud, translated by Alix Strachey:

Reprinted with permission of W. W. Norton & Company, Inc. Copyright © 1959 by the Institute of Psycho-Analysis and Angela Richards.

Index

Abend, S., 72n1, 169
Abrams, S., 89
Acting out, listening (of therapist) and, 5–6
Aggression
  displacement of, 15–16
  ego's inhibiting superego activity, 110–111
  listening (of therapist) and, 8, 13–14
  resistance and, 14–15
Alexander, F., 141
Alliance, affectionate approval as resistance, transferential fantasy of, 134–135
Analysis. *See also* Brief psychotherapy; Psychoanalysis; Psychotherapy
  psychotherapy and, xxi–xxii
  reality and, 10
  suggestion and, xxii
Analytic couch, listening (of therapist) and, 17–18
Analytic perception. *See* Listening (of therapist)
Analytic setting, transference and, 16
Analytic style, listening (of therapist) and, 29–30
Anger. *See* Aggression
Anxiety
  affectionate approval as resistance, transferential fantasy of, 133–134, 136–137
  conflict and, xii
  defensive transference of authority, xiv
  ego and, ix, x
  ego's inhibiting superego activity, 105
  therapeutic action and, 97, 100
Apfelbaum, B., 181
Arlow, J. A., 48, 185
Attention (of therapist). *See* Listening (of therapist)

Authority
analytic stance, developmental lag and, 50–54
ego conflict analysis supervision, 182–184
ego's permissive superego activity
affectionate approval as resistance, transferential fantasy of, 133–134
affectionately permissive authority, transference of, 138–144
transference and, xiii–xiv, xix, xxi–xxii, 124

Balint, M., 140, 142
Behavior control, listening (of therapist) and, 17
Behrends, R. S., 89
Bernheim, H., 38n5
Bibring, E., 34
Biphasic approach, xix
Blatt, S. J., 89
Boesky, D., 119
Bonaparte, M., 111
Brenman, M., 38n5
Brenner, C., 13, 18, 40, 72n1, 112n1, 113n2, 114n4, 118, 119, 124, 125, 134, 160, 185, 224
Brief psychotherapy
guidelines for, 196
suggestion and, xv

Carlson, A. J., 195
Character resistance concept, 119
Cognitive insight, drives and ego, xx
Collins, S., 119–120
Committee on Psychoanalytic Education (COPE), 209–212
Communication, free association and free communication contrasted, 69
Competition, listening (of therapist) and, 9
Conflict
anxiety and, xii
ego and, xii–xiii, xv, xx
Conflict-defense patterns, ego and, xxi
Conscious guilt, 119
Consciousness
ego and, 155
evolution and, 60–61
id and, xix
resistance and, xi, xiii, 32
Counterresistance
defense analysis and, xviii
developmental lag and, x
listening (of therapist) and, 8
to transference, developmental lag and, 58–59
Countertransference, 6
listening (of therapist) and, 8
outside/inside realities and, 22
Curtis, H. C., 134, 182, 188

Dahl, H., 179
Death instinct
ego's inhibiting superego activity, 108–109, 110, 111–112, 113
resistance, xix
Defenses
aggression and, 14
awareness of, xi
counterresistance and, xviii
drive theory and, xi–xii, xiii
ego analysis and, 42–43, 45–46
ego and, xiii, 39
ego conflict analysis supervision, 177–179
ego-conflict-defense patterns and, xxi
ego's inhibiting superego activity, 114
listening (of therapist) and, 6–7
memory and, 154
outside orientation and, 17
resistance and, 72n1

unconscious and, 32
Descartes, R., 159
Developmental lag, 29–61
authoritative analytic stance and, 50–54
counterresistance to transference, 58–59
defenses and, x, xv, xviii
external reality and, 54–58
Freud and ego analysis, 31–36
hypnotic technique, abandonment of, 31
id and, 49–50
listening (of therapist) and, 30
term of, 48
theory/practice and, 36–48
Displacement
ego, unconscious activity of, autonomous access to, 156–157
listening (of therapist) and, 15–16
Distortion, listening (of therapist) and, 13
Dream analysis
anxiety and conflict resolution, xii
memory as defense and, 160–170
memory as resistance, xii
Drives
defenses and, xi–xii, xiii, 43
derivatives, listening (of therapist) and, 6–8
ego and, xx, 41
ego's permissive superego activity, 132
memory and, 154
superego and, 16
Dynamic psychotherapy, guidelines for, 196–198

Ego
anxiety and, ix, x
complexity of, 155
conflict and, xii–xiii, xv
conflict-defense patterns and, xxi
defense analysis and, xviii
developmental lag and, 30
drives and, xx, 41
hypnotic technique and, 23–24, 38–40
resistance and, xix, 37–38
response of, to analysis, supervision guidelines, 203–205
self-observation and, 24–25, 60
intrapsychic activity access, 67, 72
structural theory and, ix
superego and, xi–xii, xiii, xix–xx
therapeutic outcomes and, 31–32
therapeutic role of, xx–xxi, 30, 40
unconscious activity of, autonomous access to, 153, 156
unconscious and, 23–24, 32
Ego analysis
defense and, 42–43, 45–46
Freud and, 31–36
listening (of therapist) and, 6
resistance and, 44, 45
Ego conflict analysis supervision, 175–192
constructive orientation, 186–187
guidelines for, 187–192
summary of modes, 175–186
Ego-in-defense, superego and, xxii–xxiii
Ego's inhibiting superego activity, 105–127
clarification of concept, 116–120
Freud on, 106–116
overview of, 105–106
superego analysis and therapeutic praxis, 120–127
Ego's permissive superego activity, 131–149
affectionate approval as resistance, transferential fantasy of, 133–137

Ego's permissive superego activity (*continued*)
affectionately permissive authority, transference of, 138–144
centrality of, in resistance analysis, 148–149
overview of, 131–133
supportive transference, diminishment of unanalytic effects, 144–148
Ego split, conflict resolution and, 118
Eissler, K., 66
Empathy, 6
Eroticism, listening (of therapist) and, 8–9
Esman, A. H., 132n1
Evolution, consciousness and, 60–61
Experience, memory and, 21–22
Experiential insight, drives and ego, xx
External reality, developmental lag and, 54–58

Fantasy
memory and, 20–21
resistance and, 32
Fenichel, O., 37, 39, 43, 44, 47, 52, 68, 76, 118, 223
Ferenczi, S., 38n5, 135, 138, 139, 140, 141
Fixation
ego's inhibiting superego activity, 109
external reality and, 56
Fleming, J., 24
Free association
free communication contrasted, 69
interpretation and, 35–36
repression and, 31
therapeutic action and, 94–95
French, T. M., 141
Freud, A., x, xi, xviii, 9, 13, 32, 33, 36, 37, 40, 41, 42, 44, 45, 47, 48, 53, 57, 72n1, 74, 92, 107, 108, 116, 117, 153, 181, 216
Freud, S., ix, x, xi, xii, xiv, xvii, xviii, xx, xxii–xxiii, 6, 13, 19n1, 20n2, 23, 29, 30, 31, 32, 33–36, 37, 38, 39, 40, 43, 44, 45, 46, 47, 50, 54, 55, 57, 59, 60, 68, 70, 72n1, 73, 76, 85, 93, 105, 106–116, 120, 121, 122, 123, 127, 135, 136, 138, 154, 155, 158, 160, 167, 170, 182, 187, 188, 198, 200, 215, 216, 223, 226
Friedman, L., 48n8, 66, 71, 119, 224

Gardner, R., 93
Gero, G., 72n1, 116, 122
Gill, M., 38n5, 58, 68, 72n1, 119, 181
Gillman, R., 118–119
Glover, E., 119
Goldberger, M., 223–229
Gray, P., 29, 56, 65, 68, 75, 92, 107, 123, 131, 133, 144, 156, 157, 177, 181, 182, 183, 188, 223–229
Greenacre, P., 13, 97
Greenson, R., 59
Grubrich-Simitis, I., 138, 140
Grunberger, B., 112n1
Guilt, unconscious/conscious guilt, 119
Gutheil, T. G., 32n1, 72

Hartmann, H., 30, 36, 37, 71
Hatcher, R. L., 53n12, 66
Havens, L., 32n1, 72
Holding environment, 141–142
Homosexuality, therapeutic action and, 94
Huggins, C. B., 195
Hypnotic technique, x, xi
abandonment of, 31, 38, 93

authoritative analytic stance and, 50–51
ego functions and, 23–24, 38–40

Id
developmental lag and, x, 43–44, 49–50
pleasure and, xxii–xxiii
repression and, xix
therapeutic action and, 99–100
Inhibition, ego's inhibiting superego activity, 105–127. *See also* Ego's inhibiting superego activity
Inside attention
analysand's capacity and, 22–23
listening (of therapist) and, 18–19
Insight
brief psychotherapy and, 196
drives and ego, xx
ego, unconscious activity of, autonomous access to, 156
Instinct. *See* Death instinct; Drives
Intellectualization
as defense, xi
intrapsychic activity access and, 70–71
psychoanalysis guidelines, 200
Internalization, ego's inhibiting superego activity, 106
Interpretation
ego and, xx
explaining unconscious and, 34–36
listening (of therapist) and, 7
resistance and, 37
Intervention
attention (of therapist) and, x, xiii
defensive transference of authority, xiv
Intrapsychic activity access, 65–85
clinical examples, 77–85
cooperation with self-observing activities, 75–76
motivation strengthening for, 66–75
overview of, 65–66
Irrational risk, intrapsychic activity access and, 73–74
Isakower, O., 6

Jacobson, P. B., 57n16
Jones, E., 111
Joseph, E. D., 89

Kanzer, M., 57n15, 114
Katan, M., 116
Klein, M., 52, 112n1
Kohut, H., 24, 25, 52n10, 73, 89, 144
Kramer, M., 24
Kris, E., xviii, 41, 45, 66, 67, 118n6, 181, 224
Kuhn, T., 34n2

Lewin, B. D., 136
Lichtenstein, H., 112n1
Listening (of therapist), 5–26
analysand's capacity and, 22–23
analytic couch and, 17–18
analytic style and, 29–30
behavior control and, 17
centrality of, ix–x, xii, xiii, xvii–xviii, 5
clinical examples, 11–16
developmental lag and, 30
drive derivatives and, 6–8
ego and self-observation, 24–25
ego conflict analysis supervision, 176–177
id and, 50
inside attention and, 18–19
memory and, 19–21, 160
neutrality and, 9–10
outside orientation and, 16–17
overview of, 5–6
reality and, 10, 13
therapeutic action and, 90, 91–100
Loewald, H., 89
Loewenstein, R., 70, 71, 72n1, 78

Lussier, A., 149
Lustman, S. L., 48, 59

Masochism, primary, ego's inhibiting superego activity, 111
Meers, D., 124n8
Meissner, W. W., 52n11
Memory
  experience and, 21–22
  external reality and, 55, 57
  listening (of therapist) and, 19–21
  outside orientation and, 21
  as resistance, xii, 153–170
  resistance and, 32
Modell, A. H., 89, 141, 142
Motivation, strengthening of, for intrapsychic activity access, 66–75

Namnum, A., 56n14
Neutrality
  authoritative analytic stance and, 50–54
  complexity of, 50
  listening (of therapist) and, 9–10
Novey, S., 112n1
Nunberg, H., xx, 47, 50, 68, 112n1

Object relations, ego's permissive superego activity, 143
Obsessional neuroses, superego analysis and, 121–122
Organic inertia, ego's inhibiting superego activity, 108–109
Orgel, S., 78, 112n1
Ostow, M., 112n1
Outcomes. *See* Therapeutic outcomes
Outside orientation
  behavior control and, 17
  intrapsychic activity access and, 69–70
  listening (of therapist) and, 16–17
  memory and, 21
  resistance and, 18

Passivity, listening (of therapist) and, 9
Perception. *See* Listening (of therapist)
Personality structure, therapeutic action and, 100–101
Pfeffer, A., 22
Phobias, outside orientation and, 18
Pleasure, id and, xxii–xxiii
Positive transference
  intrapsychic activity access, 68
  resistance and, xiv
Practice, theory and, xvii
Primary masochism, ego's inhibiting superego activity, 111
Projection, affectionate approval as resistance, transferential fantasy of, 137
Psychoanalysis, guidelines for, 198–200
Psychotherapy
  analysis and, xxi–xxii
  reality and, 10

Rangell, S., 72n1, 224
Rank, O., 138, 139, 141
Rationality, intrapsychic activity access and, 72–73
Reaction formation, 166
Reality
  external, developmental lag and, 54–58
  listening (of therapist) and, 10, 13, 15
  memory and, 20
Reich, W., 37, 40, 44n7
Reik, T., 6
Repetition neurosis, ego's inhibiting superego activity, 109–110
Repression
  id and, xix
  overcoming of, 31
Resistance
  aggression and, 14–15

analysis of, xiii
awareness of, xi
control of, 33
defenses and, 72n1
defensive transference of authority, xiv
ego analysis and, 44, 45
ego and, xix, 37–38
ego's inhibiting superego activity, 105, 107–108, 110, 113
ego's permissive superego activity, centrality of, 148–149
interpretation and, 37
intrapsychic activity access, 65. *See also* Intrapsychic activity access
memory as, xii, 153–170
outside orientation and, 18
positive transference and, xiv
purposes of, 32
self-observation, intrapsychic activity access, 68, 70
universality and, xxii
Ritvo, S., ix–xv
Rowntree, E., 209

Salk, J., 60
Sampson, H., 141
Sandler, J., 125
Sandler, R., xxii, 132n1, 212
Schafer, R., 72n1, 136n2
Schimek, J. G., 57n16
Schlesinger, H. J., 141, 142, 146, 182, 188
Schur, M., 109, 112n1, 119
Schwartz, L., 118n6
Scott, W. C. A., 44n7
Screen memories, 19n1, 55n13
Searl, N., 44
Self-analysis
technique and, 24
training analysis and, 23
Self-observation
cooperation with, by analyst, 75–76
ego and, 24–25, 60
intrapsychic activity access motivation, 66–75
Shapiro, T., 184
Spence, D., 126
Spiegel, L. A., 119
Spruiell, V., 149
Steele, R. S., 57n16
Stein, M. H., 10, 134, 136, 182, 188
Sterba, R., 29, 30, 37, 41–42, 45, 47, 49, 67, 73, 85, 116, 118, 224
Sternbach, O., 112n1
Stone, L., xix, 30, 37, 49, 72n1, 216
Strachey, J., xx, 36, 52, 89, 109, 111
Strengthening exercise, drives and ego, xx
Structural theory, ix
resistance and, 32
Style. *See* Analytic style
Sublimation, varieties of, 49–50
Suggestion
analytic therapies and, xxii
brief psychotherapy and, xv
intrapsychic activity access, 68
Superego
ambiguity in analysis of, xi–xii
analysis of, and therapeutic praxis, 120–127
drive defense and, 16
ego and, xi–xii, xiii, xix–xx
ego-in-defense and, xxii–xxiii
ego's inhibiting superego activity, 105–127. *See also* Ego's inhibiting superego activity
ego's permissive superego activity, 131–149. *See also* Ego's permissive superego activity
listening (of therapist) and, 9–10
transference and, xxii
transferences and, xiv
Supervision
brief psychotherapy guidelines, 196

Supervision (*continued*)
dynamic psychotherapy guidelines, 196–198
ego conflict analysis, 175–192. *See also* Ego conflict analysis supervision
ego's response to analysis, 203–205
elements of, 215–219
external reality and, 56
id and, 50
inside/outside realities and, 22
psychoanalysis guidelines, 198–200
reflections on, 209–212

Tact, intervention and, xiii
Theory, practice and, xvii, 36–48
Therapeutic action, 89–102
advantages and disadvantages of approach, 90, 100–102
listening (of therapist), 90, 91–100
theoretical and clinical context, 90–91
variety of patients and, 89
Therapeutic alliance. *See* Alliance
Therapeutic outcomes, ego and, 31–32
Third ear
id and, 50
listening (of therapist) and, 6
Ticho, G., 24
Timing, intervention and, xiii
Training analysis, self-analysis and, 23
Transference
analytic setting and, 16
attention (of therapist) and, x
of authority, 124
authority and, xiii–xiv, xix, xxi–xxii
counterresistance to, developmental lag and, 58–59
of defense, 117
defense and, xi–xii, xiii–xiv
developmental lag and, x
ego conflict analysis supervision, 182–184
ego's inhibiting superego activity, 106
ego's permissive superego activity
affectionate approval as resistance, transferential fantasy of, 133–137
affectionately permissive authority, transference of, 138–144
supportive transference, diminishment of unanalytic effects, 144–148
superego and, xiv, xxii
Transference of defense concept, superego analysis and, 117–118

Unconscious
attention (of therapist), centrality of, ix–x
autonomous access to, 153
ego and, 23–24, 32
ego's inhibiting superego activity, 108
interpretations explaining, 34–36
intrapsychic activity access, 65. *See also* Intrapsychic activity access
listening (of therapist) and, 6
memory as resistance, xii
Unconscious guilt, 119
Universality, resistance and, xxii

Waelder, R., 30, 32, 33, 107, 113n3, 124n8
Wallerstein, R., 72n1
Weiss, J., 141
Winnicott, D. W., 141
Working through
ego's inhibiting superego activity, 109, 113n3
term of, xx